Acts of Union

ACTS OF UNION

Reports on Ireland, 1973-79

ANTHONY BAILEY

Faber and Faber
London · Boston

First published in Great Britain 1980
by Faber and Faber Ltd.
3 Queen Square, London WC1

First published in the United States by
Random House, Inc., New York, and simultaneously
in Canada by Random House of Canada Limited, Toronto.

All essays in this book have originally appeared in the following publications: *The New Yorker*, *Observer Magazine*, and
Quest/78

*Grateful acknowledgment is made to the following for per-
mission to reprint previously published material:* The Bod-
ley Head: excerpts from *The Archeology of Ireland* by Peter
Harbison. Copyright © 1976 by Peter Harbison. Used by
permission of The Bodley Head, London. Central Office of
Information: excerpt from the pamphlet entitled "Northern
Ireland." Reprinted by permission of the Central Office of
Information, London. Faber and Faber Ltd.: lines from
"Autumn Journal" from the book *The Collected Poems
of Louis MacNeice*; lines from "Lament for Thomas
MacDonagh" by Francis Ledwidge, taken from the book
Faber Book of Irish Verse, edited by James Montagne;
and lines from "Mossbawn: 1. Sunlight" from *North* by
Seamus Heaney. Reprinted by permission of Faber and
Faber Ltd., Publishers, London. Seamus Heaney: extracts
from "Sweeney Astray" are reprinted by permission of
Seamus Heaney. The Honest Ulsterman: excerpt taken from
The Honest Ulsterman, Number 53, November/December
1976, by Seamus Heaney. Reprinted by permission of *The
Honest Ulsterman*, N. Ireland. The O'Brien Press: excerpts
from *The Riddle of Erskine Childers* by Michael McInerney.
Reprinted by permission of The O'Brien Press, Dublin.
A. P. Watt Ltd.: line from "Meditations in Time of Civil
War" (Part VI: "The Stare's Nest by My Window") from
Collected Poems of William Butler Yeats. Reprinted by
permission of A. P. Watt Ltd., London.

ISBN 0 571 11648 5

Manufactured in the United States of America
2 4 6 8 9 7 5 3
First Edition

TO WILLIAM SHAWN

Foreword

WRITTEN OVER half a dozen years, these pieces do not attempt to furnish a comprehensive picture of the Troubles that have once again beset Ireland. I offer them rather as aspects of my own education in Irish things. Prompted by a large dollop of Irish blood and by a feeling that what was happening in Ireland was the most important "story" a writer could examine at this time, in Great Britain and Ireland, I set about looking for ways of breaking into what, in one of these reports, I call the vicious circle of interlocked problems. I wanted to try to unravel some of the complications and mysteries attendant on the Irish question—so that I would be able to tell the difference, for example, between the O'Connells and the Collinses, the Collinses and the Connollys; so that I might discover what lay behind some of the attitudes people seemed to hold so firmly; and so that I might search not so much for solutions as for what has made solutions necessary, or has prevented them from being found. I have also indulged a need to write about what moves me in Ireland. This includes a good deal of Irish writing, here exemplified by Seamus Heaney and his poems, and the Irish landscape—in Heaney's words, "the ground possessed and repossessed"—wherein the dictates of history and geography are often, most eloquently, made manifest.

For those readers who come to this, as I did originally, with some confusion about the recent constitutional background, a few basic facts may be necessary. A paragraph from the

British Central Office of Information pamphlet "Northern Ireland" gives, I believe, a concise and objective survey:

Northern Ireland comprises six of the nine counties of the ancient province of Ulster. . . . These six counties became a separate province in 1920. The whole of Ireland had become an integral part of the United Kingdom as a result of the Act of Union of 1800. In 1920, however, the British Government, in an attempt to meet the demand for Home Rule which was prevalent in the south, provided through the Government of Ireland Act of 1920 for the establishment of subordinate legislatures and governments within the United Kingdom in Northern Ireland and Southern Ireland, and also for the creation of specific machinery—the Council of Ireland—to promote cooperation and encourage ultimate reunion between the two parts within the United Kingdom. These institutions were unwillingly accepted by Northern Ireland, but rejected by the southern Irish, who wished for independence. Consequently, the Council of Ireland never came into being; the scheme of devolution provided by the Act was introduced, with modifications, in Northern Ireland, which remained an integral part of the United Kingdom; and the 26 counties of Southern Ireland became in 1922, under the title of the Irish Free State, a self-governing state outside the United Kingdom, and subsequently, in 1948, as the Irish Republic, a fully independent republic outside the Commonwealth.

Other pertinent facts: The population of the North is roughly 1½ million, of whom just over 500,000 are Roman Catholic. The population of the South is just under 3 million; 129,000 of these are Protestant; 566,000 people live in Dublin. In the eleven years of renewed violence in the North some 2,000 people have died by bullet and bomb, fire and explosion.

Seamus Heaney has written a poem about the long Irish-British entanglement called "Act of Union." I have borrowed this thought and called this book *Acts of Union* because most of the people I deal with in it are trying, in different ways, to overcome the fragmentation and divisions that at once injure and give intensity to Ireland and Irish life.

Acknowledgments

"ON THE OLDPARK," "The House of the Chief," "Matthew and Marie," and "Irish Miles" first appeared in *The New Yorker*. "Acts of Union" was published in *Quest/78* and "The Stony Ground" in the *Observer Magazine* (which also reprinted "Matthew and Marie"). The versions printed here are in slightly different form. I am greatly obliged to the editors of these magazines, and grateful to many people in Ireland who have helped me with information and warm hospitality. If I name none of them here, it is because such public credit is not always welcome now; but I hope they know that I remember their help. This book exists because of them. Due to the considerable literature on the subject, any short list is bound to seem invidious. However, I have found particularly useful the works of E. Estyn Evans, J. C. Beckett, Liam de Paor, Conor Cruise O'Brien, Maurice Craig, and Jack White. Andrew Boyle's biography of Erskine Childers, which appeared after I wrote the essay here, is the most comprehensive account of the life of Childers *père*. The periodicals *Community Forum, Fortnight, Hibernia*, and *The Honest Ulsterman*, and the newspapers *Derry Journal, Belfast Telegraph, Belfast Newsletter*, and *Irish Times* have given me facts and background for my own questions.

Contents

Acts of Union

Chapter One

ON THE OLDPARK, BELFAST

– 1973 –

FAMILIAR FROM A DREAM, perhaps, or from a film of an occupied town in Europe, 1944, the road is dirty, treeless, lined with small grey-brown terraced houses. At a street junction it opens out in an empty, melancholy space—the width emphasized by a lack of cars, parked or moving, and a lack of people. The shadow of a solitary man appears, then disappears, around a corner. A dog, careless of vehicles or gunfire, ambles across the road, sniffing at litter. Many of the shops are closed, as if because of strict rationing or depopulation. The windows of the corner pub are bricked up, and the building itself appears hazy behind a high wire-mesh fence, one section of which juts out from the pavement into the road toward a similar fence projecting from the butcher's shop on the other side, a few yards farther along. From a car, weaving through the gap between the fences, slowly negotiating the steep asphalt ramps that have been laid in order to make all vehicles slow down, one can see that these buildings have had to be protected. Anyone with a gun or rocket launcher has a long line of sight down the road.

To the left can be seen several streets borrowed from a sepia-tinted textbook illustration of the Industrial Revolution. The streets to the right are a shade less mean. The road itself feels like a dividing line. Now come several blitzed sites covered with rubble; a house with its roof gone; houses whose windows are filled with grey cinder blocks; a burned-out factory; an anonymous filling station, its forecourt lacking pumps, weeds sprouting through the shattered concrete. Up ahead, the stranded-whale shape of a derelict cinema. To the left, an open stretch—green fields of an empty municipal sports ground built over former brick fields (shapes of slag heaps like burial mounds), and sloping down to old mill buildings, silhouetted factories, lines of grey-slate-roofed houses running southwest, and then, abruptly, only a mile and a half away, a dark wall of hills. One is conscious of being on a patch of the earth roughened to cinders, which can be blown away. One is conscious—a sudden prickly feeling—of being watched.

Opposite the sports ground a British Army observation post has been built, covered in the grey-green plastic kelp of a camouflage net. It forms a bastion of a larger building, rising behind a sloping wire-mesh fence, and gives the effect of a sort of breakwater covering the larger building's ground-floor façade. The observation post is festooned with barbed wire, backed up with corrugated steel and sandbags—a light-grey-painted Victorian building whose basically sound condition is stressed—rather than the opposite—by several bullet holes and a six-inch-deep crater gouged from the brick by a rocket. There's a plaque under the gable end, over the blacked-out, sandbagged second-floor windows, gold letters on a blue ground: FINISTON PUBLIC ELEMENTARY SCHOOL.

At 8:15 A.M., a 1971 Vauxhall sedan jounces slowly over a ramp in front of the observation post and turns off the road: the Oldpark Road, which gives its name to the surrounding Oldpark area of north Belfast, in the way that other streets—Shankill, Antrim, Crumlim, Falls—give theirs to other areas of the city. The Vauxhall parks, the only car in the side street, beyond another army observation post. And the driver, David

Russell, gets out and walks over to be frisked before starting another day as principal of what is now officially called Finiston Primary School.

Christine Lavery   P-7   Our School   16/5/73

Our school is not very big, and there are not very many people in it. We have soldiers taking over the front of it. Not long ago a rocket hit the side of the building and though no one was hurt, lots of mothers took their children away to another school, afraid of what might happen next time. There is around 250 at our school that is half the amount that used to be at our school before the trouble started.

We have to use our assembly hall for our dining room because the army use our old ones. All around the building we have corrugated iron so that no one can throw anything into the playground and after all I think we know more about Army life than we do lessons.

WITHIN THE corrugated-iron stockade, the army—A Company, 3rd Battalion, The Parachute Regiment—is to the right, in the old building. The school has drawn back into the mostly single-story 1930s structure behind—a square of classrooms, corridors, assembly hall and washrooms, enclosing a grassed yard. Immediate intimations of normality. Smell of linoleum wax and gravy. Recessed ceilings, reminiscent of a cinema lobby; pastel shades of blue and yellow paint. Prints by Braque, De La Tour, Sisley, and Manet in the main corridor, and, on a table outside the principal's office, a pair of models made by boys in P-7, the school's highest class, mostly eleven-year-olds: cereal boxes, yogurt cartons, and toilet-paper rolls turned into Harland and Wolff's shipyard, with gantries and dry docks; and an Indian compound, with tepees and campfire and prancing savages. The principal's office is in a bay projecting into the side yard: two desks; filing cabinet; a jug of pussy willow; a relief map of the world with the Himalayas like a raised blister of burned skin; the electric kettle steaming; Nancy Wallace, the school secretary, wiry and middle-aged, checking the lunch-money accounts; and David Russell reading correspondence that's resulted from a letter he wrote to the London *Times*, suggesting good-humoredly that Northern Ireland be included among the sections of the United Kingdom which have been designated educational priority areas (EPAs)—in which, among other things, teachers receive bonus payments.

Russell is fifty-three, and looks younger. His talk is full of colloquial references—to Westerns and POW escape stories, to old Ingrid Bergman and Errol Flynn movies. He is of medium height, with straight grey hair, bushy grey eyebrows, a golfer's tanned face, and, almost always, a smile. He is wearing a well-cut light-grey suit and looks like a cross between John Wayne and Humphrey Bogart. He has been principal of Finiston (which he now and then refers to as "Dodge City Academy") for three years. He has an external degree from Trinity College, Dublin. He has taught in private schools and other primary schools, including the nearby Cliftonville school, which is in a more prosperous, more stable neighborhood. After the war he spent several years in Canada, then returned because he missed Ireland. Earlier, he served for six years in the RAF, ending up in a Japanese prisoner-of-war camp. "We were flying Blenheims out of Java," he says. "The Japs took our aerodrome just after we'd returned from a fifteen-minute mission over the north coast. We destroyed our planes and got away to the beach in a Chevrolet, but our boat capsized in the surf and the natives turned us in." The POW camp provided experiences that have served him well ever since. "After that, it's hardly likely that anything that happens on the Oldpark Road is going to worry me."

On the wall behind his desk, and in the hall, are mementos from the five British Army companies that have previously used part of the school and its grounds as headquarters: plaques, pennants, and prints from the Royal Regiment of Wales, the Green Howards, the First and Third Light Infantry, and the Queen's Lancashires. Next to the Green Howards' plaque is the inscription: "Presented by the Elderly Pupils of C Company who completed their Adult Education at Finiston School in the summer of 1971." A sergeant in the First Light Infantry made its pennant, showing a bugle and two poppies; his spelling is not quite perfect. "This flag was flawn continuously over Finiston School by Support Company 1st Battalion the Light Infantry over the period 25 July–24 November 1972." The bugle is the regimental emblem. The poppies commemorate Private Rowe and Driver Kitchen, two men of the company who were killed by snipers near the school.

Although Russell's problems now may not compare with the problems he had as a prisoner of war, he has several current worries: the shrinking size of his school population, the difficulty that many of the children have in getting to school, and the possibility of violent, extremist reaction to anything he might say. Outspoken moderates are in danger from both sides. He has to talk warily, not just because he has doubts about his own point of view but because even the well-intentioned have feelings that are easily hurt by truthful comment. The doctrinaire take cheerfulness for an insult. But Russell is whistling as the hand-bell rings in the junior corridor at five past nine, and he walks quickly to the back entrance to the school to welcome the children, some of whom have walked and some of whom have been bused in, for safety's sake, from streets as close as a hundred and fifty yards away.

BEFORE THE ONSET of the most recent "troubles," in 1969, the Oldpark Road formed a fairly effective and peaceful dividing line between working-class Protestants, to the northeast, and working-class Catholics, to the southwest (though for the latter there was almost always less work to be had). On both sides of the Oldpark, many houses have no garden; toilets are in the backyards; paved entries run between the houses; the women seem to wear bedroom slippers all day long. The sort of slums, still common in Belfast, that have been eradicated from just about every other British city. However, whatever is bad in the Protestant streets is generally a touch worse in the Catholic streets—greater poverty, greater despair, and eventually a greater potential for violence. The Catholic streets are called the

Marrowbone (or Bone), from the shape they form between Old-park and Crumlin roads, bounded on the northwest by the Ardoyne district. The Bone has its own, Catholic schools, the closest of which to the Oldpark Road is St. Colmban's Boys' Primary. Russell often chats with Michael Hannon, the principal of St. Colmban's, about common problems or about Russell's hope for a Northern Ireland EPA, which Hannon supports, though nowadays, because of local tension, they don't talk face to face but over the telephone.

On both sides of the Oldpark, the troubles have caused families to move away, fleeing out of fear, intimidation, or panic. Many have moved to supposedly safer areas. (Around Finiston, a hundred out of three hundred houses are bricked up.) A number of families are squatting. Some streets that were once slightly mixed are now firmly segregated, as co-religionists bunch together for mutual protection. Two years ago, after several empty houses were set on fire and burned out, perhaps by vandals, the Protestant population of six small streets not far from Finiston packed up and moved out, and Catholic families from across the Oldpark moved in. Houses built for Protestant artisans in the 1890s were better than the slum dwellings in the Marrowbone. The new Catholic section is now called the Ballybone, since all its streets have the prefix *Bally* (Ballyclare, Ballynure, Ballycastle, Ballymena, Ballymoney, and Ballycarry); the section forms a wedge extending the Catholic ghetto into the staunchly Protestant neighborhood. It is, Russell says, three hundred yards of absolute bitterness. The move breached the so-called Peace Line of the Oldpark Road, running between the communities.

For Russell's school, this shift produced one particular problem: it was suddenly difficult for many Finiston children to get to school—just as it was for Catholic children in other parts of Belfast, where similar migrations of Protestants into once-Catholic streets had taken place. The journey to school became a trip through alien territory. Traditionally, Protestant children coming to Finiston from Louisa Street, behind the Bone, had always made a slight detour, had not used one passageway, on their way to school. But now, as they came past the Ballybone, bottles and stones were hurled, fights broke out, and children were injured. Small children would be stopped by bigger children, ordered to tell their religion, and, if the answer was "Protestant," beaten up. (The answer "Catholic" might, of course, have provoked a similar response in other sections.) For the children's safety, soldiers began to escort them—sometimes walking with them, sometimes transporting them in Saracen armored personnel vehicles, nicknamed Pigs. On these lollipop patrols, as they were called, half a dozen soldiers were killed and many injured in various parts of the city. Since the continued danger to children was one reason his school's parents were moving out, Russell nagged the city corporation to provide buses, which were in short supply at peak times (and were also being blown up, burned, and used in barricades). The army asked for the buses, too. At last, buses were provided. Fares were charged at first, but many parents couldn't afford them, and the children are now carried free. Thus, at nine in the morning half the children of Finiston are ferried to school on two plum-colored double-decker buses (marked "9—Special"), and at two-fifteen they are carried home again, on a trip that for some is as short as a quarter of a mile. (School ends an hour earlier than it did, for the buses aren't available later in the afternoon.) Some parents walk to school with their children. A few children walk home to lunch, though David Russell tries to discourage it; three small Finiston pupils were nearly hit by rifle fire the other day.

If you have information about murder, explosions,
intimidation, or acts of terrorism,
in complete confidence call Belfast 652155.
—Placard on the side of buses

AT FIVE MINUTES PAST NINE, a low, buzzing wave of children pours along the corridors, filling the classrooms. Russell welcomes many of the children by name in reply to a hundred greetings of "Good morning, Mr. Russell." His ambitions are simple. "We don't push anybody. Smart schools in better districts have parents with high expectations. We don't have many. Those parents that did have them have generally gone to the new housing estates. We're left with the children of those without much incentive. Some children are like little animals when they first come here. Some aren't house-trained. Some can't talk. They have no vocabulary, no words. No books in their houses, no magazines or papers except the racing news or comics. Some don't get talked to except by the telly. So I try for basic things. Children in this school should be happy, not afraid. They should become small human beings, trusting one another. I go on a lot about cleanliness, getting them just to wash their hands and feet. There are very few cases of vermin this year." He turns to a small boy, brings him to a halt. "Now then, Douglas, what have you done to your hand?" He examines a bandaged set of fingers, finds out how they got that way, and sends the child bustling on, grinning.

"We go in for a lot of drama. I discovered in prison camp that in any group of several hundred people there will be acting talent. There is here. And almost all kids love standing up, singing, reciting, making things up. In the last few years we've changed our methods of religious instruction, turning it into drama. The same with history. They like doing Julius Caesar landing on the Channel beach or Daniel in the lions' den— always lots of volunteers for lions."

Roll call, and collection of lunch money in the classrooms. In the youngest P-1, known as the reception class, Mrs. Eleanor Girvan, young, tall, and fashionably dressed, in her first year of teaching. In the older P-1, Miss Roberta McCallum, tall, with fine skin—"the best infant teacher in Belfast," says Russell. Mrs. Betty Emery, young and snub-nosed, in P-2. Miss Isabel Kyle, with lovely gold-red hair, in P-2/3. Mrs. Dorothy Elliott, the head of the infant school, in P-3. Mrs. Philippa Hewitt, an experienced older woman, in P-4. Miss Donna Curry, pert and pretty, also in her first year of teaching, in P-4/5. Bill Pollock, in his late forties, in P-5. The two P-6s are run by youngish men, James Moore (pronounced "Mooer") and Brian Woods, who has a shaggy mustache. P-7 is in the energetic hands of James Hutton, the vice-principal—like Russell, a former RAF pilot (he flew Hurricanes)—who has sandy hair and a small sandy mustache.

Two days a week the younger children, from P-1, P-2, and P-3, have their own assembly in the hall, which has a small stage, an upright piano, and a row of French windows. Through these there is a view of sandbags and two prefabricated wooden huts, used by the army as a sergeants' mess and an officers' mess. Gym equipment is pushed back against the hall walls— horses, climbing bars, ropes, and a trampoline, which the First Light Infantry gave the school (and the soldiers use in after-school hours). Today, Dorothy Elliott, a good-looking, bold-featured woman in her late thirties, wearing a black sweater, a grey-and-white kilt, and elegant black shoes, is in charge of the assembly. She has a soft voice with a pleasant touch of brogue. The children sit around her on the floor. She tells them how Jesus and his parents made a trip across the desert to the City of David—a story with occasional interruptions and questions: ". . . So his mummy packed spare clothes for the journey, and extra food. (And you turn round and behave yourself, Brian!) Does anyone know why they had to take food? Yes, Patricia?" Patricia, who has her hand up, says, "Because there are no cafés in the desert." "Right," says Mrs. Elliott. "And so they set out . . ." Her story takes the Holy Family with other travelers to the City of David, where they visit a big church and Jesus gets lost. The parents don't discover that he is missing until the trip home. "Joseph and Mary go round the party and ask, 'Did you see my Jesus? Did your wee girl see my Jesus?' No, she hadn't. They were very worried, just as your mummy and daddy would be if they lost you." The parents go back to the city and find Jesus in the church, talking to the ministers. The curtains of the French windows billow in the fresh, warm breeze. A fine May day, the first prolonged sunshine in several weeks.

Mrs. Elliott chooses from the volunteers—not many hands

up for being one of the Holy Family, though there's a forest of arms for joining the traveling party. She lines up Jesus, Mary, and Joseph onstage with twenty companions. At the back of the hall she places "the very important people who were ministers"—half a dozen little boys, one of them Pakistani. And those left over become desert tribesmen or people of the city through which the travelers wend their way to the church, losing their wee Jesus, miming the search for him and his discovery while Mrs. Elliott breaks up a fight among two townspeople ("Allan, will you go and sit far away from Bruce, over *there*"), not raising her voice, and provides spoken continuity: "And—golly!—look who's here. Jesus! Your mummy and daddy have come to find you."

When everyone is sitting down again, two small boys at the back who have been thumping each other are brought forward to lead the singing. Nearly as hard as they were belting each other, they belt out:

> "Tender shepherd, tender shepherd,
> Lead us to thy morning light."

THE FIGURES AS OF MAY 1973: Since the troubles began in Northern Ireland in 1969, there have been 3,000 bomb "outrages" and, as a result of the violence, 800 deaths, which include the deaths of roughly 220 soldiers. More than a thousand soldiers have been wounded. One death was that of an eight-year-old girl, whose itinerant parents were squatting for the time in a house a few doors from Finiston school. She was hit by a sniper's bullet while walking in the Oldpark Road, in front of the school, just before last Christmas. One woman who rushed out with others on hearing the shot said, "Oh, it's only a gypsy child."

"It's the easiest job in the teaching profession, being principal of a primary school," says David Russell. Certainly he makes it look easy. At some point this morning he began to cover with clear vinyl plastic a penguin, hand-embroidered onto cloth-covered cardboard by Karen Bunting in P-7, that had been on a shelf behind his desk awaiting his attention. There are frequent knocks on the door, and emissaries from each class bring in the attendance books and small tobacco tins containing the money for lunch—which here, as in most British schools, is called dinner. Mrs. Wallace dispenses the dinner tickets— yellow for those whose parents can afford the twelve pence, blue for those who can't and receive them free, pink for half price. "It's one way of telling what social category your school caters for," says Russell. Finiston's last-month dinner-money returns were, in round numbers, 350 paid or partly paid, 1,000 free. "We're lower class." The telephone rings constantly. Russell chases down a rumor on the phone with an official of the Belfast Education Authority about a neighboring school's having acquired a nursery class. (Finiston doesn't have a nursery class, and Russell feels that its recruiting powers have been undermined. Because so many families have moved away, his school has lost 250 pupils in the last three years; he fights to keep, or gain, any child in Finiston's catchment area.) A small, snotty-nosed boy is brought in, holding out to Mr. Russell a grey plastic machine gun, like a three-quarter-size Thompson.

Russell: "Do you know why I'm keeping this?"

"Yes, sir."

"Why?"

"Becus they'd shoot me."

An older girl comes in and asks if Mr. Russell will turn on the BBC school poetry broadcast for P-7. (His office radio relays to a loudspeaker in every classroom.) "Right, Anita," says Russell. "That's Anita Rowntree, the brains behind the Oldpark Mafia." Anita gives Russell an old-fashioned smile.

The phone rings, and Russell reassures a mother whose child suddenly had been upset, hadn't wanted to come to school this morning, and had been forced to come anyway. He replaces the receiver. "We don't usually have that problem. They want to come to school and they don't want to leave—they'd stay all afternoon if they could. We had one little boy who broke out last month, though. Said he was going to the toilet and then disappeared—got through the sandbags, the army checkpoint, the barbed wire, and made it home. I think he'd been watching the Colditz series on TV. No, some children insist on coming back to Finiston even though their parents have moved several miles out." He talks to a Church of Ireland minister who is on the school committee and is making an appointment to visit the school next week. The troubles have tended to reduce the number of visits from ministers, school inspectors, and other education authorities, few of whom seem quite so eager as they used to be to call on schools in areas like the Oldpark. Even the police from the Royal Ulster Constabulary station up the road find this neighborhood too dangerous, and aren't to be seen in local streets.

Things go on like this all morning. Russell talks to the secretary of the local cricket club, which is trying to get going again in its vandalized quarters on the Cliftonville recreation ground. The club can't find its motor mower, believes that the army took it, and hopes that Russell can tell them how to get it back again. After a few calls Russell discovers that the army indeed took it, "for its own protection," and now it can't be traced. But Russell gives the club secretary the number of the army claims office, which—he knows from an experience of his own, when his car hood was damaged as a result of an army bomb search—gives prompt and generous service.

Russell welcomes into the office a mother who says she's moving to a safer area next autumn; her daughter had been stoned on the way to school last week. In five minutes Russell persuades her to leave her daughter's name on the school's books until September, so that she can change her mind about withdrawing the child. He says, "I can always ring the head of the other school and they'll accept her at once. But things may seem better to you then." It develops that the girl doesn't want to leave Finiston, is in tears at the idea. The mother is talked round.

Russell next confers with a young woman in the local office of the Northern Ireland Community Relations Commission. She seems to think she's talking with a reactionary and rabidly Orange headmaster, for he says, laughing, "Oh, we're not like that—we're just trying to get them to grow up not throwing stones at little Catholics, washing their feet, and not thinking sex is dirty. Drop in sometime—there's always a kettle on the boil."

The kettle is boiling, and Mrs. Wallace makes instant coffee, adding a cup for the major in command of the paratroopers, who drops in looking bleary—he has been on duty all night.

Mrs. Elliott brings in a little girl from the reception class, Patricia Faulkner, who is five and a half years old. A plump, round-faced child dressed in a grey long-sleeved sweater, a grey pleated skirt, a shirt, and a wool tie. Visibly the child of someone who means her to be a schoolgirl. "Patricia has written out something lovely," says Mrs. Elliott, holding Patricia's hand. Russell takes a pale-blue exercise book with wide-ruled lines and reads aloud some of Patricia's lines:

> "Here they are in sun
> At the top of the hill
> Mummy Daddy and
> the children all like the sun.
> they stop now to look
> down the hill. They can see
> the farm and a man with some
> Cows   the cows are going to
> the station   look   says Jane
> I can see the sun on
> the sea."

Patricia's teacher, Mrs. Girvan, had stuck a big red star underneath. Russell finds some change in his jacket pocket, and gives it to Patricia for a reward. Asked what she is going to buy with it, Patricia says, "A chocolate biscuit."

SOME BELFAST SCHOOLS have been used as arms dumps, unbeknown to their staff. The Irish Republican Army has used some Catholic children to carry bombs and ammunition. One five-year-old at another school recently brought her teacher a bag full of detonators and gelignite. "Thank God," says Russell, "we haven't had that." However, a five-pound bomb was found outside his office during the Easter holidays a year ago. And for several weeks in 1971 the school was under siege by a rioting crowd from the Bone; there was a constant bombardment with bricks and stones, and the factory across the road was set on fire. Bursts of rifle fire now and then hit the old school building, and most of the windows of the classrooms in the senior corridor were smashed. This was before the army moved in; for a fortnight troops sent up to protect Finiston school slept under their Saracens in the Oldpark Road. Since then a thirty-foot-high sheet-steel-and-wire-mesh fence has been built alongside the senior playground, and windows are less frequently smashed. The school has been evacuated a dozen times because of bomb scares and excessive shooting. On these occasions, as when the rocket hit, there has been no alarm. Russell has sent word down one corridor and taken it himself down the other for everyone to get to the infants' playground, behind the school. "No panic, just an orderly retreat." But he's of two minds as to whether forming up in the playground (at which no shots have been directed, so far) is safer than staying in the classrooms. Sometimes when firing is heard and a boy says, "Miss, are we going to get shot?" he's told, "You'll get shot if you don't get on with your spelling." And they stay put.

A COMPANY consists of one major, two captains, three lieutenants, one company sergeant-major, and a hundred and thirty other ranks. At the moment they are halfway through their four-month tour of duty in Northern Ireland. They have had one man shot in the stomach while patrolling the Oldpark Road, and they don't mean to lose another if they can help it. That means not relaxing for a moment, not letting your hair down, staying on the *qui vive*. On a sunny day, it's easy for even a soldier to be lulled into a feeling that all's right with the world. Then a sniper shot cracks out. So the paras, who strike Russell as super-efficient, even a little chilly in their professionalism, have their reasons for wearing black cork on their

faces for patrols, and draping barbed wire on the hoods of their
Land-Rovers. In the last year, their battalion has rounded up
the leading officers of the local IRA company. This morning,
as Russell came through the school gate, the young para on
guard reported with pride that the night before they'd uncov-
ered 13,000 rounds and sundry weapons in a search operation
in Wilton Street, off the Shankill Road. Several members of an
extremist Protestant group had been arrested.

For four months, except for four days' home leave, the
paras are on duty all the time. It is like life on shipboard—
watch on and watch off, seven days a week, twenty-four hours a
day. One platoon mans the observation posts overlooking
streets and intersections in the area—two square miles—that the
company is responsible for. A second platoon patrols, partly in
Land-Rovers but mostly on foot, searching cars, checking anything that arouses suspicion. The third platoon guards the base.
No going out to the pubs or taking girls to the pictures. The
British Army's role is to assist the Royal Ulster Constabulary to
maintain law and order in a time of extraordinary strife. This
means an attempt at complete impartiality, going after both
sides' bombers and gunmen, protection racketeers and assassins.
It means a stress on impersonality, partly for their own protection, partly to underline the fact that they are here as an
arm of British law, trying to stamp out violence and reestablish
peaceful conditions in which perhaps the people of Northern
Ireland can work out their future. The difficulty of their task is
expressed in the military maps of the city, where the Catholic
streets are shaded in lime-green and the streets of Protestants
in an orangy-beige.

Soldiers are now in parts of two Belfast primary schools
besides Finiston. Schools have the advantages of being mostly
empty during weekends and holidays, and they possess facili-
ties—showers, kitchens, parking lots, and recreation areas—that
a large body of men requires. Schools tend to be situated at
focal points in a community. In Belfast, moreover, the school
population has been shrinking (down from roughly 47,000 in
1963 to 42,000 at this point), so the schools have had some

room to spare for the army. In the Oldpark area, the soldiers were first based at St. Colmban's school, on Glenview Street, in the Bone. But once early gratitude for the army's presence died away, there was a greater hostility toward the British soldiers in the Bone than there was in the Protestant streets of the adjoining area. The St. Colmban's staff members say, "The locals felt better about attacking the soldiers up at Finiston than here at their own school." And the paras say they are happy at Finiston. Their company commander spent his last Belfast tour, two years ago, in a bombed-out factory on the Shankill. He and his men now have the use of the older part of the school, and they also use the hall, for gym in after-school hours; the staff room, for Sunday church services, including Mass; and the central courtyard, to train for tug-of-war competitions without being sniped at. One of the best things about being at Finiston, the paras' major feels, is that after patrolling the sullen neighborhood they can come back and hear normal sounds of children—bells ringing, plates clattering at lunch, the noise of play. He says, "It's really a tonic."

Serving in Belfast is a strange job for a soldier. Some of the paras are Ulstermen, some are Catholics, some are blacks. The flow of recruits into the army has dropped off, apparently because of the Northern Ireland situation, but the paras' morale seems high; many of them intend to sign on again, and feel they are accomplishing the most significant military job available at the moment. However, there remains a good deal of puzzlement. The background to the troubles is tortuous enough for historians and political scientists. Anyone taking a really long view, casting a cool, almost anthropological eye on the migrations of Celts, Picts, Irish, Welsh, Scots, Britons, Normans, and English from one side of the Irish Sea to the other, back and forth at numerous times in the last few thousand years, may well wonder what the devil the descendants of the migratory waves are going on about. Faced with football-mob fanaticism, harnessed to bombs and machine guns, it's hard to keep in mind the current miserable conditions of existence that—coupled with several generations of oligarchical misgovernment—give that fanaticism some support.

The paras see their friends wounded or killed, and it isn't war. The enemy is elusive. He is—the soldiers feel—overprotected by the law. They say, "We know where the gunmen are, and if Whitelaw, the Secretary of State for Northern Ireland, cleared out for a few days and let us go to work, we'd clean them up." They feel the resentment on some of the streets; they're never sure who is friend and who is foe. The sight of a paratrooper's red beret makes some Belfast citizens imagine all sorts of brutality, and though the paras are not young thugs, they are young, strong men who now and then get fed up with the hanging around; their feeling that they'd like to have a bash at the bastards who are causing all this becomes overpoweringly strong. It is necessary for them to keep telling themselves —and their officers to keep telling their men—that many people are in fact reassured by their presence, and the presence of other military units, in the streets.

There are sudden flashes of hospitality—cups of tea for a search party, an offer of payment to the army carpenter who comes round to repair a kicked-in door. A woman will pause while hurling bottles and abuse to whisper "We're only doing this because the boys are watching. Don't take it to heart." The paras attempt to steer a middle course while seeking out the murderers who find employment on both sides. They are occasionally rewarded by detecting a wanted man, despite his aliases, or uncovering a cache of arms. They try to do what in normal times a local policeman might do for those who need help—calling an ambulance, writing a letter, helping solve community problems (as they did in pressing for buses to ferry the children to school). They can also perhaps take credit for the fact that it has been quieter on the Oldpark since they've been there.

The soldiers of A Company have done their best to domesticate the old Finiston building. Classrooms serve as dormitories for the three platoons, with double-decker bunks instead of desks, the rooms dark for day-round sleeping instead of sunlit for schoolwork. The tall, clerical Victorian windows are partly blocked with sandbags, and the remaining glass is covered with crisscrossed tape and grey paint. High up in the plaster a bullet hole or two can be seen, where sniper fire has penetrated. Some men are flat out, asleep; others clean their boots or read paperback Westerns. It is a fort. Upstairs, wall and staircase windows are bricked up. The soldiers have used a hundred tons of sand since they arrived, improving the sandbag walls that form staggered, mazelike approaches to ground-floor doors and windows. The downstairs corridors have been partitioned with hardboard to make a company office, quartermaster's stores, and a military-operations room. Ammunition cases serve as shelves and filing cabinets. There are *Penthouse* nudes on one wall, looking prissy, and a photo on the opposite wall of Princess Alexandra, who is patron of the regiment, smiling primly. A WANTED FOR MURDER poster. Jokey notices and photographs with added captions ("Take a shower with your platoon sergeant," says Tired & Lonely).

Officers and men share the same washrooms and eat the same food—better food than they get at home, so some of them say. There is a room full of battered armchairs, a color TV, and a snack bar presided over by two amiable Pakistani caterers; one of them knew the company commander in Cyprus, before the major rose from the ranks. A few bookshelves hold fifty crumpled paperbacks. Two movies are shown every week: this week's are *Ned Kelly* and *Shaft*. The paras no longer have to polish their brass or clean their webbing with Blanco, as British soldiers did until a few years ago. The paras, in fact, darken their badges so they won't reflect the sun. The paras maintain their own equipment and semiautomatic rifles. They check in and out the tools required for a search party—jimmy, pick, shovel, hammer, screwdriver, and wirecutting pliers—from the quartermaster's stores. They wear berets, camouflage parkas, and grey-green flakproof waistcoats, and as they go out to the observation posts, known by the Hindustani word *sangars*, or to patrol the streets of the Oldpark, they say to one another, "Keep your head down."

WHEN THE SOLDIERS first came to Finiston, the children couldn't take their eyes off them. The eleven-year-old girls in P-7 giggled at the sight of all the young men. The boys soon talked familiarly of Saracens, *sangars*, and "aggro." Now, though the children aren't allowed in the old building, the soldiers occasionally drift through the school. Russell found A Company's cook taking P-2 the other day, while Mrs. Emery (who felt ill) had a rest. "He was working on one group with their reading, and had another group practicing their handwriting." The para medical orderly uses Russell's office in the evenings to study for examinations he didn't take in secondary school. The medic bandages children's cuts and hands out medicine to local women. Officers come in to talk to classes about skiing or about their tour in Germany. One Welsh soldier (known as Twenty-six, because he shared the surname Jones with half his company and the last digits of his army serial number were 26) used to draw Batman and Dracula for small boys, and, though he'd often expressed a desire to get out of bloody Ireland and back to Wales as soon as possible, once told a teacher that he would like to send his children to Finiston. The Scots medic in the First Light Infantry spent a lot of time in the hall at dinner teaching one child how to hold a knife and fork. The soldiers make friends with the children easily, perhaps partly because they feel that children aren't yet biased and that they themselves aren't showing bias in being friendly with kids. They know how to joke with children, and quite fondly tease the little girls. They bring in boxes of chocolate biscuits to share around a class. They run football games after school or during holidays, organizing matches between the top of the street and the bottom of the street. One led physical training classes in the hall during his four months. Another hung curtains in the French windows in the hall, and painted its walls.

At midmorning break in the infants' playground, two small boys start a fight. New drainpipes are being laid on loose stones in a ditch along Torrens Avenue, and some of these stones are thrown. A head is cut open. One child is sent off for medical attention. The offenders are chastized and dispatched to the senior playground, with a threat from Russell: "If there's any more of that stuff, I'll send you both to Eton." (The children seem to think that Eton is a junior version of Long Kesh, the local Alcatraz for terrorists.) Some Belfast teachers, including those at St. Colmban's, say in the past couple of years there is a pronounced decline in disciplinary standards. Some secondary schools have a great problem with violence and vandalism, particularly in out-of-school hours. Psychologists are worried about the permanent effect on Belfast children of constant adult violence. Yet one local teacher, G. H. Slevin, has written in the first issue of *Community Forum*, a magazine put out by the Northern Ireland Community Relations Commission, that he is convinced the symptoms of violence "will disappear as quickly as they appeared." He added, "If the violence were to stop, the so-called scars on children's personalities would be shown up as no more significant than those sustained during ordinary play."

Russell says that 99 percent of Finiston pupils behave well at school, 80 percent out of it—those who go home to care and affection. There is the occasional playground fight, but he sees no evidence of viciousness or of increase in fear—no sudden stammering, nail-biting, bed-wetting, or shaking. In Northern Ireland, standards of literacy are generally higher than in Southern Ireland; children are generally more articulate and vocal than in the United States; the number of passes in Ordinary and Advanced level examinations continues to go up, despite the troubles, gradually catching up with the percentage of passes in England and Wales. Russell acknowledges a slight waning in class concentration and scholastic achievement at Finiston in the last few years. With the school day an hour shorter than it was last year, before the buses were laid on, much time has been lost. The brighter children—generally of more ambitious parents—have been taken away to safer areas. But this has left smaller classes, so teachers are able to give more attention to the slower children who remain. Russell believes, moreover, that school is a refuge from the reality of the streets. Some of the boys now and then draw a Saracen or Land-Rover, but the troubles aren't much in evidence in the children's work. Mrs. Elliott says, "In most drawings, it's still Nazi war planes bombing American convoys. Little girls draw little girls skipping between apple trees in front of houses with smoke curling up out of the chimneys." Russell says, "Away from school, the children witness things no child should see, but by some miracle a protective mental shell forms." A good proportion of the children are already at home in the midst of violence, illness, poverty, and cruelty. Many go to bed at eleven, when their fathers come home from the pubs. These children watch late-night thrillers on TV. On the other hand, many of the children have never had so much attention. They are taken on trips and excursions by the army and by teacher-training colleges. English societies invite them over for holidays. Russell and his vice-principal, Hutton, take groups to Liverpool and Edinburgh, though it is sometimes hard to persuade the parents to let their children go. Many parents believe their children are highly strung—"have wee nerves," as they say in Belfast. But Russell finds very few children at Finiston who don't love to sing, act, and recite, who don't want to show you with pride what they've learned or made. "Resilience" is a word quite a few people use in Belfast, and Russell uses it too. "These kids are resilient."

THE IRISH QUESTION: "I'm a British subject, and proud of it," says an education official in Belfast. "But in France, if someone asks me where I come from, I say Ireland. We're all Irish here."

The *Belfast Telegraph* carries the Killarney race results. St. Patrick's Day is a school holiday throughout Northern Ireland. The Irish rugby team has players from both North and South. Russell spends his holidays in Donegal, in the Republic. His daughter is married to a clergyman of the Protestant Church of Ireland and lives in Dublin.

In the middle of Belfast, a prominent sign directs drivers to the motorway with the word DUBLIN.

A good many Northerners feel that Southerners pay lip service to unification but that in fact Southerners are apprehensive that if the border should be removed, Northerners would soon be running the whole country. All that Presbyterian industriousness.

A good many Southerners are hoping for the success of a

plan put forth earlier this year by Conor Cruise O'Brien, the
Irish Minister of Posts and Telegraphs, for the North to watch
Eire television and the South to watch the BBC.

"Ireland's my country," said one Belfast teacher. "And yet
when I go into a hotel in the South and see all those priests
drinking and laughing and acting as if they owned the place,
I have the horrors. Popery! Clerical dominance! It's a real
worry."

A remark attributed to a nineteenth-century British politician:
"Just when you begin to understand the Irish question, the
Irish change the question."

THE CHILDREN ARE coming in from mid-morning break, carrying skipping ropes and plastic footballs back to classroom cupboards. The cupboard doors and classroom walls are covered
with the children's maps, charts, pictures, and graphs. In P-2,
the story of the potato. In P-7, a colorful diagram of columns
climbing up, up, up—1970, 1971, 1972: "Fatalities in N.
Ireland." In P-7, Jeffrey Haddock is sitting at his desk in the
front row looking at a page about "sets" in his math workbook
and thinking about his dog, who died yesterday. In P-3, small
groups are reading out loud, helping one another. In P-6,
there's much activity with Modroc, the up-to-date construction material for model-making that seems to have replaced plaster of Paris and "paper-mash," which is what papier-
mâché is called here. In P-1, there are little satchels on the floor,
potato crisps on the windowsill, a crate of empty milk bottles.
In all the classes, some children are tidily dressed; some wear
things that are too big or too small, wrists and ankles showing;
some are in clothes from corner shops and some are in hand-me-
downs of good quality, which Russell collects from better-off
schools and keeps in a store cupboard, to be handed out
to children who seem to need them. The children do a lot of
work in project books, compiling essays, pictures, maps, and
photographs on subjects that interest them: Florence Nightin-
gale; Finiston School; the shipyards of Belfast. Russell says,
"Many of the children don't know the date of Waterloo, or
even the name of the Prime Minister. But they can tell you

what a medieval Japanese costume looked like, because they've just finished a project on Japan."

There's still an official primary school curriculum: "Religious Education, English, Mathematics, Geography, Nature Study, History, Music, Physical Education, Arts and Crafts, Needlework, and [in a few schools] Irish." In P-7, Hutton has pinned up a traditional-looking timetable allotting various hours to various subjects, but he treats this as a very rough guide. More often than not, one group in his class will be studying sets while another is model-making, another is writing poetry, and another is working on a project connected with a trip to Scotland. Lectures by the teacher and textbooks have been a good deal replaced by "discovery methods"—groups working on joint activities that may bring together in various ways aspects of traditional subjects, with each of the children pursuing his own strongest interests. Russell says, "I haven't completely made up my mind yet about all this. I don't think all the old methods will be thrown away. Some children need strict bounds within which to work. The new methods leave some teachers pretty much at sea. There's a lot of dabbling that goes on under the name of innovation. In one Belfast school, they've taken the doors off all the classrooms."

AT ELEVEN-FIFTEEN, the school assembles in the central hall for an anti-smoking lecture, given for the Belfast Health Department by a genial Seventh-Day Adventist. His visual aids are a cartoon film, featuring the Devil as Old Nick O'Tine, and a ventriloquist's dummy with two jars of nicotine-soaked cotton wool that can be removed from within. Five of the Finiston teachers smoke. Russell has taken it up again after quitting several years ago, but says he's giving up during the next holidays. Some of the questions the children ask the lecturer are:

"How many days does it take to stop smoking?"

"Is cancer worse than any other disease?"

"How long does it take to die of cancer?"

"How do you know if your mother and father are going to die of cancer?"

HEADLINES AND SUBHEADS from the *Belfast Telegraph*, May 17, 1973:

WOMAN HIT IN BELFAST SHOOTING

LETTER BOMB INJURES RESIDENT MAGISTRATE

TRIPLE KILLING—EIRE DRAMA

AIRPORT BOMB CHECK

MURDER BID: OFFICER FOR TRIAL

FATHER AND SON ON GUNS CHARGE

HOAX HALTS TRAFFIC

MAN INTIMIDATED RUC MAN—SENTENCED

RIOTING IN NEW LODGE

MURDER BID: YOUTH CHARGED

"TAKE SOLDIERS HOME" MOTHER SEEKS SUPPORT

"STOP SEARCHES BY TROOPS"—REPUBLICAN PRISONERS

"NO LETUP IN WAR ON TERRORISTS"

"MONEY FROM U.S. GETTING INTO WRONG HANDS."

TWO JAILED FOR FIVE YEARS IN THREAT CASE

TWO WHO FOUND GUN AND KEPT IT JAILED

FOUR GET ONE-YEAR SENTENCE ON GUNS CHARGE

BOYS HAD HOME-MADE GUN

REMAND ON GUNS CHARGE

"SICK" MAN STOPPED TAXI BEFORE MURDER

INQUEST TOLD HOW MAN WAS SHOT IN FRONT OF HIS WIFE

"I WAS ON IRA DEATH LIST"

MAN CLEARED OF BLOWING UP ARMAGH HALL

"IT WOULD BE nice to know why the Ulster schools are still segregated," one army officer said. At the beginning of this term fifteen furious mothers stormed into Russell's office and demanded their children's leaving cards. They understood, mistakenly, that Russell was allowing a large number of Catholic children to attend Finiston school. Russell talked them round. A month or so later, Russell asked another group of mothers what they would think if twenty Catholic children did in fact turn up at Finiston next term. (He can't be sure that they won't, if Catholic families move into some of the empty houses near the school.) The mothers surprised him by saying, "It's the only answer."

In 1830, the Roman Catholic bishop of Kildare said, "I do not know any measures which would prepare the way for a better feeling in Ireland than uniting children at an early age, and bringing them up in the same school." The 1923 Education Act (Northern Ireland) decreed that education was to be the secular responsibility of local school committees; there was to be no religious discrimination. This provision united the various Ulster denominations in opposition to the Act. The March 1973 Constitutional Proposals for Northern Ireland, put forward by the British government and well-received by middle-of-the-road opinion in Ulster, say in regard to education, "If the tragic events of recent times are not to recur, means must be found to create a greater sense of community in the minds of the rising generation. One of the obvious factors in the situation is the high degree of educational segregation. . . . While . . . it is the Roman Catholic church which maintains a separate system, it is by no means to be assumed that, in practice, all Protestant parents would be happy to see a completely integrated school system, involving as it would the teaching of Protestant children by Roman Catholic teachers, some of them members of religious orders."

The gulf is deep, and has some obvious causes. The Catholics for a long time were gerrymandered out of adequate political representation. They have borne the brunt of unemployment. And the Protestants, because they know that the Catholics have indeed had good reason for deep dissatisfaction with the State of Ulster, are terrified of Catholic *cohesion*—the unity established among the Catholics by their church, their schools, and the injustice done to them. The Protestants reply with flagstaffs bearing the Union Jack or the St. Andrew's Cross, Orange parades, and paintings on the gable ends of their houses showing King Billy on his white horse—King William of Orange, who in 1690 led the forces that defeated James II and his Catholic army at the Battle of the Boyne. This gulf has in other ways been deepened and exploited by generations of

Ulster politicians, who have found great personal benefit in maintaining what, to all intents and purposes, has been an intermittent working-class civil war. They have encouraged the belief of Catholics and Protestants that they are fundamentally different from one another. (Catholic children ask their parents, "What does a Protestant look like?" Some Protestants will tell you that Catholics do look different—have "definite racial characteristics, such as smaller eyes.") Both sides take their religion seriously. On either side, many want to believe the worst about one another. Protestants are sure the Catholics have plans to take over certain areas of the city. Catholics believe that the Orange lodges are loaning money to Protestants for house purchases when neither side can get conventional mortgage loans. Protestants say that Catholics get most of the houses on the new public housing estates.

Now and then the gulf has been bridged. In 1932 the Protestant unemployed rioted in support of the Catholic unemployed. In 1969, Prime Minister Terence O'Neill said, "It is frightfully hard to explain to Protestants that if you give Roman Catholics a good job and a good house, they will live like Protestants." No one has tried very hard to make that explanation, however condescending it sounds, until recent years. Now many on the two sides would like to get together, but militants make it dangerously difficult. There is some integration in sports and art —youth orchestras, for instance, have Catholic and Protestant players. And in education, at least at the very top and bottom, one can catch at a few straws of hope. The five new education area boards include representatives of both Protestant and Catholic schools. Of forty play groups so far started in Northern Ireland, two (sponsored by the National Society for the Prevention of Cruelty to Children) are integrated. After that, the educational divide begins, and ends only in university. The Roman Catholics have their own two teacher-training colleges, one for either sex, though their students last January got together with those of the coeducational, nominally nondenominational but actually Protestant Stranmilis College of Education to debate the question of segregated schools. At the moment fewer than 2 percent of Catholic children attend the state schools; the number of Protestant pupils who cross the line into Catholic schools is even smaller. Catholic schools are "maintained" by the state to the extent of receiving their running costs and 80 percent of their capital expenditure from the public purse. Of the 1,500 schools in Ulster, only half a dozen are making significant attempts at integration.

However, circumstances have made for integration in a few cases, as at Vere Foster, a Belfast primary school in the Ballymurphy area, two or three miles from Finiston. There, suddenly, the surrounding streets became Catholic. Once a school with an almost totally Protestant population, Vere Foster now has a majority of Catholic pupils. The teaching staff has been quietly adjusted to suit—which is good for Catholic teachers, who don't usually stand much chance of getting jobs in state schools. (The change at Vere Foster doesn't seem to have impressed the IRA, which recently fired a rocket at an army post in the school.) For the time being, educational authorities don't feel that integrated schools can be forced on Northern Ireland. If they come naturally, fine; otherwise it's best to take advantage of any positive interplay between the two school systems.

Much of the time there are in fact a few Catholic children at Finiston. One Catholic child is there now because his mother is living with a Protestant man in a nearby street. David Russell hopes the child will stay. Last year Finiston had five boys who'd previously been at a Catholic school, but their mother has now moved on, taking them with her. Russell himself is not sure the time is right for any ostentatious attempt at educational bridge-building in the Oldpark area. Though there's no great difference between the people on one side and the people on the other, they believe there is; tension remains strong. Sometimes the children meet on holidays, at sponsored games or parties, but then they go back to school and the iron curtain descends again. They think they have to fight each other. However, as Russell came to the school the other day, he saw three Finiston children waiting at a bus stop on one side of the

Oldpark Road, and three little Catholic children walking past the Catholic church on the other. These children had all been brought together on a Community Relations Commission holiday scheme, but Russell assumed there might well be a confrontation, and stopped just beyond them to watch. One of the three small Catholic boys looked up and down the road to see if anyone he knew was watching, and then called out, "How are you, Bruce?" Bruce called back, "Hello, Seamus!"

FINISTON PARENTS: It's the colorful or desperate minority who attract attention, the women with trim curtains in well-washed front windows who follow Mrs. Warren's Profession; the men who fight and march for the ultraloyalist Ulster Defense Association; mothers who die of malnutrition, leaving the kids to cope with drunken fathers. But the majority, though moderately fond of bingo, booze, and TV, are responsible and law-abiding, and see that the children get to school. Most of the men are employed, holding such jobs as lorry drivers, pipe-fitters, and roofers.

AT TWELVE-TEN, it's time to inspect hands for cleanliness, dispense the dinner tickets, march to the hall. Hutton, the vice-principal, looks in briefly to see that the queue is orderly. He chats with Mrs. Maginnis, one of the ladies dishing out, and learns from her that the mother of a particular child who hasn't come to school today is ill; Mrs. Maginnis knows the neighborhood. The food is cooked and brought in hot from another school whose kitchen isn't, like Finiston's, in army hands. Today it's meat pie, ice-cream scoops of mashed potato, spring greens (generally declined), and gravy. For dessert, jam roly-poly and custard. The children eating lunches they've brought with them sit at some adjacent tables; there are cheese sandwiches and oranges, and lots of packages of potato crisps and cans of soda. Hutton says, "Many mothers spend more on this sort of lunch than they would on school dinners. They're not good economists."

None of the teachers eat school dinner. They eat sandwiches

or drink from thermos flasks of soup in the staff room, above the principal's office. One of the young women teachers generally makes instant coffee or a pot of tea for everyone. The chairs are tatty, the wallpaper was up-to-date in 1935, and the pair of watercolor landscapes over the gas-fire are thoroughly banal, but the atmosphere is merry. Mrs. Elliott discusses tactics for handling the clergyman's visit next week. "We'll take him to your class first, Roberta, so he can see the drawings they've done of birds and butterflies. He'll ask the children, 'Who made the birds and butterflies?' They'll say, 'God did,' and then Clarke Brolly, if I know him, will pipe up with 'Where did He get the butter?'" As she talks there's a dull, back-of-the-ear thud, like a door being slammed against pressure. "That's a bomb," says David Russell, and there's a moment of contemplation—where it went off (probably the Ardoyne), what damage has been done, the mind flicking quickly over shattered glass, shattered limbs—before conversation resumes. A few of the younger women talk about a pair of shoes Eleanor Girvan bought in London; one of the men asks Russell if he's had any news of the stage lighting equipment on order from the Education Authority now for six months. "Not a word," says Russell. "I think they're waiting to see if we sink or swim." He looks particularly buoyant as he speaks.

One thing that Russell is proud of is the way his staff has stood up to the troubles. One woman teacher left a year ago, the stoning, shooting, and bottle-throwing coming on top of great personal troubles—a sick husband, a child injured in a car crash. The other teachers—four men, seven women—are clearly enthusiastic about Finiston and its principal. Russell complains that the teacher's colleges won't send him student teachers, because they think it's too dangerous on the Oldpark. He personally recruited Mrs. Girvan and Donna Curry last year, when they graduated; both of them were in tears when Russell told them that, because of Finiston's shrinking numbers, the Education Authority considered them redundant and they would have to be transferred at the end of the school year. They're both pretty, and the male staff will miss seeing them, though Finiston will still have Isabel Kyle's flaming red hair, Roberta McCallum's lovely complexion, and Betty Emery's miniskirts, which strike David Russell's eye as going about as short as they can go. He says, "My father used to say, 'When you stop noticing that, you might as well pack up and die.' "

All the teachers live in suburbs or safer, middle-class sections of Belfast, and getting to school has been a problem for them. Several, while waiting at bus stops, have had stones and bottles thrown at them; walking up Oldpark Road they've been harassed and abused. Now they drive or get a lift in a colleague's car. But driving isn't always easy. Mrs. Elliott was stuck in a long line of traffic on the way to school the other morning; every car was being searched at an army checkpoint. She had the radio on, and the BBC announcer was warning London drivers about slow conditions on the Kingston bypass. She thought, The Kingston bypass—another world! When Mrs. Girvan was in London, she went into a store on Oxford Street and automatically opened her shopping bag to the view of the first man inside the door; then she realized no one in London was checking to see if there were bombs in bags. "There was a period when we were pretty weary," says Hutton. "Every day you could hear bullets, and there were wee bomb scares. It took an effort to carry on. Now we're used to it, we're cheerful, but I think it has got to us. It seems never-ending. We all suffer from battle fatigue. We don't plan far ahead. We do things at the last minute. And we're a wee bit jumpy." Mrs. Elliott went on holiday to Majorca, and in the hotel there was a loud noise during the night—a door slammed, perhaps—but she was half-way down the hall, heading for the back playground, before she realized where she was. Some teachers have received threatening phone calls.

Yet whereas many schools, such as St. Colmban's, across the way, have had difficulty acquiring and hanging on to their staff, Finiston has not. Its teachers all want to stay. They enjoy the smaller classes. They like the children, deprived and backward though some of them may be. Mrs. Elliott says, "It's something visitors notice, but we now take for granted—this school is full of very pretty children." A hundred and thirty-three are boys, ninety girls—a figure that can be explained by the old belief that more boys are born in times of war or by assuming that more parents of girls move out of the Oldpark.

Russell has left the staff room—his laughter can be heard at the foot of the stairs—and Hutton says, "David keeps this place going. He's built into it a great feeling, which he's got us all to share. I'm convinced the school would have folded without him."

BELFAST WAS ONCE a town of distinguished character. In the eighteenth century it had for a while a reputation for radical, egalitarian thought. Now this city of 395,000 human beings is a place of memorials and landmarks. "That's where McGurk's Bar stood . . ." "That's where the Abercorn Restaurant blast occurred . . ." "Down there is Farringdon Gardens, a whole street of houses burned out . . ." Reminders everywhere of loss, death, mutilation, blindness, pain, individual agony, and family grief, not easily wiped away. With so much flattened, burned out, or in ruins, it is a city perfectly ripe for planners, redevelopment, motorways, ring roads, giant housing projects. Many walls left standing are covered with the graffiti of violence. For new arrivals, it's a shock to halt at a street crossing and stare into the muzzle of a semiautomatic held by a soldier in a Land-Rover waiting for the light to change. Pairs of armed vehicles patrol the streets. Soldiers on foot patrol the sidewalks.

The entry to all the side streets of the city's center is controlled by steel fences topped with barbed wire, with gates through which pedestrians enter for inspection, and turnstiles through which they come out. Wider gates have to be unlocked for those cars that have reason for access; the cars are then thoroughly searched. One effect of this is to produce de facto pedestrian precincts, in which people can walk without fear of traffic. Moreover, in the main downtown streets the parking of unattended cars is everywhere prohibited—because bombs have been left in parked cars. Parking meters have been removed. A few important buildings reinforce the ban with rows of concrete-filled oil drums in the former parking spaces by the curb. Main street traffic flows smoothly. However, in the evening the center streets are almost empty. There is an unnatural lack of population, as if plague were keeping people indoors, and the emptiness makes the few who do have an errand feel edgy and suspect.

As it is, most banks, offices, and shops have had to take off-putting precautions. Their windows are now either filled with toughened, opaque glass or crisscrossed with tape to prevent splinters in a blast. The doors are generally locked ("Please knock and wait") or guarded by men who inspect women's bags and frisk the men. Porters in hotels don't rush to take the suitcase of a stranger until he has identified himself at the desk. People hasten by a car momentarily parked for unloading and give the driver sharp looks. No one delivers consignments quite as fast as salesmen in Belfast.

For all this, trade is picking up again. One student's mother works as a buyer in a Belfast department store, and she is annoyed that she has been taken off commission and put on salary; business has since picked up, and she would be making more money under the other arrangement. Bartenders, salespeople, waitresses, cashiers, and booksellers are immensely helpful and friendly, whether because it's good for business or from genuine pleasure in their job. The camaraderie of the blitz is often real. An old man walking down a nearly deserted side street at 6:30 P.M. nods good evening to a total stranger walking past him, then cocks his head at a sudden sound and says, passing on the news, "*Bullets.*"

AT 1:30 P.M. the mail is brought into Russell's office by a paratrooper. Russell looks through the open window at the sun bouncing off the corrugated steel fence three feet away and says, "It's a gorgeous day." He has just heard on the phone that there will be five unexpected new pupils next year—their mother is moving into an empty house up the street. He has covered Karen Bunting's penguin with vinyl, and is now searching for a suitable edging material. From a transistor radio in the front yard, where a para mechanic is working on a Land-Rover, comes BBC 1 pop music—"Cece-lia, you're breaking my heart . . ." (In spite of all this, Russell often forgets the army is here in his school.) In the mail are a few responses to a survey of the neighborhood he's helping to make in order to find out whether, when the Oldpark settles down, people who have moved out will be willing to move back. One says maybe. One says no. Some families are squatting in empty houses, which the owners refuse to re-let but are willing to sell. Since people can't get mortgages in the Oldpark area, Russell hopes that the Northern Ireland Housing Executive will buy the houses and rent them out. He's working at holding the community together, for he needs the children for the school, and he feels the school can provide social cement. He has persuaded a number of local women to donate their time to the school, helping with meals, serving tea, clearing up, and holding community meetings and group parties at the school in the evenings. But the Oldpark is blacked out around the school at night, and when the senior classes recently put on a play, *The Other Children*, people could be lured to the school for only one evening performance—although, Russell says, the play was good enough to run a week.

Out in the paras' yard now, there is a click of bolts as a patrol comes in and rifle chambers are cleared. The transistor is putting forth the Youngbloods, a song about peace and coming together. A bunch of young paras start kicking a football around; the ball is chased by a small black-and-white mongrel that has adopted them. Russell is on the phone again, sorting out a foul-up in arrangements for buses taking children to a city sports ground; though the Oldpark playing fields are just across Oldpark Road, Finiston children were attacked on them, and the Catholic schools alone now use them.

The attendance officer arrives, breezily asking Russell, "Anything for me to do?"

Russell mentions a family that has been troubling him. "His mother just isn't sending him to school. We've held fire because a youngster broke a bottle over his head, but his mother has gone on exploiting this. They need a scare thrown into them."

Although the attendance officer has the power to bring children to juvenile court or the parents before a magistrate, he does either only as a last resort. He more often acts as a welfare officer, recommending children with problems to the educational psychologists. Last week he took a child to juvenile court, ostensibly for truancy but in fact to get the child away from complete neglect at home—no food, no heat.

"Now, look like a Catholic," says Russell with a laugh as the attendance officer sets off for some calls in Catholic streets. The attendance officer smiles wryly; a Catholic welfare officer was shot dead a few weeks ago while making a call. He says, "I don't feel like dying for school attendance."

THERE ARE TWENTY-SEVEN CHILDREN in P-7, down from thirty-five last year—the smallest class Hutton has ever had. The short school afternoon goes quickly. One boy is working on the class newspaper, writing a report of last week's soccer match between Linfield and Coleraine: ". . . then the Coleraine goalkeeper got edgy." Two boys are using Modroc to make mountains, a watershed, and a reservoir. The father of one of them—the boy who made the Harland and Wolff shipyard model in the corridor outside Russell's office—is a professional model-maker at Harland and Wolff. A boy neatly dressed in blazer and grey flannels is looking at a book about the United States; he has a bad stammer and loves ballroom dancing (he won a junior cha-cha competition last month); his family is emigrating to California in the autumn. The boy sitting next to him is tracing a personnel carrier from an infantry recruiting pamphlet; he means to join the army when he's older. "Too dangerous," says another lad. "No, it isn't," says the would-be soldier. "If you join the Royal Irish Rangers, they send you to Germany."

None of them seem optimistic about the troubles ending; when you're eleven, four years is a good deal of your life. The shooting is a result of "politics," and "it's all stupid." They have various solutions. The boy who wants to join the army says,

"Put a soldier in every house." His neighbor says, "See what they want. They always want something different." The troubles are constantly around them. Sometimes they are playing in the street and a bullet cracks by. They take cover—run behind a wall, or scamper to a nearby door and knock. Most people let them in. Sometimes they get searched by the army. The worst time was when *they* threw bricks and bottles from opposite the school; it went on a week. Now and then there's an adventure for one of them, a trip downtown to sit in Russell's car while he delivers some papers; the car can't be left unattended or the army might force open the doors to look for bombs. One boy woke up the other night to see armed men in his room: paras, who searched the house and took his father away for questioning. But none of them have yet acquired quite the glory of Clarke Brolly, in P-2. Not long ago he got into the Oldpark cinema, which is supposed to be boarded up, and dropped a light bulb out onto the road. It went off with a pop, and the army opened fire. Clarke Brolly yelled out, "Stop! I'm only a little boy."

Hutton encourages singing and poetry; he says, "The boys and girls prefer writing poems to writing prose." Half a dozen of them take turns singing or reading in front of the class. One pale little girl, Phyllis Coates, does all the housework at home; her mother died last year. She has black hair and wears a red dress with a white collar. She recites a poem she has written:

A NIGHT ON THE OLDPARK

Bin lids Clatter! Clatter
Screams and Shouts
People running
Whistle blows
The crack of a gun
The army stop and look for somewhere
Safe to hide
Gates creak   Soldiers run
Men shout evil words.

"Someone's hit," they scream out loud
The dogs bark
Cats meow
Glass tankles on the ground
Oh, what a din.
Women and children run for home
A prowling cat slinks alone on a wall.

IN ELEANOR GIRVAN's P-1 they're getting ready to tidy up for the end of the day. One little girl called Elizabeth Scarborough is sitting with a doll on her lap, and when she's told it's time to pack up, she comes and holds Mrs. Girvan's hand. Clasps it tightly.

"Tell me about your dream again, Patricia," says Mrs. Girvan, who is wearing big round sunglasses. In a low voice Patricia tells about a monster that came to the bedroom and took the wee baby. A rambling, scarcely audible account of her nightmare, in which the teddy bear saves her. "Where's your teddy now?" asks Mrs. Girvan.

"My daddy threw him in the dustbin because he had a rip in his back."

The children have frightening dreams, Mrs. Girvan says. They draw disturbing things now and then, such as blood coming out of the mouth of a baby. Family background is probably more to blame than these particular troubles. Margaret is another child whose mother died last year—malnutrition—and her father is down and out (there's no heat in the house during the winter and the welfare officer is hoping to take her into care). The father of Ian, a small boy in a brown sweater by the blackboard, is presently up on an arms' charge. On her first day at Finiston Mrs. Girvan asked the children what their fathers did. Ian stood up and proudly said, "My father fights the Fenians up the Oldpark Road."

Eleanor Girvan isn't without hope that the troubles will end, but she's afraid that the last few years have reanimated this savage virus the Irish have in their blood; they won't easily get it out. "It was curious being in England on holiday, and no one asking what religion you were. Here it will be fifty years before they have integrated schools. The extremists are alike on both sides, and share a profound ignorance of one another. *Ian*—stop putting that chalk on Mary's neck!"

Mary doesn't seem to mind, but Ian is brought before the class to demonstrate Mrs. Girvan's point that some children know extremist Protestant battle songs at least as well as they know nursery rhymes. He sings "The Sash Thy Father Wore," beginning, "It was old, but it was beautiful . . ."

"It's been marvelous here at Finiston—I'll hate leaving," says Mrs. Girvan. "I went to various schools for interviews, and they had cold atmospheres compared to this. Of course I'm lucky having just eleven in the class. I can let them talk *and* give them some discipline. This is the only place some of them are ever going to get it."

The children line up by the door, bags in hand, satchels over their shoulders. They wait for Mrs. Girvan's word before filing out into the corridor toward the waiting buses. Ian kisses Mrs. Girvan and says, like a lover leaving, "See you tomorrow."

BACK FROM SEEING the children off, Russell sits in his office with Hutton and Mrs. Elliott. They are sharing a package of potato crisps—every schoolchild's favorite snack—while they discuss which songs and hymns will be sung at Friday-morning assembly, and work out how to get two boys home who have stayed after school to practice their cricket in the inner courtyard. The troubles have made it necessary to warn parents several days in advance when children have to stay after school for any reason; if the children usually go home by bus, other arrangements have to be made for the parents to collect them or for the teachers to give them a lift home. The fact that many children don't walk home past shops has been bad for the local sweetshops' business (and perhaps good for the children's teeth). The troubles have restricted the area in which local children can play—they complain that there's barbed wire everywhere in the park by the reservoir. The swimming pool on the Falls Road, a Catholic area, is no longer safe for them to use.

Russell feels changes in himself brought on by the troubles. Not only has he started smoking again but he has got down off the political fence and started working for the new, moderate, nonsectarian Alliance party. However, handing out first-aid leaflets to the staff and pinning up bomb-warning posters along-side road-safety posters, where the children will see them, he occasionally feels less generous about mankind. "People ask me, do I think human beings could behave like this elsewhere—for instance, start shooting one another in Birmingham. My answer is yes, they can. From what I've seen here, I believe that if you scratch any of us you'll find an animal underneath."

He goes to the open office window and yells out, "Hey, Ella! How about some for us?" Ella, a vivacious lady in her forties, is pouring tea and handing out cake to the paras in the yard.

"You look happy," Russell says when she comes into the office and dispenses the tea and cake there.

"Ah," she says, smiling, "it's all those young men, keeping me young." Ella has a son with a Ph.D. in physics, and she helps run the recently started neighborhood social evening, held on Thursday nights at the school.

Hutton has been looking at a framed photograph of Russell handing a silver tray to an army major, and he recalls the cere-mony when the First Light Infantry departed. There was a sherry party in the staff room, and afterward an assembly in the hall, attended by the troops, at which the children sang "Amazing Grace." Some of the teachers were near tears, and some soldiers, too. Then, with several hundred people watching in the street outside, the soldiers formed up in full battle equip-ment, packs and arms, ready to march out. Their major made a brief speech and said that he would like them to remember the two young men they were leaving here, dead. The bugler played the last post. The company's flag was lowered and pre-sented to Russell for the school to keep, and Russell, who is rarely at a loss for words, was for a few moments too moved to speak.

Outside in the paras' yard, two lads from P-7 who live on an adjacent street are helping to fill sandbags. A few paras wan-der through the school, chatting with the cleaning ladies. Rus-sell puts down the phone after a call from a member of the

Primary Principals' Forum, a group he has helped organize to promote interest in primary schools. (In recent years secondary schools have been getting more government money.)

Russell says that most men who are going to get a principal's job have one before they're forty. Several years ago, he had felt that his easygoing attitude toward the teaching of religion and his irregular church attendance had harmed him with the clerical members of the school committees, which pick principals, and he had just about given up hope of such a post; he had begun to study law, with the idea of becoming a barrister. Then, after seven years at Cliftonville primary school, he got this job, at the age of fifty. He earns a modest £3089 a year ("Modest for a golfer like me," he says), but he loves what he is doing, and with his and his wife's salaries combined, the family gets by. His salary worries him less than the disparity between the rewards of his profession and those of other responsible ones. "I have a friend who used to fly a full bomb load over Germany and, like me at the time, thought himself lucky to be getting fifteen shillings and threepence a day. Now he's earning eleven thousand pounds as an airline pilot, and his union wants more."

AT FOUR P.M. most of the school is quiet; the classrooms are empty. The afternoon sun angles down onto the desks, and in the leaning columns of light, bright specks of dust stirred up by the departed cleaners continue to spin. In Russell's office the para medical orderly and the local Community Relations Commission officer, who is a Catholic, are having a discussion that is somewhat at cross-purposes. Russell is wondering if it will turn into an argument.

"You don't realize the pressures these people are under," says Brendan Henry, the Community Relations Commission officer—a big young man with black hair, huge eyebrows, broad, strong features. "Not just ordinary intimidation but environmental intimidation. Those Catholic families who moved into the Ballybone moved from streets that weren't just unsafe— they were unfit to live in. The families were looking for something secure and something simply better than what they had—something no government of Northern Ireland has ever provided or given them a chance of getting."

"I've had three friends killed in the streets of Belfast, and five wounded," says the medical orderly, who has a squirrel-like face and wears glasses. "And all for nothing. No one minds dying for a cause, but there's no cause here."

"The government has never built anything here," says Henry, who taught at St. Colmban's several years ago. "A million-pound sports complex has gone up near Queens University, in South Belfast—not on the Falls or the Shankill. Here, no clinic, no community center. There's one social worker. I'm the only contact most people have with the administration, apart from the dole and the welfare. To most people in the Bone, the army is just another aspect of government power. They don't appreciate the searches, the frisking. And now on top of everything else they're threatened with plans for redevelopment and ring roads. The planners ask *me* what people down here want. I tell them to come and open a local office for a few months and find out—let people have a chance to meet them, tell them."

"You know yourself that 98 percent of the Catholics in the Ardoyne say they want peace," says the medic. "But they go on sheltering these terrorists—Communists, some of them—who want to destroy the country. And then a soldier is shot in the stomach, out in the street, and the women stand there and laugh." He is furious.

"One thing," says Henry, "the troubles have produced working-class people who are doing something for themselves for the first time—like getting into community organizations, starting the Bone Enterprises to make playground equipment and lobster pots. They're not apathetic, the way they used to be. They realize the inequalities. And now with proportional representation, the local elections, and elections for the new Assembly, people can start to concentrate on real problems, like housing, and industrial development, for jobs—not unreal problems like the border."

"It's the level of hate that's surprising," says the medic. "On my last tour here I worked in the hospital, and sometimes you'd get people refusing to lend a hand when a blown-up person was brought in and he wasn't the same religion they were."

"Oh, people have sunk low here," says Henry. "That's a basic fact you have to face."

For the last few minutes, Russell has been loudly turning the key in his desk drawer, conspicuously locking up for the night. This moment of semi-agreement seems to him a good moment to break into the conversation—which, in one form or other, he has heard before. He knows both sides, understands the frustrations of both sides, and knows that a willingness to listen is a way of keeping the peace. He says, "Brendan, it only took two or three particular families to move out of our streets for it to be quiet. It's pretty happy right now. How many would it take to move out of the Ballybone?"

"Oh, the same—two or three. A hard core. The rest follow the leaders."

Russell stands up. He puts the penguin sampler made by Karen Bunting on the mantelpiece. During this discussion he has framed it with blue masking tape. He drives home to have tea before going out to spend the evening canvassing for the Alliance party.

IN THE BONE, some of the houses are sixteen bricks wide. Unemployment has been as high as 40 percent. The average family has six children. On winter afternoons, when it gets dark early, there is a terrible feeling of being shut in, of hopelessness. It was a phrase in history books—"the Irish poor." They still exist. But perhaps the vicious circle in which they play a crucial part, providing momentum for cause and effect, cause and effect, can be broken up into segments, each to be tackled with goodwill, cheerfulness, and, God, what patience. Russell hopes so.

ON FRIDAY MORNING the whole of Finiston school assembles in the hall. The children march in to the African hymn "Kumbaya." Russell stands on the stage with a local minister, who leads the prayers. Mrs. Emery plays the piano to accompany the children and the staff as they sing "The Old Rugged Cross" and "Lord of the Dance." Two girls from P-6 come to the front to sing a song from *Fiddler on the Roof*, "Sunrise, Sunset." In this, there is an allusion to a betrothal, which leads Russell to tell about a Jewish wedding he went to in Montreal when he was living in Canada. At the end of the wedding, the bride and groom smashed their wineglasses. He asks the school, since he has often wondered about it, if anyone knows why they did this. No one does. But the unanswered question and the suggestion of smashing things leads him naturally to something else he wants to mention. Yesterday two boys in the infants' playground were throwing rocks and stones. One boy had to have a cut stitched up. "Now," says Russell, "is rock-throwing allowed at Finiston School?"

There is a loud chorus: "No, Mr. Russell."

"Is there going to be any more rock-throwing at Finiston?"

Louder still: "No, Mr. Russell."

They sing the old round "One man went to mow, went to mow a meadow" as, under Russell's eye, they leave the hall, a class at a time, each accompanied by its teacher. And when the sound of singing is dispersed throughout the school, and the last child has left the hall, Russell jumps down from the stage and goes out, singing too.

Chapter Two

THE HOUSE OF
THE CHIEF

– 1974 –

PAINTERS WERE at work in the downstairs room Mrs. de Valéra used to call *Grianan*, Gaelic for "the place of sunlight." The late-autumn sun fell over Phoenix Park and through the windows of the Great Reception Room onto the immense orange, white, and green carpet woven—with the design of a phoenix at the center—by forty women in a Donegal fishing village. "Phoenix," here, is the result of an Anglicization that has stuck, arising in the first place not from the mythical bird but from the sound of the Gaelic words *fionn uisce*, meaning "clear water," for a spring there. The lake in the grounds of the house is fed by four such springs, and Phoenix therefore became the name of the house that stood here in the mid-seventeenth century, when Henry Cromwell, the Lord Protector's fourth son, lived in it as lord deputy and governor general. The name carried over to the royal park created in the 1660s on the restoration of King Charles II—a park then, as now, verdant, well stocked with deer and pheasant, a great green slice out of

Dublin. Above the carpet, sunlight ricocheted off the Waterford-glass chandeliers, flecking an allegorical plaster-work on the ceiling that shows Time rescuing Truth from the assaults of Discord and Envy and a plaster bas-relief over the mantelpiece of Marcus Curtius on horseback about to plunge into the abyss for the salvation of Rome.

In the official anteroom the sun lit the objects resting on a small table between the windows: a tiny orange, white, and green flag taken to the moon and back by a U.S. rocket crew, and, encased in plastic, a fragment of lunar rock from the Taurus Littrow canyon, closely resembling a piece of aerated fudge. In the outer, formal study, twin shafts of sunlight fell on a floor-to-ceiling bookcase behind the President's desk, spot-lighting Volumes VIII and IX of the *Catholic Encyclopedia*, and *The Great Hunger*, by Cecil Woodham-Smith. In the inner, working study, the sun bathed a desk where Erskine Hamilton Childers, the fourth President of Ireland, sat making notes for a speech for the opening of the Navan Road Sports Center. Through the window could be seen a stretch of lawn; a section of white balustrade, with a gap where some steps led down to a lower lawn; a policeman's head; cars passing on the road through Phoenix Park to Castleknock and Blanchardstown; and the escarpment of the Dublin hills. A gong rang—with Oriental, imperial, country-house reverberations—for lunch. The President, a short, handsome man of sixty-seven, with a high, professorial forehead accentuated by brushed-back grey hair, stood up.

SOME ENGLISH VICEROYS are said to have liked the house because it reminded them of distant colonial posts. Some architectural historians are put in mind of the White House in Washington, but there is probably no connection other than the fact that James Hoban, the White House architect, was Irish-born. Concealed now in the wide-spreading, formally proportioned, light-painted stucco Georgian mansion is the mid-eighteenth-century Ranger's House, built for the Right Honorable Nathaniel Clements. By the end of the eighteenth century, when the British government tried to present it to the patriot Henry Grattan, it was in such bad repair he refused to accept it. In 1815, Francis Johnston, an architect, improved it, adding the wings and refronting the south portico. One viceroy during the nineteenth century was the Duke of Marlborough, whose son Lord Randolph Churchill had offended the Prince of Wales and therefore had to forgo London society for a time and bring his family to Dublin. Thus, between the ages of one and four, Winston Churchill lived in a small lodge on the vice-regal grounds. The nearly three years in Ireland seemed to convince both Lord Randolph and his son that they understood "the Irish question," on which they both thereafter made bold, not always well considered pronouncements. In 1882, the next viceroy, Earl Spencer, saw some men apparently wrestling in the grounds; what he in fact saw was Lord Frederick Cavendish and Mr. Thomas Burke—respectively Chief Secretary and Undersecretary for Ireland—being assassinated by a patriotic group of Fenians called the Irish Invincibles. (In London, some years later, young Churchill reflected how fortunate it was the Fenians hadn't got him when, two years before, he had fallen off his donkey in Phoenix Park.) In 1911 a new domestic wing, in Queen Anne style, was built for the state visit of King George V, and it is in the less grandiose private rooms of this that the Presidents of Ireland and their families have lived since the withdrawal of the last representative of the British Crown. The vice-regal lodge has been renamed *Arus an Uachtaráin*, Gaelic for "the House of the Chief." The chiefs to date have been Dr. Douglas Hyde, Seán T. O'Kelly, Éamon de Valéra, and President Childers. Also in the grounds of Phoenix Park are the papal nunciature, the Dublin Zoo, the residence of the U.S. ambassador, and a race course.

UNTIL HE WAS ELECTED President in May 1973, Mr. Childers was *Tanaiste*, or Deputy Prime Minister, and he, his wife Rita, and youngest daughter Nessa lived in a comfortable, by no means fancy, semi-detached red-brick house on Highfield Road, south Dublin. His telephone number at that address is still in the

Dublin area section of the current Irish telephone directory—the
only Childers—sandwiched between the Child Study Centre and
Childminders. There are almost five pages of Murphys. The
President sometimes dips into a volume called *Genealogies of
the English Kings,* in which the Childerses can trace their
descent from Edward III. Less remote than the Plantagenet
monarch is Leonard Childers of Carr House, near Doncaster,
in Yorkshire, who bought and bred the first great Arab stallion,
the Darley Arabian, which had been brought into England
around 1704. In the outer study there is a small bronze of the
Darley Arabian's son, Flying Childers, winner of the Five Hundred Guineas in 1721. The Darley Arabian was the great-great-
grandsire of Eclipse, from whom have sprung most of the great
racing horses since then.

The Childerses have furnished five members of British or
Irish parliaments. Their ancestor Lord Thomas Erskine served
as Lord Chancellor of England in 1806–07; earlier, in 1792, he
appeared on behalf of Tom Paine, then in trouble for his
pro-revolutionary book *The Rights of Man.* Hugh Childers
founded Melbourne University, was Chancellor of the Ex-
chequer under Gladstone, made the first speech in the Commons in favor of Home Rule for Ireland, and led the campaign
that brought to England the secret ballot. The President's
paternal grandfather was an eminent scholar of Pali and other
Oriental languages, but both he and his Irish wife died in their
thirties. They left, among other children, Robert Erskine
Childers, the President's father.

Though the first Erskine Childers was born and educated in
England, he was brought up by and spent all his holidays with
his mother's family, the Bartons, who lived in a large country
house thirty miles south of Dublin in the Wicklow hills. In
1903, on a trip to Boston with the English artillery company
he had served with during the Boer War, Childers met and
swiftly married a New England woman, Molly Osgood. The
President's mother (who was crippled at an early age, and spent
a good deal of her life bedridden) brought into the Childers
family a notable inheritance of her own. Through the Osgoods,

the President is descended from John Alden, cooper of the *Mayflower*, and from John Adams, second President of the United States. Molly Osgood's father, the Boston physician Dr. Hamilton Osgood, first introduced Pasteur's rabies serum to America. (The Cunard Line put Dr. Osgood's rabbits in a first-class cabin by themselves.) The Osgoods gave Erskine and Molly Childers a fifty-foot Norwegian ketch, the *Asgard*, as a wedding present. It was in *Asgard* that the Childerses, in 1914, ran a cargo of rifles and ammunition from the North Sea for the use of Irish insurgents; quite possibly some of those rifles were used when, eight years later, during the civil war that followed the treaty between British and Irish representatives setting up the Irish Free State, Robert Erskine Childers, the President's father, after the verdict of an Irish military court, was taken into the courtyard of Beggar's Bush barracks, in Dublin, and shot.

OUTSIDE IRELAND the name Erskine Childers means most to those who sail small yachts, are knowledgeable in the literature of the sea, or are addicted to thrillers written around the turn of the last century, in what is sometimes called the heyday of Edwardian optimism. But probably few of those who react enthusiastically to the words *The Riddle of the Sands* are aware of the fact that the author of that book was an English-public-school-educated civil servant who became an Irish revolutionary, and that his son is now the President of Ireland. Because he has the same name as his father, the President is often taken for the author of *The Riddle of the Sands*. In 1972 the *Providence Journal* ran an article about the father illustrated with a photograph of the son. Unlike the father, the son has never taken up sailing; he is an energetic gardener and mountain walker. But he keeps, on bookshelves in the working study, among the other books his father wrote, half a dozen of the various editions that *The Riddle of the Sands* has gone into since it was published, in 1903, by Smith, Elder—his prized copy being a battered first edition, spine broken, binding torn, stuffed with clippings and letters.

The Riddle of the Sands has been issued in Nelson's Six-penny Library; as a Collins Classic; by Penguin and Signet; in Rupert Hart-Davis's Mariners' Library; by Sidgwick and Jackson in London; by Dodd, Mead, and Dutton in New York; and in a deluxe illustrated edition by the Imprint Society in Barre, Massachusetts. It is the sort of book that gives those who come across it the cozy and exciting feeling of becoming the member of a special group. Those who make a practice of reading it regularly, perhaps once a year, like to compare their favorite passages and show off their knowledge of the book by asking one another obscure questions: "What cargo was Bartels' barge carrying?" or "What was the name of the ship's carpenter who repaired the rudder of the *Dulcibella* at Flensburg?" Small-boat sailors tend to say that it is the best book to do with small-boat sailing that has ever been written. Even those who know little about sailing find that they are dragged into the book willy-nilly along with the narrator, Carruthers, who to begin with doesn't know much about it, either. But it is also simply a very fine thriller, which had contemporary writers like John Buchan greatly praising it.

Carruthers joins his friend Davies aboard a small converted lifeboat on what he thinks will be a late-season yachting holiday, but turns out to be an uncomfortable voyage of discovery along the North Sea coast of Germany, ferreting out the channels and creeks behind the East Frisian Islands and falling upon what they eventually realize are German preparations to invade England. There is much rowing with muffled oars on compass courses through thick fog. There is a girl with slim brown wrists—the daughter of an English traitor.

When the book appeared, it not only excited readers but also—Childers's intention—aroused the British Admiralty to examine its coastal defenses and muster craft suitable for use in the narrow seas. For that matter, spurred by the book, several British officers made unofficial coastal reconnaissances of their own and ran into trouble with the German authorities. And apart from the book's message, its novel detail, and its power as a yarn, its attraction resides in a transparently genuine, romantic patriotism. Carruthers refers to the *Dulcibella* at one point as "that frail atom of English soil, their first guerdon of home and safety." The book marked the high-water of its author's pride and belief in England, the sort of rapture which—though not exactly careless—is full of buoyant concern. His later passion involved much graver stuff.

President Childers first read *The Riddle of the Sands* when he was ten. In recent years he has found that the book is a splendid icebreaker—people talk to him about it, how they first read it, and how many people they've told about it, and in the process reveal far more of their own personalities than they would in normally constrained conversation. For a long time film producers came nearly once a year to discuss making a movie of the book [a project finally accomplished, with qualified success, in 1978]. The BBC has done it as an afternoon radio serial. The President thinks of the book as a talisman, for it has brought him into contact with people he wouldn't otherwise have known, and has opened doors for him. In the early 1930s when he was advertising manager of Mr. de Valéra's new newspaper, the *Irish Press*, and was struggling to sell advertising space, he asked for an appointment with the world sales manager of the Dunlop Rubber Company, Sir George Harrod. Sir George agreed to see him. He shook hands with the young salesman, perched himself on the edge of his desk, and began to recite word for word a chapter of *The Riddle of the Sands*. Naturally, after that, he bought space.

TO THE SPRING-FED LAKE in the grounds of Arus come flocks of wild ducks. At the same time every day, four swans parade across the grass to the guard's lodge and peck at the door until the guard comes out to feed them. There are deer in the park, many rabbits and squirrels to be seen, and foxes, more furtive, who have been killing the geese in the zoo and adding insult to injury by eating them outside the keeper's office. These animals so far have managed to coexist with the President's young dogs, whom he takes for early-morning walks—Cashel, a standard poodle, and Daragh, an Irish wolfhound named after an early Irish king. According to the President, Irish wolfhounds have been a traditional Irish export; one appears on the frieze of the Acropolis, and Roman legionnaires coveted them.

Some afternoons the President rows out to the island in the lake. There, in a tradition formed by such political leaders and fellers of trees as Washington and Gladstone, he tackles the thick underbrush and tree overgrowth, clearing the ground for new planting. As Minister of Lands, Forestry and Fisheries from 1957 to 1959, he encouraged new plantations and forestry parks on the largely denuded Irish hills. Trails have been created in new and old forests. He and his wife Rita often don boots, oilskins, and backpacks and take weekend-long hikes. He has climbed every mountain in Ireland, and many in Europe, but his favorite climb remains the ascent of the Scagh, a hill behind Glendalough House, on the Barton estate at Annamoe, where like his father he spent childhood holidays, where he goes now on many weekends and holidays, and where one day he hopes to retire. (His younger brother Robert, recently retired from the newspaper business in Britain, is living there now, helping their father's cousin Robert Barton, who is ninety-three, run the estate farm.)

The President also takes pride in less utilitarian cultivation, such as the ornamental Victorian water garden at Glendalough House, and the fine formal garden of Arus. In the Arus garden a long, graveled walk known as the Queen's Walk is lined by two rows of trees, the first having been planted during a visit of Queen Victoria. Since then a tree—generally a maple, an oak, or beech—has been put in for every head of state or royal person to visit Arus, among them the Duke of Connaught, Edward VII, George V, King Baudouin, and Queen Fabiola. Mrs. Childers recently took along the Queen's Walk a party of children from Belfast, both Catholic and Protestant, and explained its history to them. One small Protestant boy wanted to know where was the tree they had planted for King Billy— that is, William of Orange, whose forces defeated the Catholic army of James II at the Boyne in 1690. The President's knowledge of the history of Ireland and his unceasing reflections on his father's role in helping to create the Irish republic are sometimes joined by a sense of wonder at his own position as First Citizen. Some evenings he and his wife stroll along the Queen's Walk and along the terrace on the south side of Arus, the lawn rolling away to their left and, on their right, the tall windows of the grand downstairs rooms lit from within, and they pause, and he asks himself with some amazement, "Are we really living here?"

FOR A WHILE he was reluctant to become a candidate for the Presidency. Despite the honor and the privileges attached, the post is hedged about with limitations. Mr. de Valéra introduced the present Irish constitution in 1937, becoming Prime Minister after its enactment, and he didn't want his office to be overshadowed by that of President. The Irish Presidency is roughly equivalent to the Crown in a constitutional monarchy, possessing little power of initiative. In normal times, the President's job is to follow the advice of the Prime Minister and the Dáil, or Parliament, in appointing ministers; to sign bills into law; to grant commissions to officers in the armed forces; and to receive the credentials of foreign ambassadors. In an emergency, if parlimentary government breaks down, he has the important job of holding the state together. During his seven-year term of office, he may not leave the country without the government's permission. He is allowed to run for a second term but no more. He may be impeached for "stated misbehaviour." Although in theory any citizen of Ireland over the age of thirty-five is eligible for the post, a candidate requires nomination either by twenty Dáil deputies or by four county councils, and this in fact restricts the job to practicing politicians.

In the last Irish government, headed by Jack Lynch, Childers was Minister of Health and Deputy Prime Minister. He had a reputation as a stalwart member of his party, Fianna Fáil (a poetic Gaelic name meaning "the Soldiers of Destiny"), and had served in the Dáil longer than all but two other deputies. He also had the distinction of being the only Protestant on the Fianna Fáil front benches. However, Fianna Fáil lost the 1973 general election, and it was clear that the coalition of the Fine Gael and Labour parties, headed by Liam Cosgrave, would be in power for some time—some observers thought for at least two terms. Thus, although he regretted the unfinished business he left at the Ministry of Health, Mr. Childers took into account the fact that he was then sixty-seven. Perhaps it was time to make room on the Opposition front benches for a younger man. Furthermore, Mr. de Valéra's second term as President was up. So Childers agreed to run for President.

His opponent, Thomas O'Higgins, had run Mr. de Valéra a close race for the Presidency in 1966, and was the candidate of the coalition parties in power; he started as the favorite. Mr. Childers had an English education and a gentlemanly English accent; he didn't speak Irish or have, as do many Irishmen in public life, a Gaelic spelling for his name. For all that, he came across very well on television. Some voters who had never supported a Fianna Fáil candidate before were impressed by the patient, cultured voice, the suggestion that here was someone who wouldn't easily fly off the handle. Perhaps the man wasn't very Irish, but—just now—was that a bad thing? Childers wasn't afraid to say publicly that he was against violence as an answer to political problems; he spoke for peace and conciliation. And—to the surprise of many used to the retiring nature of former, venerable Presidents and familiar with the limitations imposed on the post by the constitution, all of which had given the job a predictable tone—he spoke about expanding the dimensions and character of the Presidency, giving it a more active, thought-provoking place in Irish life. In any event, together with the votes of Fianna Fáil diehards, he collected those of many women impressed by what he had accomplished as Minister of Health. Perhaps, being a Protestant, he was thought to be a good person to deal with the fearful Northerners, giving them the feeling that the South wasn't altogether the Catholic church–dominated state it is sometimes made out to be. Perhaps, having put one party in power, the Irish electorate showed a sophisticated desire to redress the balance a little by giving the other party the Presidency. And perhaps, for some, there was the magic of the name, his father's name. For Mr. Childers won the contest, 635,867 to 587,771—a margin of 48,096 votes. He was inaugurated as President in St. Patrick's Hall, Dublin, on June 25, 1973. As it happened, this was his father's birthday.

THREE PHOTOGRAPHS of the President's father hang in Arus an Uachtaráin. In the upstairs drawing room of the private wing a fuzzy, enlarged snapshot from just before the First World War shows him between his two sons, smiling happily, the three sitting in deck chairs on the shingle of a Sussex beach. In the same room, another photograph of about the same period shows him alone, smiling faintly, wearing the high, stiff collar of the time and a jacket whose collar is cut very distant from the neck. In the President's working study, a similar photograph of somewhat later date has him with no smile at all. Apart from the suit, collar, and tie, the straight, neatly parted Anglo-Saxon hair, you might see in it the face of an American Indian brave: strong nose, dark eyes, hollowed cheeks under high cheekbones, ears that stuck out, downturned lips— the face of a man who could bear torture.

There are glimpses to be had of the youth who became that man, trained to the high, abnegatory standards of late-nineteenth-century British government. At boarding school and college, despite a slight limp, he was an eager outdoorsman, rower, sailor, and climber. Bertrand Russell and Edward Marsh, later Winston Churchill's private secretary, were with him on a college-vacation reading party in Wales, and Marsh wrote, not altogether contentedly: "Childers has turned us all into fishermen." Together with a fierce devotion to any subject that interested him went a pedantic streak; Childers's long-windedness lost him one college-debating-society election ("The intolerable gas of Mr. Childers" was how his opponents put it). While up at Trinity College, Cambridge, he took debating positions against trade unions, against luxury in modern society, and against Home Rule for Ireland. Although he went back to Glendalough House for most vacations, sailed in Arklow Bay, and walked in the Wicklow hills, his political views were largely imperialist. In 1893 he spoke twice in one week against Home Rule. Self-government within the Empire was all very well for Australia and Canada, he felt, but "the case of Ireland was exceptional because of its proximity, and the national aspirations of that country were incompatible with our own safety." (Gladstone's Irish Home Rule bill of that year passed the Commons but was overwhelmingly defeated by the Lords—which, until the Parliament Act of 1911, had the power to thwart legislation.)

From college, Childers went to a post of high prestige in the British civil service. His colleagues on the official staff of the House of Commons admired his absorption in his work, though they noted a complementary absent-mindedness. During the long parliamentary vacations of that period he made arduous voyages in small boats like the *Dulcibella*. Then, in 1899, he volunteered for the Boer War. He enjoyed a job that few others could stomach—looking after the horses of his artillery troop on the ship which, rolling and pitching, took them to South Africa. Gung-ho, he was afraid that he wouldn't get to the front before the war ended.

And then came a change. Perhaps the war itself brought it about, for, as he noted in his book *In the Ranks of the C.I.V.*, published in 1900, it was "a liberal education. . . . to have lived with and for two horses day and night for eight months!" He appreciated the courage of the Boers and the cleverness of their tactics; he wrote a letter to the *Times* of London commenting respectfully on the strategy of the Boer general, Christiaan de Wet, and he was later commissioned to write the volume of the *Times History of the War in South Africa* that was particularly concerned with guerrilla activities. Another influence for change was his marriage. Molly Osgood was a tiny, auburn-haired, strong-willed woman, at that point able to walk slightly as the result of an operation. He married her in Boston, within five months of meeting her. And though he remained after the success of *The Riddle of the Sands* a committee clerk of the House of Commons, set up house with his wife in London, and joined a club (he was put up for the Reform Club by his friend William le Fanu and his fellow writer Arthur Conan Doyle), the liberalizing process continued. While writing of warfare, he made time to read scores of books on Irish history. In 1908 he toured western Ireland with his cousin Robert Barton, who had cast off his own Unionist, landowning, ascendancy ties to join Sinn Féin, a separatist organization dedicated to the cause of Irish independence. Although the mid-nineteenth-century horrors—insecurity of tenure, the great potato famine, the misery of starvation and emigration—had been greatly alleviated through land reform, religious emancipation, and the extension of the franchise, the Irish desire for Home Rule had not, as British Conservative ministries had hoped, "been killed with kindness." Tardy reform merely encouraged belief in ultimate reform, and—among some—in revolution.

Erskine Childers came back from that trip a convert to Home Rule, and though he now had two sons and could have made a prosperous career as a novelist, he chose instead the cause of converting others to his new way of thinking about the government of Ireland. In 1910 he resigned from the staff of the House of Commons. His book *The Framework of Home Rule* was published in 1911; in it he made a long, powerfully argued plea for dominion status for Ireland. He did not advocate complete separation, which Sinn Féin intended, and which, he said, "Ireland does not want." But he noted that "if another Home Rule bill were to fail, Sinn Féin would undoubtedly redouble its strength," and he gave his services to a special Commons committee set up to draft amendments to the new bill. In fact, by 1914 Home Rule was at last in the offing, but so was world war, and the Protestant majority in Ulster were taking advantage of England's predicament by arming volunteers to make plain their refusal to be "handed over" to the South.

Backed by liberal English and Anglo-Irish friends, and with his wife among the crew, Childers sailed the *Asgard* to the Bel-

gian coast to pick up rifles and ammunition for the Southern
Irish Volunteers. On the voyage back to Ireland there were exciting moments. They sailed through the British fleet, ready for
war, being reviewed at Spithead by the King; they were hit by
severe gales in the Irish Sea, and when some tackle carried away
aloft, Childers—though the eldest aboard—went up the mast
to lash it down. But on the appointed morning (forty-eight
hours before Austria delivered its ultimatum to Serbia), with
Molly Childers at the helm, they sailed into the small harbor
of Howth, just north of Dublin.

The immediate repercussions of this voyage—the arming of a
thousand Irishmen; British troops sent to seize the arms, of
which they captured only nineteen; and shooting in Bachelor's
Walk, Dublin, when the troops were jeered and stoned on
their way back into the city and three onlookers were killed—
were overshadowed by the outbreak of war in Europe. Childers immediately joined up. For though the implementation of
Home Rule was postponed because of the war, he believed
that England's fight to defend Belgium and the rights of other
small nations could only be to the advantage of Ireland. He
was then forty-four, and despite the fact that he had never
flown or taken a photograph before, he was soon aloft on
aerial intelligence missions for the Royal Naval Air Service.
He took part in the first Naval Air Service air raid, on Cux-
haven, in 1914. For a while he flew Sopwith seaplanes off a
converted Isle of Man pleasure steamer, photographing Turkish
fortifications in Palestine. For a year he was navigating and
intelligence officer for a squadron of fast forty-foot motorboats,
carrying one torpedo each, reconnoitering the Belgian coast. At
the war's end he held the rank of major in the RAF, had won
the Distinguished Service Cross, and had twice been mentioned
in dispatches.

To those who had known him well before the war, Childers
after it seemed a different man. While he was flying low over
Turkish fortifications and patrolling the coast of Flanders, the
Howth rifles had been put to use. The Easter Rising of 1916
had taken place, the blood sacrifice that Padhraic Pearse, the

poet and nationalist, had thought necessary to remind the Irish of their nationhood and right to independence. "Life springs from death," Pearse had said. He and fifteen others were executed, and a new generation of young Irish patriots—including a tall, ascetic, New York-born, half-Spanish mathematics teacher, Éamon de Valéra, who had fought in and survived the Rising—was brought to the fore. Childers was Secretary to the Irish Convention of 1917, set up by Prime Minister Lloyd George to work on an improved Home Rule scheme, and he was disappointed by its failure. The war itself, an immense slaughter for the sake of freedoms and security that proved so ephemeral, gave him no long-lived sense of victory. Demobilized in 1919, he moved with his wife and sons to Dublin. There he offered his services to Michael Collins and Arthur Griffith, two of the leaders of Sinn Féin, which had won a considerable victory in the general election of December 1918 (many of its candidates were in British prisons, which helped), had then refused to send any members to Parliament in Westminster, and had set up its own assembly, the Dáil, and its own government. Childers went as part of the Irish delegation to the Paris peace conference—a delegation that was given neither official standing nor any satisfaction. In the summer of 1919, the militants of Sinn Féin began to take violent action against British rule. There commenced the period of ambush and reprisal, assassination, arrest, imprisonment, terror and counterterror, execution and outrage, known as the Troubles.

The third photograph of the President's father—the one in which he is not smiling—dates from this time.

ON A SIDE TABLE in the upstairs drawing room lay two anthologies edited by John Hadfield—A Book of Beauty and A Book of Joy. The President had been reading them with a view to finding some little-known poems to read in public. Although he doesn't write poetry, he accepts with alacrity any invitation to recite it. He spent a recent evening in Dundalk, an industrial town ten miles from the Ulster border, reciting to the Dundalk Literary and Debating Society a number of Irish and

English lyrical poems from the seventeenth to the twentieth centuries. He read poems by Marvell, Herrick, Byron, Keats, and Walter de la Mare. He remembers W. B. Yeats coming to tea one day with his parents and a discussion taking place as to whether poetry should be recited or chanted. Yeats often chanted his own poems. The President sometimes obliges at private dinner parties with a solo of "The West's Awake," but he doesn't sing in public. He has a clear recollection of nights when he was very young and they lived in London: his father standing in the children's darkened bedroom, lit by the glow from a low-burning gas fire, reciting poem after poem to his sons.

Born in London, the President was naturally a British subject, but he grew up believing that he was Irish too. His father's mother, Anna Barton, came from a family that had settled in Ireland in the seventeenth century, and the boy thought that in moving to Ireland his father had been able to adopt the nationality of his Irish forebears. In fact, his father's death had preceded by two weeks the enactment of citizenship provisions of the Constitution of the Irish Free State in 1922, which gave Irish citizenship to those who desired it and qualified for it on that date, and thus to their children. When the President discovered this, he was fighting his first election for the Dáil, and his opponents were claiming that he wasn't Irish. He was quickly naturalized, under a 1935 act allowing citizenship to be speedily conferred for service to the nation, but this has never quite settled the matter. There are people today in Irish politics who will say of the President, with a note of grievance, "He's not an Irishman. He has no connection at all with the Irish people."

Part of the trouble is that he lacks a visibly "Irish" manner. He has none of the spontaneity, the easy wit, the surface charm, and the demonstrative, careless passion. He has instead an old-fashioned courtesy and a cautious, donnish air, of which one element seems to be a mind working constantly and somewhat abstractedly, preoccupied with things above or beyond the matter or person immediately confronting him. He talks familiarly of Norfolk relatives, of Cambridge friends, of holidays on the Wiltshire downs; he and his family can come and go easily across the Irish Sea. Certainly a thoughtful man, "a thorough gentleman," according to many Irishmen. A long remove from savage indignation. The eyes quizzical, the smile a trifle hesitant. Perhaps a slightly rueful look, as of one who knows that to be a diehard is to be more intensely popular—at least with an enthusiastic minority—whereas ecumenical tendencies have always been constrained here. His predecessor as President, de Valéra, was at one point nearly thrown out of the Gaelic Athletic Association (which believed that the only "pure" Celtic sport was Irish football) for attending a Lansdowne Road rugby game. Furthermore, where Mr. de Valéra was born a Catholic and remained a dedicated member of that faith all his life, Mr. Childers is a Protestant. So, of course, were other notable Irishmen: Jonathan Swift, Wolfe Tone, Robert Emmet, Isaac Butt, Charles Stewart Parnell, and Yeats. But that doesn't help with the fiercer Irish-Irish, who see Childers's Protestantism as one more Anglo-Irish or Ascendancy characteristic.

This Anglo-Irish business is a curious thing, interwoven with problems of accent, education, poise, religion, family, and the date and method of original settlement. Some so-called Anglo-Irish families have lived in Ireland for longer than America has been settled by white men. Some Norman, or Anglo-French, families first put down roots there not long after their Viking uncles discovered the North American continent, but they still strike their more Gaelic co-inhabitants in Ireland as un-Irish. Some perhaps cynical historians claim that the friction in Ireland stems from the fact that the indigenous Celts were neither assimilated by new settlers nor—like the North American natives, the Indians—sufficiently destroyed. Some modern Irishmen are hard to tell from their English contemporaries; they may get their accents from Oxford, their clothes from London, their weekly intelligence from *The Economist* or *The Observer*, and yet be Irish at the core; while others, in moist tweeds and with strong brogues, are considered for devious historical or sentimental reasons to be part of the old Ascendancy class. A good deal of Ireland in the east of the country seems almost ordinarily "British": small Morrises or Vauxhalls are parked by semi-detached pebble-dashed houses; the economy and the currency seem a good deal dependent on that of the United Kingdom (interest rates rising and falling together, the coins and notes of the same shape and denomination though of different superficial design); and high rooftop antennas enable householders to enliven their television watching with British programs, such as the nuptials of Princess Anne and Captain Phillips, which emptied the streets of Dublin.

And yet a young man walking in the city streets can meet the eye of a pretty girl, who smiles at him in passing, and meet the eye of the next, equally pretty, who immediately crosses herself. A man in politics is up against similar, but pricklier, contradictions. There is an abrasive them-and-us, tenants-and-landlords situation, not much ameliorated by the fact that those on one side now have the ability to cast off most of their inherited burdens, and those on the other often feel an obligation to pitch in and help their historically oppressed compatriots. A profound distrust remains. An Irish-Irishman feels that an Anglo-Irishman—or "West Briton," as he may be called—just *doesn't understand:* has no real connection with land hunger, potato famine, starvation, disenfranchisement, or (despite Yeats) the collective consciousness of gaiety, beauty, and violent suffering suggested in the words "Holy Ireland." Moreover, despite this aboriginal attachment, many Irish have an inferiority complex vis-à-vis the Anglo-Irish; the Anglo-Irish have the burden of this, of taking it into account, of putting up with it.

In the corridor of Arus running south from the front entrance, linking the state reception rooms, stands a ceremonial green harp in a glass case. The President sometimes wears a lovat green tweed suit, and with it a green tie bearing a small Erin's harp, the national symbol; and, looking up from his desk in the outer study, often glances at a fine crayon portrait of Padhraic Pearse, who believed in the revitalizing influence of the Irish language. But like his father and 70 percent of the Irish people, Mr. Childers does not speak what under the 1937 constitution is called "the first official language" of Ireland. However, he can read it a little, and took the presidential oath in Gaelic. Moreover, he knows Irish history as a scholar of it, and though in some ways he is a moderate Republican—recommending, for instance, Frank Pakenham's *Peace by Ordeal* rather than Dorothy Macardle's more partial *The Irish Republic* as essential for understanding the 1919–22 period—he takes a firm position on a basic Irish question: Did frequent invaders and alien settlement make the Irish the sometimes violent people they are, as the President believes, or did the essentially savage Irish bring out the worst in their conquerors? Even if you feel that it's six of one and half a dozen of the other, there is much evidence that a sea change affected those English who were dispatched to rule the other island. Maurice Craig, in his fine book *Dublin 1660–1860*, recalls "Swift's complaint that the English government always sent us holy and godly men, but by an unfortunate chance they were always waylaid and murdered by bandits on the road to Chester, who took their clothes and letters of appointment and so arrived in Ireland." Swift thought the English should be "ashamed of the reproaches they cast on the ignorances, the dulness and the want of courage, in the Irish natives; those defects, wherever they happen, arising only from the poverty and slavery they suffer from their inhuman neighbours."

AT GRESHAM SCHOOL in Norfolk, Erskine Hamilton Childers, aged fifteen, kept a signed photograph of Éamon de Valéra on his chest of drawers. At home during the school holidays, he found his father and mother entirely taken up with the cause of Irish independence. Arthur Griffith, the head of Sinn Féin, had wanted the elder Childers to work for the cause in England; he was exasperated by the meticulous manner in which Childers worked, and he never got over a suspicion that Childers, with his background of British intelligence service, might be an English spy. But Michael Collins, the organizer of the Irish Volunteers and Minister of Finance in the Sinn Féin government, took to Childers and made him one of the five directors of the National Land Bank. Molly Childers looked after Sinn Féin funds and papers. Their home was now and then raided by the Royal Irish Constabulary or by British troops, but the invalidism of Mrs. Childers caused personal searches to be less than thorough. People on the run were sheltered, and foreign visitors were often brought there to get Sinn Féin's point of view from one of the Childerses. (Or the opposing point of view from Molly's mother, Mrs. Osgood.) And despite the coolness of Griffith and the resentment of some other Sinn Féin workers for one with so formal and English a manner, Childers worked most days from seven A.M. till after midnight, publishing, writing, and eventually editing a daily cyclostyled sheet called the *Irish Bulletin*. This presented the nationalist attitude and was sent daily by post to some nine hundred newspapers and prominent people in England. It was often quoted in the House of Commons.

At this time, guerrilla war had broken out in Ireland. Murder was opposed with murder, terror with terror—all, for the most part, over the apathetic majority of the Irish populace, for whom Home Rule would have been acceptable enough. On one side, the Republicans fought without uniform; on the other, the mostly local and unenthusiastic constabulary were bolstered by British soldiers and the hastily recruited Black and Tans, dressed in part police, part civilian clothes, and so named after a famous pack of hounds in Limerick, where their first detachment was stationed. Childers wrote a series of articles on British atrocities and excesses for the London *Daily News*. In March of 1921, he was appointed Minister for Publicity in the Sinn Féin government. In the general elections of May 1921, his son, young Erskine, canvassed for Sinn Féin candidates, while he himself was returned as a deputy for a Wicklow constituency, pledged to attend not the Southern Ireland parliament just set up by the British but the separatist Dáil. The British general Sir Nevil Macready noted, in a tone of "Where but in Ireland?" wonder, that open rebellion, martial law, a general election, and peace proposals were all taking place at once.

At the London conference called in October of 1921 to negotiate a treaty and finally settle the Irish question, both sides wanted to bring about peace, but less reconcilable were the Sinn Féin hopes for independence and the British insistence that Ireland, given Home Rule, remain within the Commonwealth. De Valéra had been elected President by the Dáil, and he appointed Erskine Childers secretary to the Irish delegation. De Valéra said once that he had a higher regard for Childers than for anyone else he had ever met in politics—that Childers was an exemplary combination of thinker, writer, man of action, and idealist. Moreover, his civil-service training and his experience in constitutional procedure would be of great use in the treaty negotiations. In terms of representing De Valéra's own point of view at the London conference, Childers was therefore a good choice, but as someone who would get on with the rest of the delegation, led by Griffith and Collins, he was not. Griffith had studied Hungary's fight for independence, and he was known to feel that something similar, perhaps involving a dual monarchy, would be acceptable. De Valéra, on the other hand, wanted nothing less than real independence—with no oath to the King—and a form of "external association" with the British Empire.

Basil Williams, an old friend who had served on the staff of the House of Commons and in the Boer War with Childers, said of him at this time, "Physically he looked almost a wreck—thin and deadly pale and with white hair. His mind was as alert and bright as ever, but it seemed a hectic brightness, with almost all his old sense of humor and of proportion vanished, at least when he spoke of Ireland." Childers didn't go with the other delegates to social occasions, such as evenings at the house of the Irish portrait painter Sir John Lavery—whose wife was smitten with Michael Collins. He kept a cold eye on the conference business and warned the women secretaries of the dangers of the big city. And his relations with Griffith, the

joint leader of the delegation, had worsened. Griffith had re-
tained his distrust of Childers as, if not an *agent provocateur*,
an English radical politician making a new career for himself
in Ireland—an interloper. He had always been put off by Childers's precise manner and superior air; now he was overwhelmingly irritated by Childers's constant cough. Things reached
the point where Griffith would stop talking when Childers
came into a room and would resume his conversation only
when Childers left. Childers was writing long memoranda back
to De Valéra in Dublin—perfectly accurate, as it turned out,
but discomforting to some of the delegates.

And in the negotiations, faced by Lloyd George, Churchill,
and Lord Birkenhead, among others, the Irish had a hard fight.
They were eventually pushed by Lloyd George, who seemed to
be threatening renewed war, into a compromise settlement
involving a "Free State" within the Commonwealth and an
oath of allegiance to the King as head of the Commonwealth.
The delegation split, but Griffith and Collins persuaded the
others to sign; they were convinced that peace, the Free State
they had gained, and hope of final independence to come were
worth the oath.

In Ireland, most people clearly agreed that Griffith and Collins had done well, and in the debates that followed in the
Dáil, a majority of the deputies seemed to think so, too. De
Valéra did not. His belief in absolute Irish independence would
not allow him to take an oath to the King. The Dáil debates
grew fierce, with Childers making cool, detailed criticisms of
the treaty, and his opponents infuriated by what they thought
to be irrelevant nit-picking. Griffith at one point exploded: "I
will not reply to any damned Englishman in this assembly!"
Some might have been reminded of Grattan's Parliament,
which gave Ireland semi-independent government from 1782 to
1800 and which Childers had described in his *Framework of
Home Rule:* "Time and talent were wasted . . . over points
of pride, trivialities which seemed portentous to over-sensitive
minds; metaphysical puzzles. . . . Meanwhile the sands of
time were running out." Hearing Childers going on imper-

turbably about constitutional clauses and subsections, the journalist Desmond Ryan was reminded of the French revolutionary thinker Saint-Just: "The house was on fire around him but he argued on." The extreme Republican minority began to feel that argument was getting them nowhere, and their militant wing decided that violence was necessary. The sands ran out; the fire blazed up. Civil war began.

IN THE SUMMER of 1922, the poet and painter George Russell suggested to Lady Gregory, patron and playwright, an idea for a play "about how the generations for seven hundred years fought for the liberation of beautiful Cathleen ni Houlihan, and when they set her free she walked out, a fierce, vituperative old hag." The play, had it been written, could have been a tragicomedy or a straight tragedy. Withdrawing from Ireland, the British saw the deaths and atrocities continuing as the Irish began to assassinate one another, and they said, "We told you so—that's the way the Irish behave when left to themselves." The Irish replied, with some justice, that the divisive terms of settlement the British had demanded were a good deal to blame, and that the British in the previous centuries hadn't exactly given them much experience in self-government.

Certainly, although it was a dangerous time for many Irishmen, sometimes fighting brother against brother, it was even more so for the single-minded English-born editor of *An Poblacht*, the weekly bulletin of De Valéra's newly constituted Republican Party, in which in every issue Childers denounced the treaty and the Free State provisional government. In turn, the Free State government and the Dublin press denounced Childers, accusing him of inspiring the Republican rebellion. Childers himself, serving with the Irregular Republican forces, refused to recognize that his position was more precarious than that of any man in Ireland—that, as the writer Frank O'Connor later said, "in a family row it is always the outsider who gets the blame." Perhaps, too, there was something in Desmond Ryan's impression that the author of *The Riddle of the Sands* enjoyed soldiering and its attendant dangers; he had volunteered for the Boer War, the Great War, and now this war. In his reminiscences of this time, *Remembering Sion*, Ryan recalled Childers quoting from *Moby Dick* the mariner Bulkington, just landed from a dangerous four-year voyage, who almost at once pushes off again on the *Pequod* "into the cold malicious waves," believing it better "to perish in that howling infinite, than be ingloriously dashed upon the lee, even if that were safety!"

Together with his cousin David Robinson, another "damned Englishman" who was in charge of the so-called cavalry, Childers traveled with the Southern Brigade of the Irish Republican Army, printing his weekly bulletin for distribution to Irish and foreign papers, jails, embassies, and other Irregular columns. It was printed on a portable press set up wherever the brigade moved or (as was usually the case) retreated, in farmhouses and village homes, in the city of Cork and mountain hamlets west of Macroom. For a time he served in the same unit as nineteen-year-old Michael O'Donovan, who under the name Frank O'Connor wrote—among many splendid books— *An Only Child*, an autobiography, in which he left a record of these years. O'Connor was disappointed by his first sight of Childers, "limping and frowning; a small, slight, grey-haired man in tweeds with a tweed cap pulled over his eyes, wearing a light mackintosh stuffed with papers." Not only Childers's accent made him seem peculiarly English. He reminded O'Connor of an elderly parson, "conscientious to a fault and overburdened with minor cares. . . . His thin, grey face, shrunk almost to its mould of bone, had a coldness as though life had contracted behind it to its narrowest span; the brows were puckered in a triangle of obsessive thought like pain, and the eyes were clear, pale, and tragic."

Childers had a fanaticism that was new to O'Connor; he looked at everything in terms of whether it would help achieve an independent republican Ireland. He was an abstracted, bewildering companion in arms. His bad cough kept him awake, and he read all night—books such as *The Deerslayer* and

Twenty Years After. Robert Brennan, a Sinn Féin leader whom the Childerses had hidden in their home, found that Childers was a "Wrong Boxer"—a devotee of a mystery story popular in London a few years before, and the object of a fairly long-lived cult. O'Connor, deep in Dostoevsky, wondered why Childers didn't read more improving literature. But he also noticed that Childers fixed the bedside light so that it didn't disturb the others. When there was a shortage of beds, Childers gave up his bed and spent the night wandering around town. Brennan one night came on him coughing violently in a cold barracks corridor, his feet bare, clad only in pajamas, afraid that he would wake the other men.

While the Dublin papers were spreading the impression that he was a secret agent covertly running the war, organizing ambushes, raids, and explosions—the archenemy planning the ruin of Ireland—Childers, the expert in guerrilla warfare, was often ignored by the Irish Irregular staff. Then, as now, there was a natural resentment toward a person from a different background who had arrived by a different route at a passion similar to one's own, and who expressed that passion in a well-modulated English accent. It was in fact easier in some ways to be an Irish Republican by birth, by fate. But if Childers felt that he had made a great sacrifice—of his Chelsea flat, of his London club, of his British civil-service career—to get to that position, he didn't show it. Despite the Dublin condemnations of him, he wrote for the Republican bulletin moving, generous pieces when his former colleagues, now his enemies, died—first Arthur Griffith, worn out, and then Michael Collins, killed in an Irregular ambush. Childers was generally armed with a pistol Collins had given him, a miniature .22 which he kept fixed to his braces with a strap and safety pin. Frank O'Connor watched him one day reconnoitering the so-called front line, strolling along a road and walking coolly across a railway bridge that was covered by Free State machine guns, studying the lie of the land and apparently oblivious of danger. O'Connor thought this was partly the attitude of a professional soldier, "who always knows by instinct when and where to take cover," and

partly that of an absent-minded schoolteacher, "who is so worried about what to do with Jones Minor's peculiar habits that
he has no time to worry about himself."

The habits of the Irregular army might well have exasperated
the professional soldier in Childers. After one abortive raid,
he said to O'Connor, "I'll never understand this country. I
thought I was going off to a bloody combat, and instead I
found myself in Mick Sullivan's feather bed in Kilnamartyr."
He had difficulty in getting his colleagues to give him useful
work: when the printing press was abandoned, he offered
to address envelopes. And yet when Robinson—realizing that
Childers was the one man the Free State government intended
to get rid of—wanted O'Connor and another lad to take Childers by fishing boat to France, the Irregular leaders refused to
allow it. "One of these, pulling rank, said, '*Staff Captain*
Childers is under my command.' Childers's fate was decided
that afternoon."

THE PRESIDENT spends much of his free time, on weekends and
holidays, at Glendalough House, near the village of Annamoe,
as he has done since he was a child. There, thirty miles south
of Dublin and six miles in from the coast, on a green plateau
amid the rugged Wicklow hills, the Bartons have farmed for
the last hundred and fifty years. The estate, fifteen hundred
acres of woods, arable crops, and fields given over to dairy cattle,
is entered through granite gateposts just outside the village.
A graveled, tree-lined drive winds between fields to a grey
stone house on the flank of a hill. The house takes its name
from the sixth-century monastic settlement founded by Saint
Kevin at Glendalough, five miles away. The back wing, hugging
the hillside, dates from the late seventeenth century, while the
upstanding front wing is Victorian Tudor. Behind the house
are ornamental water gardens, a summer house, a network of
paths, a pond, and plantations, all laid out in the 1870s. And
near the side door stands a tall pine tree, planted in 1881, the
year Robert Barton was born.

Barton, a cousin of the President's father, was his companion
on that trip to western Ireland that helped convert him to

Home Rule; he became Minister for Agriculture in the Sinn
Féin government of 1919; and he is the only surviving signatory
of the Anglo-Irish treaty of 1921. During the Troubles, people
on the run often sought refuge at Glendalough House, one of
the great Unionist houses in Ireland to have gone Republican,
and it was occasionally raided by British troops. Mr. Barton was
captured, given a three-year sentence, and imprisoned in England, but released to attend the treaty conference. (Earlier,
in March 1919, Barton had escaped from Mountjoy Prison in
Dublin, leaving a note for the governor saying that the accom-
modations hadn't been all he had expected.) Charles Barton,
Robert's father, had been a justice of the peace and high
sheriff of the county.

The Bartons had taken the President's father into their home
after the boy's parents had died, and when in turn the future
President came to Glendalough House as a child before the
First World War, he climbed the same trees and fished in the
same lake as his father had done. He saw more of his father then
than he ever did thereafter; they went for long walks, looking
at animals, birds, and plants, and he was encouraged to ask
what things were. He remembers how excited he felt landing
from the ferry boat at Kingstown (the Anglo-Irish name for the
port of Dun Laoghaire) and climbing aboard the Bartons' big
white Daimler Silver Knight—suitcases in the boot—and then
the drive. When they reached the long hill from Kilmacanoge
to Roundwood, where the valley has since been flooded to
make a reservoir, he knew that his Irish holiday, a magic dream,
had really begun again. The year he was nine, George Russell,
who believed in the little folk, came to stay at Glendalough
House and in the garden said to the boy, "Look, do you see the
fairies?" Young Erskine thought that he did, but he asked his
mother if it was all right to see them. His mother and father,
after a short discussion, decided that it was.

Between the wars David Robinson, the former "cavalry"
leader, helped manage the Glendalough estate. Now the President's brother Robert, retired from the newspaper business, is
helping Robert Barton run the farm.

The house is large. Even now, in winter, the front Victorian

wing is unheated; anyone venturing into the large, high-ceil-
inged rooms—where there are stuffed deer heads, a gondola
seat, a Flemish tapestry, and South American Indian curiosities
collected by Mrs. Barton, who died last year—has to remember
to close the doors, against drafts. Beside the back doorstep
rest two prehistoric Celtic grain grinders—hollowed, dishlike
stones, each cradling a smaller round stone. And on Sunday
afternoon in late autumn, when the President has come in from
a tramp in the hills behind the estate, it is snug in the small
back sitting room. Fire in the fireplace; a smell blended of
tweeds, muddy shoes, pipe smoke, and tea cakes toasting in
the kitchen; Mr. Barton not saying much but with a lively look
in his old eyes; the two Mrs. Childerses, wives of the brothers, pouring tea and passing cucumber sandwiches; and talk
about the land, the condition of tracks and fields and trees.

NOVEMBER OF 1922. The Republicans had lost the war. Childers
believed that it was now a matter of ending it on the right
terms. De Valéra had set up an Emergency Republican Government to rival the Provisional Free State Government, and
Liam Lynch, chief of staff of the Republican forces, told Childers to make his way to Dublin and offer the Republican government his services. So he and Robinson set out across Ireland
from the mountains west of Macroom, in County Cork, sleeping by day and traveling by night. It is a shame that such a good
writer never had a chance to record that Buchanesque journey.
According to Frank O'Connor, who pieced together part of their
adventure, they were unwelcome guests in some places and
were promptly sent on their way. In others, various Republican
heroes struck picturesque attitudes of defiance to the Free State,
and sometimes, matching the deed to the gesture, gave Childers
and Robinson a temporary roof over their heads. Sometimes the
two got lifts on farmcarts. Robinson fell while cycling on a borrowed bike and broke a shoulder bone. North of Clonmel, a
town in Tipperary, they made a dangerous crossing of Slievena-
man Mountain at night. It was November, raw, drizzly, paths
slithery with mud and hillsides with damp moss and ferns, the

nights noisy with wind in the trees and water rushing down becks and falls. They made their way across Kilkenny and Carlow, across the Wicklow hills to the apparent safety of Glendalough House. Perhaps because it was home, it felt particularly safe.

Robert Barton, taken off to prison, had left word that if Childers turned up he was to be hidden, but Childers, worn out, slept in his old room. He sent word to De Valéra in Dublin saying he was available. And word also reached the Free State forces. On November 10, the house was surrounded by Free State troops. Childers rushed from his room holding the revolver Michael Collins had given him. Six Free State soldiers leveled their arms at him, but a woman servant interposed herself; no shots were fired.

Childers and Robinson were placed in adjoining cells in the prison of a Dublin army barracks. According to O'Connor, a previous prisoner had dug a tiny hole through the wall, and Childers and Robinson passed chess moves to each other. They played—with chessmen cut out of newspaper—on boards chalked on the floor. Childers knew there was no hope for him. The Free State government had set up army courts because the ordinary system of law—of judges, juries, and witnesses—was unable to handle the problem of the Republicans without danger of intimidation or favoritism. The army courts were empowered to try prisoners and punish unauthorized possession of arms and ammunition with severe penalties—with fines, imprisonment, deportation, or death. From the Free State point of view, it was a rebellion, not a civil war.

The capture of Erskine Childers set off in the press a renewed clamor against "the Englishman." Winston Churchill, who had sat across the London treaty table from Childers, said in a speech at Dundee (in extravagant words he later withdrew): "I have seen with satisfaction that the mischief-making murderous renegade, Erskine Childers, has been captured. No man has done more harm or shown more genuine malice, or endeavoured to bring a greater curse upon the common people than this strange being, actuated by a deadly and malignant hatred for the land of his birth." On the morning of November 17—the day on which Childers was brought to trial before a military court—four young Irregulars who had been captured with revolvers on them in a Dublin street were executed. That same day Kevin O'Higgins, Free State Minister for Home Affairs, spoke of Childers as guilty of "outstandingly wicked activities."

Childers refused to recognize the legality of the court. He claimed to be a prisoner of war. Although he was prepared to "suffer gladly and happily," he presented a handwritten statement to refute the suggestions that he was a spy or a double traitor. He recounted the facts of his life: English father, Irish mother; his upbringing; how he had changed from being an imperialist and a Unionist to being a Liberal and a nationalist; how he had served in the Great War and lost faith in Home Rule and chosen to work for, and be a citizen of, the Irish Republic; how he had worked for the treaty delegation, taken a strong stand against dominion status, which he had favored years before and gone beyond, and had come for the first time into conflict with his colleagues. And he went on (at least as he recalled it in a version of his statement he made a day or two later, for he had kept no exact copy of that presented to the court):

The slow growth of moral and intellectual conviction had brought me to where I stood, and it was and is impossible and unthinkable to go back. I was bound by honour, conscience, and principle to oppose the Treaty by speech, writing, and action, both in peace, and when it came to the disastrous point, in war. For we hold that a Nation has no right to surrender its declared and established independence and that even a minority has a right to resist that surrender in arms.

I take the fullest responsibility for any influence I may have had on my fellow-countrymen. That influence has been grossly and ridiculously exaggerated by our enemies in order to discredit our cause through me, but such as it has been I am proud of it.

I have fought and worked for a sacred principle, the loyalty of the nation to its declared Independence and repudiation of any voluntary surrender to conquest and inclusion in the British Empire. That is the faith of my comrades, my leaders, and myself. Some day we shall be justified when the nation forgets its weakness and reverts to the ancient and holy tradition which we are preserving in our struggle, and may God hasten the day of reunion amongst us all under the honoured flag of the Republic.

The court sentenced Childers to be shot. An unsuccessful attempt was made by his counsel to get a writ of habeas corpus for him and eight other prisoners. Perhaps if his old colleague Michael Collins had been alive, the sentence would not have been carried out. But Kevin O'Higgins, the Free State Minister for Home Affairs, whom Yeats called "a great man in his pride,/Confronting murderous men," had already approved the execution of *his* old friend Rory O'Connor, which took place two weeks later. He was not to grow suddenly merciful toward an Englishman he had described as striking ghoulishly at the heart of the nation. Childers wrote daily to his wife, saying on one occasion: "I have been told that I am to be shot tomorrow at 7. . . . It is best so, viewing it from the biggest standpoint. . . . It is such a simple thing too, a soldier's death. . . . I die full of intense love of Ireland. . . . I hope one day my good name will be cleared in England. I feel what Churchill said about my 'hatred' and 'malice' against England. How well we know it is not true. What line I ever spoke or wrote justifies the charge? I die loving England and passionately praying that she may change completely and finally towards Ireland."

But he had after this a day of waiting, and another, and another, which was the last. He was allowed a brief visit from his family, and young Erskine—then sixteen—saw his father for a few minutes. Childers asked his son whether he wanted to take part in politics when he was older. Young Erskine said yes. Childers then said that because he was going to die, he wanted his son to swear that he would seek out and shake the hand of all those who had signed his execution warrant, that he would truly forgive them, and that he would never allow the mention of his father's death to be used as a way of inciting bitterness about the civil war. There must never be a tragedy like this in Ireland again.

On the night of November 23, 1922, Childers wrote to his wife: "The guard was relieved at eight, and the men going off all said goodbye and God bless you, and I to them. They wanted souvenirs, but I have very few, some books and some signatures. It will be the same with the present lot—in case I am unable to record it—all friendly and infinitely considerate. So we, 'Children of the Universal Mother,' touch hands, and go our ways in the very midst of the horror of this war of brothers."

He added a postscript at dawn, two hours before his execution: "My beloved country, God send you courage, victory, and rest, and to all our people harmony and love. It is 6 a.m. You would be pleased to see how imperturbably normal and tranquil I have been this night and am. It all seems perfectly simple and inevitable, like lying down after a long day's work."

At 7:55 A.M. on November 24, Childers was marched into the yard of Beggar's Bush Barracks, in Dublin. He told the officer in charge that he did not need a blindfold. He shook hands with each member of the firing party. He then walked to where he had been asked to stand, but when he turned to face the nervous riflemen, he thought the distance was too great. He said, "Come closer, boys. It will be easier for you."

AT SCHOOL, the President's ambition had been to become a doctor, but when he went up to Cambridge in 1923, to Trinity College, where his father and grandfather had been, he decided to study history. While at Cambridge, he met and married a girl, like his mother, from New England—Ruth Ellen Dow, a journalist from Exeter, New Hampshire, who was covering the Irish revolution for the *Boston Globe*. Only too soon he had a degree in modern history, a young wife, the burdensome name Erskine Childers, and life ahead of him. In Ireland the civil war had ended in May of 1923 in the defeat of the Republicans. The history graduate had memories of running messages for the Irregulars on long night bike rides from the Four Courts into the countryside around Dublin, and he had the omnipresent memory of his father's fate and the pact they had made: no bitterness; shake hands. Moreover, he had the feeling, which he has never lost, that his father was a saint.

The young Erskine Childerses went to France. Through his American connections he got a job as Paris manager for the C. C. Drake Travel Service of Chicago, for whose wealthier clients he arranged safaris to hunt black-maned lions in Abyssinia, barge trips on the Danube, and rides on sacred white elephants in India. He also performed more prosaic tasks, selling train and boat tickets, sometimes to writers and artists such as James Joyce and Gloria Swanson. The agency ran five Hispano-Suiza limousines, driven on occasion by some of the more respectable White Russian princes.

Childers returned to Ireland at the end of 1931—and to jump from the Paris of the 1920s to the Ireland of the 1930s was to move from a cosmopolitan and vital present into a petty, parochial past. Ireland remained poor, and in the economic shadow of England. The civil war had imposed upon the new Free State two parties, which perpetuated the divisions of that period. As Frank O'Connor wrote, neither group had seen at the time of the civil war that what they "were bringing about was a new Establishment of Church and State in which imagination would play no part, and young men and women would emigrate to the ends of the earth, not because the country was poor, but because it was mediocre."

In 1932, however, after ten years in the political wilderness, De Valéra led into office his Fianna Fáil party, which he had founded in 1926. Actually, in 1927, when he had taken an Opposition seat in the Dáil, De Valéra had had to bend—somewhat Jesuitically, according to his opponents—his high-principled objection to the oath of allegiance to the British Crown. (He signed a piece of paper but declared it of no significance.) But once in office he abolished the offending oath. Debts to Britain were consolidated into a single payment—a sum decided by De Valéra—causing the British to retaliate with taxes on imports from Ireland. There was an uncomfortable period of economic strife and political chilliness. The new Irish constitution adopted in 1937 declared Ireland to be a sovereign state. (In 1949, after neutrality during the Second World War, the country took the name of the Republic of Ireland—the last step, as far as the British were concerned, in leaving the Commonwealth.) It could be said that finally De Valéra had won the civil war. His opponents (who rarely numbered much less than half the country) noted that in the process of "winning," De Valéra was forced to take stern action, including special courts and imprisonment, against those Republican militants who believed, and, in some instances, still believe that the civil war goes on.

Back in Ireland, Childers had gone to work for his father's old chief as advertising manager of the *Irish Press*, the daily paper De Valéra had started to provide his party with publicity. And though the legend of his father as an English spy or Republican malefactor had not quite died away, Childers found that in Fianna Fáil, at least, the name Erskine Childers was no hindrance; it was the name of a hero. In 1938, the son was elected to the Dáil for the constituency of Athlone-Longford. He was a deputy for this and other constituencies until June of 1973, when he resigned his seat on becoming President.

Although he inherited something of his father's well-mannered aloofness, and seemed to be a rather solitary man in a gregarious profession—not at all a hustings man or one of the boys to joke or drink with—he gained a reputation as a party stalwart, someone Fianna Fáil could put up to speak when the going got tough; unflappable; devoted to De Valéra; and sometimes most usefully one of the few Protestants in the party. He slowly worked his way up, first as a Parliamentary Secretary to the Minister for Local Government, then Minister himself—for Posts and Telegraphs, for Land and Forestries, and for Transport and Power—and eventually, from 1969 to 1973, Minister for Health and Deputy Prime Minister. An unflamboyant, conscientious political career, in which he was called upon to make speeches about bacon one moment and Irish timber the next; to travel abroad to promote Aer Lingus and drum up markets for Irish products; to attend meetings in remote country districts and speak good French at European conferences, finding useful his knowledge of the Irish abroad (the Ulstermen who had become United States presidents, the Irish who had become Russian generals and South American leaders); to open industrial estates and make the introductions at banquets held by folklore societies; and to work hard on the nitty-gritty of government—creating regulations to govern the width of roads and types of nonskid materials, improving postage-stamp design, boosting the Radio Eireann Symphony Orchestra (perhaps thereby expressing his suppressed long-held ambition to be a conductor), and failing, like his predecessors and successors in Posts and Telegraphs, to make any great improvements in the Irish telephone service, which has more deafening clicks, misconnections, and crossed lines than any other in Western Europe. He developed airports and encouraged rural electrification and was probably the most successful Health Minister Ireland has had, commissioning new hospitals, psychiatric hostels, and old peoples' homes, encouraging home-help schemes for the aged, increasing the number of district nursing posts, establishing area health boards, and giving medical card holders (generally the less well off) the right to choose their doctors, thereby removing an element of social discrimination. Childers gained a reputation for skill at absorbing the necessary details and getting into the paperwork ("He actually answered his letters"), but he credits a great deal of this to the sense of public service he acquired from his parents—the notion that a life spent trying to make the world a better place was the happiest of lives.

Twice out of office, for periods of three years each, he first worked as a manager of an engineering-machinery firm and during the second helped set up an electronics factory. He brought up a large family, with two sons and three daughters by his first wife, who died in 1950, and another daughter by Rita, whom he married in 1952. His mother continued to live in Dublin till her death, in 1964, at the age of eighty-seven. The Osgood medical tradition, which in the President produced not a doctor but a Health Minister, has cropped up among his children: his son Roderick is assistant professor of cardiology at the University of Chicago, and his youngest daughter, Nessa, now eighteen, intends to become a doctor. (Roderick's elder brother Erskine Barton Childers is a senior United Nations' official.)

IN THE OUTER STUDY the President sits at his desk, thinking about Ireland—the least well off of the "developed" countries but more prosperous than it has ever been. Net immigration, with not so much emigration now; still relatively slow of pace, with the advantages of a late entry into the industrial age, open roads, a wealth of countryside, and people who have not ceased to go to church. The fact that it is a small rural country has benefits in terms of scale, of social qualities, and of those human characteristics enhanced by man's role as a hand-working, agricultural being. Consequently people who come from larger and livelier countries think how quiet and lovely it all is. But then if you watch the television news (or for that matter, any Irish play), you see the violence and the drunkenness, which are still Irish, too. And the urban age, with its attendant problems, is growling toward Ireland. A third of the visits now made to Irish doctors have to do with problems of mental health, and in Ireland, as elsewhere, tranquilizers are increasingly prescribed to enable people to sleep or relax.

The President sits in his stiff-backed chair, white linen handkerchief poking from white shirt cuff, grey hair brushed back from domed forehead. His calmness is exemplary. But he also sees a job for himself as someone who can stimulate what the Irish think and do about the complexities of modern life. He believes that what people do on their own, and in their "spare" time, is going to count for more in the future than what government can do for them. He reads and quotes from Dennis Gabor, René Dubos, and the Vatican II document on the duties of the laity. He wants to encourage people—young, old, and middle-aged alike—to work in their own communities, because to work in a small group, feeling you belong somewhere and are serving the interests of a particular place, is to have the best possible chance of happily escaping and counteracting contemporary deracinating rat-race pressures. Since he has been President he has invited to Arus more than a thousand people sympathetic to these ideas. He has talked with the officials of all the Irish voluntary organizations, with a view to finding out how they can become more effective, and how he can help them. On two days out of every three, he and his wife have gone to visit festivals and events, to open clinics and community centers, to attend plowing contests and first nights of local opera societies, and to present the prizes to children in a tiny Cavan village that had won a national competition for solving local environmental problems.

BEING PRESIDENT of Ireland is somewhat like being both Queen Elizabeth of England *and* Prince Philip. Like the monarch, the President has official privileges, honors, and duties, and strong constitutional constraints on what he can do and say; like her consort, he can promote causes he favors and speak advisory words, as long as those actions are unpolitical. As a former politician who enjoyed the day-to-day working of politics, he admits to certain frustrations now that he has been elevated above party matters. He has to answer many pointed questions with "that's a political matter," or "that would have to be approved by the government." However, he has been outspoken, particularly in television interviews, in rejecting violence as a way of solving the problems of Ireland; he knows he speaks for 99 percent of the Irish people. He believes the reunification of Ireland is inevitable, in time, within the European community. He believes the presence of British troops in the North is necessary right now. And although he cannot actually mediate between the North and the South, Northerners come to see him—whether groups of Belfast schoolchildren or individuals such as the former Ulster Prime Minister, Lord O'Neill of the Maine—for a walk around Arus and a chat over tea. He frankly and publicly approves actions such as those of the Belfast Protestant family that recently moved in with a Catholic family to protect them from intimidation by other Protestants.

His position requires qualities possibly instilled by British public-school training. A stiff upper lip and a wry historian's view of human nature help him bear the attention he and his family receive, and the accompanying mirth, Irish wit, and savage abuse, some of which gets into print, but which for the most part is roared out into the smoky air of bars and public meetings. Taking sides, as the Irish do, with passion—the passion of the guts and senses rather than that of intellectual argument—anyone saying of the President, "Oh, he's a fine, courteous man, just what the country needs," is immediately confronted by someone saying hotly, "Are you crazy? The man's quite mad. Nothing at all Irish about him." Dublin political gossip has been enlivened by the new life in the presidential house (whose recent past was so quiet and stuffy), with consequent wild rumors about new Rolls-Royces and the impending construction of heated swimming pools and five-thousand-pound discotheques for the President's daughter Nessa. The fact that he is a Fianna Fáil man (though his present concerns clearly match those of the Fine Gael–dominated government) leads to slightly malicious suggestions that the government has not been encouraging any presidential initiatives because they don't want a man of the other party garnering goodwill. The scuttlebutt in print finds useful handles in the presidential pastimes, such as hiking. After President Childers's oilskins and Wellington boots disappeared while he was visiting the Killybegs festival, the Irish fortnightly *Hibernia* published a comic ballad on the subject, attributed by *Hibernia* to "a Donegal postman," and by those in the know to the editor of *Hibernia's* sardonic back page.

The dynastic element in Irish politics is as apparent now as it ever has been. The present Prime Minister, Liam Cosgrave, is the son of W. T. Cosgrave, head of the Irish Free State from 1922 to 1932. Garrett Fitzgerald, the Foreign Minister, is the son of Desmond Fitzgerald, Robert Erskine Childers's predecessor as Minister for Publicity in the Sinn Féin Revolutionary Government. The present Attorney General, Declan Costello, is the son of John A. Costello, Prime Minister from 1948 to

1951. And Thomas O'Higgins, the President's opponent in the presidential election, is the nephew of Kevin O'Higgins, Minister for Home Affairs at the time the President's father was shot, who was himself assassinated in 1927. Little wonder that after the wedding of Princess Anne and Captain Phillips, Irish newspaper columnists were asking when Nessa Childers would be getting married. (People say of her, "I hear she's quite a girl," the way they do of the Princess, as if they are surprised she is human.) But for all his reputation for being correct and aloof, most people in Ireland refer to the President as "Ersk," and most are, for the Irish, almost gracious in making allowances for his un-Irishness. One veteran political observer says, "He's never been impolite to anyone, but it isn't held against him."

ON THE TWENTY-FOURTH of November every year a small group meets in the Republican plot of Glasnevin cemetery, in north Dublin. Family, close friends, and survivors of the Irish Troubles gather to stand silently for ten minutes by the grave of Robert Erskine Childers. At Howth, every summer until recently, a modest ceremony was held to commemorate the landing of arms from the *Asgard*. The *Asgard* herself has been preserved, so far, as a youth training ship, and in 1972, on the fiftieth anniversary of Childers's death, a fund was established to endow a fellowship in marine biology in his name at the University College of Galway. The President himself has spent a great deal of time in recent years making a complete bibliography of his father's writings. Last year he authorized Andrew Boyle (who has written biographies of various eminent men) to write a biography of his father—a task that had been started by A. P. Ryan, a writer for the London *Times* who was in Ireland during the Troubles, but who died before getting far into the book.

President Childers's own life has been balanced constantly between the necessity of memory and the necessity of deliberate forgetfulness—his devotion to his father and what he stood for on one side, and on the other his obligation to fulfill his promise to forgive, to eschew all bitterness. He remembers going for long walks with his father when he was small; then the five years, during the Great War and its aftermath, when he saw little of his father; and then, in school holidays in Ireland, those intense three years in which his father rushed in and out, to him a hero. He does not talk easily about his father's death, though he is now some fifteen years older than his father was when the elder Childers was executed. He gives the impression of being still moved by it, but through long habit of keeping all his emotions under strict control, choked back, in this matter. What happened then should never be allowed to happen again—although in a way, as he knows, in Belfast, in Londonderry, in the countryside along the border, with bombs and snipers' bullets, it still happens: a man falls, a child is blown apart, a woman is maimed for life.

If asked about his father's death, Childers prefers to emphasize his father's consideration for the men about to shoot him. Magnanimity is not the most celebrated Irish virtue. Maurice Craig has pointed out in an introduction to a Dublin guidebook that the column on which Nelson used to stand outside the general post office, on O'Connell Street, was blown up in 1966: "We are not magnanimous enough to have left Nelson, or even his Pillar, standing where they were." But silence— a conscious putting aside of one's personal past in a country that is exceptionally aware of its painful history—is a form of magnanimity that could bear emulation.

IN THE OLD vice-regal lodge, now Arus an Uachtaráin, the House of the Chief, President Childers walked past the room where the painters were at work, on his way to the family dining room, while the sunlight fell on the phoenix carpet and the last reverberation of the gong sounded in the corridor, and among the delicately molded plaster ceiling figures, Time went on rescuing Truth from Discord and Envy.

Chapter Three

MATTHEW AND
MARIE

– 1977 –

MARIE BOYLE met Matthew Ferguson two autumns ago at a large manufacturing company in Belfast, where they both work. She is twenty, a clerical officer. He is twenty-three, an accountant in the finance department. They met during a staff tennis tournament, and they went on bumping into each other for a month or so on the courts and in the firm's cafeteria. Then, with the weather getting colder, Matthew asked Marie if she would like to learn to play bridge—he would teach her. But the first evening a lesson was planned they found themselves going to a movie instead—*Lady in Cement*, Marie remembers, starring Frank Sinatra. This was the first time they actually "went out" together; that is, it was an occasion outside the company, Matthew paid, and they held hands. After the film, in an espresso café on Botanic Avenue, near Queen's University, they talked around a subject that had been in their minds since their first meeting and now gave an edge of Ulster sharpness to the questions that a young man and woman on a date anywhere in the world might ask each other: Where were you born? Where do you live? Where did you go to school? How many brothers and sisters do you have? Matthew had already concluded, from her name and looks, that Marie was a Catholic, and she, on a similar basis, had concluded he was a Protestant. The answers they gave each other proved them right. Matthew had not gone out with a Catholic girl before. Marie's experience of Protestant boys was equally blank, and as Matthew's hand nervously touched her hand on the formica tabletop, she thought, Daddy's going to kill me when he finds out about this.

Neither Matthew nor Marie told their families at this point that they were going out with each other. (Their names have been changed, as have those of other couples in their situation, and the names of ordinary people involved with them.) Marie is the oldest of seven children. She was born and brought up in Andersonstown, a fairly modern and almost totally Catholic district in west Belfast, but since 1970 she and her family have lived in Bangor, a town on the coast ten miles from the city. There they have a bigger house, with four bedrooms, in a quiet street with mostly Protestant neighbors. But they moved not only for more room but to get away from the Troubles, which have particularly affected the working-class areas of Northern Ireland—the region of the United Kingdom with the highest unemployment and the lowest average wages.

Such older Belfast districts as the Falls and the Shankill, named after their main streets, have been identified with particular religions for over a hundred years—the Falls Catholic, the Shankill Protestant—but in the last eight years or so, streets between them that were roughly mixed have become one or the other. Even in more modern areas, such as Cliftonville, Ballymurphy, and Andersonstown, intimidation and fear have caused shifts of people; the planners of relatively new municipal housing estates have seen their hopes for a peaceful mixture dashed. The result is that Belfast is split into wedge-shaped slices that are Catholic or Protestant, virtual "ghettos"—the term is used by the residents with a certain pride—in which those who belong feel a communal warmth and those who do not are aware of an almost tangible hatred. The exceptions to this are such areas of middle-class homes as those along the Malone and Antrim roads, where, at least on the surface, a more or less suburban privacy and tacit tolerance prevail. The move to the suburbs and to nearby towns like Bangor has caused the population of Belfast to fall from about 400,000 to roughly 360,000 in the last ten years, as people get away from decaying nineteenth-century slums and the contemporary violence that springs partly from such housing conditions.

Marie's father has worked his way up to a responsible job in an insurance firm, where he is one of the few Catholics employed. (Catholics form roughly 35 percent of the 1½ million people of Northern Ireland.) Marie's mother, now in her mid-forties, has been fully occupied since she got married in bearing and bringing up children—she has made most of her children's clothes from birth through adolescence. Marie went to a Catholic primary school and a convent grammar school, made her first communion, was confirmed, and has always gone to confession once a week. At eighteen, after a year at secretarial college, she joined the company where she now works, handling the correspondence for export sales. She is a pretty girl, with pert features, close-cut reddish hair, and grey eyes; she generally wears a tiny gold cross on a chain around her neck.

Before Marie met Matthew, she felt that her immediate family—her parents and brothers and sisters—was her world; other relatives, in various country villages, were rarely encountered. Matthew, on the other hand, has been aware from childhood of a close family network of grandparents, aunts, uncles, and cousins. His father and mother died in a car crash when he was ten. Matthew and his younger sisters Fiona and Lesley were brought up by an aunt and uncle in a small terrace house—his home ever since—in Newtownards Road, a staunch Protestant working-class district not far from the city center. In some of its streets, many houses are empty, ready for demolition, with bricked-up windows and doors to keep out squatters. In others, with similar rows of slate-roofed, grimy-brick houses, life goes on, sometimes taking a stand for pride and gentility with a polished brass knocker, a scrubbed step and windowsill, and a vase of flowers framed between the curtains.

Matthew went to state primary and secondary schools. In principle these are open to all children, but in practice, because the Catholic church insists on running its own schools (to whose maintenance costs the government contributes), the state schools are almost exclusively Protestant. Matthew—brighter than most, and interested in mathematics—stayed on at school until he was eighteen. He was accepted for the first job he applied for, in the company accounts department where he now works. He is a solidly built young man, with wavy light-brown hair and a quiet manner. He goes to church twice on Sundays (to the Church of Ireland, which used to be part of the Church of England and conducts the same services)—in the morning with his aunt and uncle, in the evening with his grandparents. Both his aunt and grandfather work in a small hardware shop. Another of Matthew's aunts married a Catholic twenty years ago, and though she is said to have a happy marriage, the family connection with her has weakened. Matthew's grandfather did not speak to her for years. It was mainly because Matthew feared his grandfather's reaction that he didn't dare say anything at home about the girl he was going out with.

Marie's parents, however, soon got curious about the young man who was taking their daughter out two or three times a week. Marie mentioned his first name but not his last; she fended off further questions. The anxieties that parents have when their children start going out with the other sex are naturally greater in Northern Ireland. Besides the customary dangers of drinking and of driving, there is the fact that many pubs are patronized almost wholly by people of one religion or the other and may thus be targets for terrorists, while some city streets are not safe to drive on at night. The city center is a fortress of barricades, barbed wire, checkpoints, and police and army patrols; all people entering the center are frisked, their bags and cars thoroughly searched. After dark the center is desolate: a few stray dogs; no pedestrians, though plenty of parked cars belonging to people crowded into pubs and clubs.

There are only two routes through the city between north and south that people feel confident in taking; a wrong turn could bring them into a no-man's-land of shattered streets, demolition sites, and army barricades erected—so it seems—to keep warring tribes apart. Flame-retardant blankets are on sale, prominently displayed, in hardware stores. The ground-floor windows of many offices and hotels have wire screens over them, or have been filled in with concrete blocks. Yet the atmosphere is convivial in many pubs and hotels—perhaps the more so because of the blitz-like conditions without. Once one is past the door—with its buzzer system, inspection grille, frosty sign reading REGULAR CUSTOMERS ONLY, and searches by security men—the friendliness and hospitality are immense, at least for one's own kind and complete strangers; in other words, not for a Northern Irelander of the "other side." Matthew and Marie felt the need to be careful, and sought out neutral places, which are not common. In some places young people frequent, Catholics come one night, Protestants the next. Outside the safe, impartial territory of the company, Matthew and Marie felt restricted to several cinemas and theatres, and the few remaining big hotels, where Marie would sip a Coke or sherry and Matthew would drink lemonade-and-beer shandy. (He worries about alcoholism.)

A month after things became serious between them, Matthew drove out to Bangor to pick up Marie for an annual staff dinner-dance. She was still getting ready when he knocked at the door, and he was led into the front room by one of Marie's younger sisters. There, sat down on the couch, he had the impression of being inspected by eight pairs of eyes. Marie's mother asked politely about the dance. Fortunately Marie wasn't long, and Matthew escaped from the unspoken inquisition. For a little while after this Marie's parents seemed to avoid the subject of Matthew. Perhaps they hoped it would all blow over, and the less said the better. Then there was a sudden change.

One Saturday afternoon in February—there was to be a Valentine's Day party that evening at the St. John's ambulance unit where Matthew does volunteer work—Marie's father called her into the living room. Her mother was there. Her father said, "Marie, it's time we knew more about this fellow. Where does he live?"

Marie took a breath. This time, though she knew what would happen next, it couldn't be dodged. She said, "He lives off Newtownards Road."

It was a long row. "Newtownards Road"—full of diehard Protestants—confirmed her parents' fears. Her mother shouted at her and then fell furiously silent. Her father did most of the talking. The rest of the family was brought into the room to listen. Her father said that Marie was putting all of them at risk by going out with Matthew. It made it dangerous for him at his work. It meant that any of her brothers and sisters could be made the target for a bullet or bomb. Didn't Marie care about them at all? Didn't she care about keeping her family safe? She must promise never to see this Protestant boy again.

Marie said she wouldn't promise, that she was going to continue seeing Matthew. But her parents kept on at her. Her father reminded her of what had happened in the last few years to people of different religions who had associated with one another; girls who had been tarred and feathered or had their heads shaved; couples who had been brutally murdered; dreadful threats. Marie's mother said, "There's always the chance of a bomb under your daddy's car, or a machine gun opening up as he goes to work." Did Marie want to bring all this down on them? Her mother said to the other children, "Look at your sister—she doesn't care about you. She only cares for this fellow from Newtownards Road."

So it went on. Marie felt her parents wearing her down. In many ways she understood their feelings. They were older; they had lived through times when Catholics felt oppressed, were kept in second place, had to lie low to improve their chances, and didn't trust the intentions of the Protestant majority. Matthew represented those they feared: he was a *Protestant*. That was enough. There was also the teaching of the church. In her mother's eyes, Marie was being seduced from her faith and was laying herself open to the chance of eternal damnation. And on top of all that was their understandable anxiety about what might happen if word got around. Naturally, they wanted to keep their family safe.

Her father said this was to be her last evening out with Matthew. Marie was to tell him that she had too many other things to do after work. Her mother said Marie would get over it, even if it seemed dreadful now; there were other boys in the world.

On the way home that night after the party, Matthew said, "You've been very quiet this evening. What's the matter?"

Marie poured out the story, including what her parents had told her to say.

Matthew asked her if that was what she wanted, and she said no, but that was how it was. She was crying as she added, "They're so upset. I promised them."

MARIE AND MATTHEW tried for the next month to be "just friends." But they saw each other all the time at the firm— passed by each other in the corridors, and talked on the telephone, because Marie's office needed information from Matthew's department. It was hard. When they began to go out together again, they told each other that it wouldn't be serious; they would see other people, too. But it didn't work out that way. For the first time, Marie was deceiving her parents—letting them think she was with other friends when she was seeing Matthew. She was involved in the local Legion of Mary, and Matthew picked her up after her branch meetings. He drove her once a week to guitar lessons at the technical college, and afterwards left her a little way down the road from her home. The deception was a strain, and Marie hated it. When she and Matthew went out together, they both kept thinking they would run into people who would tell on them.

At Easter, they went on a day's excursion to Dublin. Marie told her parents that she and a girlfriend were going on a staff outing together. She and Matthew had a lovely day. The Irish countryside, north and south, was as always beautiful, and now fresh with spring. They walked in Phoenix Park. They sat and looked at the Liffey. They had tea at Bewley's in Grafton Street. They were happy. They didn't talk about religion or families. They thought they would get married but would put off telling anyone till Marie's parents looked like they were coming round, and then Matthew and Marie would find the right moment to tell them jointly. The Troubles might pass; everything might improve.

Matthew dropped Marie just down the street from her house at eleven-thirty that night. She found her parents and two of her mother's unmarried sisters, just arrived from Portadown for a holiday, waiting up for her. Her mother was weeping hysterically. The aunts had seen Marie and Matthew earlier that evening at the railway station. So it all came out. Marie's mother had been in a state for several hours and now said she was leaving home because she couldn't take any more. Marie's father shouted at her that she was ungrateful, selfish, deceitful—she was killing her mother. Marie declared she was going to marry Matthew.

While Marie's mother sobbed, one of the maiden aunts said, referring to Marie, "Why doesn't she come back with us to Portadown for the week?"

Her father said, "I'd like to finish off that Protestant boy."

The other aunt said tactfully that perhaps it would help if Marie had a long talk with the sisters at the convent school she had attended.

Her mother now fell silent, and though this usually might have worried Marie more than anger, she refused to let her mind dwell on it. She wasn't going to give in this time. She thought about Matthew ordering tea and tea cakes in Bewley's. She remembered how his raincoat, neatly folded, had fallen off the little rack under his chair. She had picked it up and put it with hers. Matthew would now be falling asleep after their day together. She could hear her parents and her aunts going on and on about Portadown and the boy from the Newtownards Road and the sisters at school and the parish priest, whom they proposed to call on the next morning. Had they all gone mad?

THERE IS A traditional Ulster song called "The Old Orange Flute," which—like many traditional things in Northern Ireland—casts a long light on Matthew and Marie's situation. The song tells of a young Protestant weaver, Bob Williamson, "a stout Orange blade" who played the flute in the Twelfth of July parade, which each year celebrates William III's victory over James II at the Battle of the Boyne—renowned, in retentive Irish memories, for preserving the union of Ireland with England under Protestant kings. However, Bob Williamson proves not so stout after all. He marries "a Papish called Bridget McGinn" and turns Papish himself. When the local lads get upset about his treachery, he has to flee across the county border with his wife and possessions. His old Orange flute loyally goes on playing the Protestant repertoire—"Croppies Lie Down," "Kick the Pope," and "The Boyne Water"—and, though finally burned as a heretic by a council of priests, plays to the last:

> While the flames roared around it they heard a great noise,
> 'Twas the old flute still whistling "The Protestant Boys."

This song manifests some of the elements that give Northern Ireland its character: a widespread belief that historical events are of contemporary importance; a general intransigence, often taking the form of a stubborn patriotism; and a common inability to treat any subject as purely secular. Much energy is expended by scholars and pundits on whether the evident division in Northern Ireland is basically religious, political, or cultural. It appears that in fact all sorts of accumulated old differences are maintained and enlarged for reasons of social distinction and self-esteem, and are used by both politicians and clerics when they want to enlist their supporters; then the labels Nationalist and Loyalist, Catholic and Protestant, are handed out, and people wear these labels proudly.

Though it would be difficult to prove that people in Northern Ireland are more religious than others elsewhere, it *is* known that they go to church more than most people in Western Europe: something like nine out of ten Catholics in Northern Ireland attend Sunday mass; more than five out of ten Protestants are believed to go to church on Sundays. Belfast appears to have more church buildings than similar-sized cities: steeples still create much of the city skyline; at sidewalk level, church noticeboards are conspicuous. One Belfast cinema was converted a short time ago not into a supermarket or bingo hall but into a church. Although many Protestant ministers complain about Catholic church interference in politics in the Irish Republic, Northern Ireland is remarkable for the number of Protestant clerics who are politicians. One of the best known is the Reverend Dr. Ian Paisley, M.P., whose strident Calvinist voice can be heard from the pulpit of the new Free Presbyterian Church in Ravenhill Road, which is reckoned to be—apart from the cathedrals of Liverpool and Coventry—the most expensive ecclesiastical structure built in the United Kingdom since the Second World War. Many newspapers, like Paisley's weekly *Protestant Telegraph*, have obvious religious affiliations; religious bookshops are common. Indeed, in a city where clerical dog collars and REPENT YE MUST sandwich boards are a frequent sight, local people find nothing exceptional in religious graffiti, such as a slogan painted on a wall off University Road: SAM TODD FOR GOD. Todd is a star player for the Linfield soccer team, whose supporters are Protestant, and whoever scrawled this message was presumably drawing attention to the close link that Linfield supporters believe exists between the Almighty and His team.

If one splits open the vicious circle of interlocked problems in Northern Ireland—which is something that the printed word allows one to do, though in daily life the circle is a vortex, whirling mercilessly—one can see that a large segment of it is education segregated along religious lines. A few play groups have attracted both Protestant and Catholic infants. A few state grammar schools and some private schools have a small number of Catholic students. But problems arise from these minglings, beyond bullying and name-calling. Catholic children attending state schools have been refused confirmation by their bishops. Some Catholic students in state schools are told by their parents not to mention the fact that they go to mass on

Sundays. A proposal for an experimental mixed school was effectively blocked by a Catholic bishop's refusal to allow a Catholic chaplain to give religious instruction to Catholic children who might attend it. A group called All Children Together, which is working for unsegregated education in Ulster, was refused permission to use a Catholic church hall for a meeting. It is, by and large, the Catholic church that insists on separate education, and in many cases the Catholic clergy is prepared to back up the insistence with threats to Catholic parents of hell-fire and purgatory; but undoubtedly the segregation has the support of many Protestant ministers and teachers. One young Catholic woman who taught for a while in a Belfast state school did so under an assumed name, without telling her colleagues she was Catholic. After she left and the truth came out, there was a great uproar; several teachers said they would have objected to her presence among them if they had known.

The system tends to perpetuate two somewhat archaic visions of citizenry and loyalty. Teachers go to training colleges run by the state or by the Catholic church, and intellectual border-crossing is not encouraged. Catholic schools teach the Irish language and promote a nationalist Irish allegiance. Protestant schools exalt the binding tie with Britain. Both visions obscure the fact that Catholics in Northern Ireland have not voted with their feet to move to Southern Ireland (where economic opportunities and social benefits are fewer), and that Ulster Protestants also feel a very strong attachment to their country—they are at once Irish *and* British. Although the Gaelic natives of Ireland (the descendants of aboriginal Irish and of Celtic invaders) have been infiltrated by Vikings, Normans, Scots, and English over a good twelve hundred years, and some Anglo-Irish families date their arrival in Ireland to the twelfth century, roughly a century after the Norman Conquest of England, the popular Irish view is that anyone from the British Isle to the east is an invader—particularly those who came from Scotland, full of the fire of the Reformation, in the seventeenth century. In fact, some of the Scots—including many of Gaelic descent—who settled in Ulster before the *Mayflower* reached

America were Catholic. Cromwell, infamous in Ireland, was equally ruthless to Scotch Presbyterians and Irish Catholics, and he also expelled all Anglican clergymen from their Irish parishes in order to install his own men. Protestant Ulstermen have led campaigns for Irish independence. Protestant Irish of English ancestry have fomented rebellions in the South against British rule.

Yet the simplified view of history has its effect, and whatever the lines that have been crossed in the past, undermining generalizations, there is no doubt that the lines are now distinct, and often take the form of barricades. Intermarriage between English and Irish was possible before the Reformation. With those who have arrived since, particularly those from Scotland (despite their own Gaelic ancestry), little mixing has occurred; the two tribes have grown apart. There are Catholic names, like Seamus Murphy and Sean Flanagan, and Protestant names, like Ian Forsythe and David Simmons. O'Reilly is Catholic, Reilly Protestant. (Anthony Trollope entitled a book *The Kellys and the O'Kellys*.) The segregation has gone on for so long it has become genetic. Ulster people, at any rate, can recognize Catholic features and Protestant features: differences in shape of eye, height of cheekbones, color of hair. Sandy hair like Matthew Ferguson's is Protestant, carroty red is Catholic. Protestant men have a confident swagger; Catholic men a lighter, jauntier step. Catholics are smaller. Protestants have conspicuous shoulders. In Belfast, moreover, the locals can, with a Henry Higgins–like precision, relate accent to home address within a street or two, and that enables them to tell which side someone belongs to.

To an outsider, both Catholic and Protestant seem to speak in a mixed Irish-Scottish voice, its modulations having more to do with education and occupation than with religion; all use, whatever their class or income, "whenever" for "when," and constantly apply the diminutive "wee"—for example, "Here's your wee receipt," or "Don't forget your wee umbrella." ("Wee" seems to have little to do with size. A shipowner collecting his new 300,000-ton vessel from Harland and Wolff's shipyard might well be told, "Here's your wee tanker.") Each side has nicknames for the other: Catholics are Micks, Taigs, or Fenians; Protestants are, curtly, Prods or Blacks. They start to use these as children, after school, when they encounter children from the other side; sometimes of course the children from the two sides feel bound to fight. Since they hardly know one another, each side has persistent misconceptions about the other: to Protestants, all Catholics have twelve children and live in squalor; to Catholics, all Protestants behave like participants in a drunken football crowd. Each side has its own signs and symbols (the Harp of Erin; King Billy on a white horse), its own exhortations ("Up the IRA"; "To Hell with the Pope"), and its own days for parading and celebrating.

The Protestant drums beating during the Twelfth of July parade, commemorating King William's victory at the Boyne, arouse in Catholics apprehension and old grievances, dating from a long period of Protestant domination of Ulster life. This domination resulted in the gerrymandering of political constituencies and in discrimination in employment and public housing—all designed, Catholics felt, to keep them an inferior caste. The gradual elimination of these abuses—as the Northern Ireland government was prodded into reforms by the civil-rights movement of the late 1960s, by some of its liberal-minded supporters, and by an anxious British government in Westminster—persuaded many working-class Protestants that they were losing their edge. They were encouraged in this view by the sermons of their ministers and by editorials in such papers as the *Protestant Telegraph*. Papism was on the march; the Pope would soon be running the Belfast shipyard; they were going to be dragged into a united Ireland, where *they* would be the minority. They don't like what they see or hear of the South: divorce prohibited under the Irish constitution; contraception illegal; Catholic bishops attempting to block government health schemes; beggars in the streets of Dublin. Northern Protestants are convinced that the Catholic church is trying to beat them by weight of numbers. Indeed, several priests have publicly suggested that Catholics keep up a high marriage and birth rate in

order to outbreed Protestants, and have thereby enhanced
Protestant fears—even to the point, some observers feel, of
"justifying" the assassination of individual Catholics by Protestant psychopaths or gunmen, who tell themselves they are
reducing the chances of a Catholic majority. (Catholic births
average four per family in Northern Ireland, Protestants three
per family. But more Catholics quit the country, mostly for
England, because of limited opportunity, and so far the ratio
between the two sides has stayed roughly the same.)

Protestant fears are also intensified by what has happened to
the Protestant population in the South: it was 343,000 in 1901
and 144,000 in 1961, and is estimated to have been declining at
10 percent per decade since then. The Southern Protestant is a
member of a dying species. There are various reasons for this,
but undoubtedly one factor is that more than a quarter of the
Southern Protestants marry Catholics, and most allow their children to be brought up as Catholics: Bob Williamson's "treachery" goes on. Thus, although the Catholic church officially dis-
approves of mixed marriage—to such an extent that priests
have been known to declare that a Catholic woman is better
off marrying a drunkard than a Protestant—Protestants feel that
mixed marriages are one more Roman weapon in the long battle to overthrow the Protestant ascendancy. They believe the
Catholic church's position on mixed marriages is one of im-
plicit superiority: Bob is expected to be converted, or "turn,"
or at any rate allow his children to be Catholic. This makes for
great bitterness.

Most mixed marriages appear to involve Protestant men and
Catholic women, perhaps because Catholic women strike Protestant men as more submissive or as better homemakers. Some of
these marriages result in conversions, but most, it is felt, simply in the husband's going along with what, as a result of her
upbringing, his Catholic wife more decidedly wants. And consequently many Protestants feel all the more strongly opposed to
mixed marriage. Even if they didn't have a strong Calvinist
predisposition to abhor Rome and condemn any sort of union
with it, Catholic success in this respect would give them cause

to do so. A recent Presbyterian church statement on mixed marriage said: "Greater problems arise where the man or woman is a member of some special sect or of the Roman Catholic church." Presbyterian ministers have refused to take part in joint marriage services with Catholic priests. Anyone who steps outside the lines is a traitor. In 1968, a leading Protestant politician, Phelim O'Neill, M.P., was expelled from the Orange Order—a form of Protestant religious and political brotherhood —for attending a community service in a Catholic church two years before.

No official figures are kept on the numbers of mixed marriages in Northern Ireland. From records kept by one Catholic and two Church of Ireland dioceses, it seems that more mixed marriages are taking place in Catholic churches than before. However, it also seems that in recent years fewer of all marriages occurring in Northern Ireland have been mixed. (In the rural Catholic diocese of Armagh, which spans the border between Northern Ireland and the Republic, 3 percent of the marriages taking place in Catholic churches in 1974 were mixed; in Belfast the figure for mixed marriages taking place in all churches and registry offices may be 10 percent.) Although nearly everyone in Northern Ireland knows of a mixed marriage somewhere in his own family, it is assumed that fewer mixed marriages are occurring than before the Troubles, particularly among working-class people, because of the hardening of ghetto frontiers and the greater dangers involved. Even among middle-class and well-educated young people, it has become more difficult to make contact across the religious divide. At Queen's University, the students are split roughly fifty-fifty, Catholic and Protestant, and for the most part have thoroughly nonsectarian ambitions and anxieties—to do with their studies in quantum mechanics, say, or the novels of D. H. Lawrence. But students have noticed that co-religionists now seem more inclined to band together; they tend to sit with their own side in the libraries or in the students' union dining room. These are undergraduates who have been at primary and secondary school through the years of renewed Troubles since 1969.

Yet Queen's is still common ground, where boy and girl may meet with less of the tribal impedimenta hanging over them, and despite a recent bomb or two in University Road and several murders in 1977 resulting from an IRA campaign against businessmen with offices in the area, the university neighborhood with its cafés, pubs, cinemas, and theatres is safer than many other parts of the city—though restaurant goers still favor the tables at the back, away from windows and what in a terrible instant may become splinters of flying glass. The indications and effects of violence are ever-present: daily headlines of assassination and terrorism; patrolling Land-Rovers manned by flak-jacketed soldiers, weapons at the ready; loose paving stones —in ill-repaired sidewalks outside bombed buildings—that tip under pedestrians and eject a stream of accumulated rainwater. Yet Belfast, at least for its middle class and its students, remains a city with two good newspapers, a serious fortnightly magazine, a thriving theatrical and artistic life, an excellent annual arts festival. New buildings rise; hotels are repaired, bombed, repaired again. One hears fewer sirens than in New York. There are said to be fewer murders proportionally than in Detroit. There are more traffic fatalities than deaths from terrorism. But violence has perhaps not been reduced (as a previous British Home Secretary hoped) to "an acceptable level." It appears to be organic; one will have to produce different people in Northern Ireland in order to do away with it.

For people who are in a sense different already—who, it is evident, are not easily lumped with one side or the other—the risks are clearly considerable. Their existence is a rebuke to the fanatics in each camp. The dangers are more constant in working-class areas; in some streets no mixed couple would now dare to live. Many who were born and brought up in such districts have cleared out to England upon marrying someone from the other side. One couple who ran into difficulties are the Millars—to give them the pseudonym that was used for them in a study on intimidation done for the Northern Ireland Community Relations Commission in 1973. Mr. Millar was a Protestant, Mrs. Millar a Catholic, and they lived for eleven years in a public-housing development a few miles north of the city. Then, in mid-1971, trouble began. Some of their neighbors were involved in sectarian disputes, but the Millars were subjected to abuse and intimidation from both sides. Their car tires were slashed; their house windows were broken; obscenities were painted on their walls and footpath; they were cursed and threatened. They abandoned their home and moved in with relatives, but were soon forced to move on by further threats of physical violence. Since a safe area for Mrs. Millar was a dangerous one for her husband, the family split up: the children stayed with their mother while their father got a room of his own in a Protestant area. However, they were fortunate enough to be able to get a mortgage and buy a house on a private estate farther from the city, where they are now living together again.

Similar cases are known. One mixed family moved four times because of intimidation, and the husband, a Catholic who worked on building sites where most of the laborers were Protestant, eventually became so frightened that he took his family to England. One mixed couple were petrol-bombed out of their house in the Shankill Road and machine-gunned in the Falls Road house they next moved into. Following that, the man was badly cut up in what he believes was an attempt to murder him. Some mixed couples have tried to defend their property—for instance, by putting barbed wire in the garden—but most feel that such actions would merely advertise their predicament. Some never answer the door at night. The ring of the telephone can be terrifying: a threatening caller, whose name you don't know, knows who *you* are, where your wife works, and where your children go to school. And, of course, moving isn't always a complete escape. One working-class Protestant who is married to a Catholic woman now drives a taxi on the Falls Road. In the eyes of those he has left, he has turned, like Bob Williamson. His children go to a Catholic school, and although he is secure among Catholics and is doing well (taxis tend to run on sectarian routes, crowded with passengers, and are highly profitable), he is trapped in the Falls Road area, ter-

rified to leave it. One Shankill man whose family had run a
grocery store in the Shankill Road for twenty years had to move
out when he married a Catholic. He moved to Stranmillis, an
improving middle-class district, but even there he and his wife
have been subjected to snide looks and nasty gossip, and they
continue to worry about what else might happen.

For behind the looks and the words is always the chance of
death. Again, no figures exist for the numbers of mixed couples
who have been murdered, but there have been several tragic
cases. The methods used on occasion remind one of the savage
practices of the Gauls—of punishments meted out in the Ger-
manic forests to those threatening the solidarity of the tribe.
On September 2, 1972, a Protestant propaganda sheet called
Loyalist News asked, "What prominent member of the SDLP"
—an almost entirely Catholic political party—"is keeping company with a Protestant female from Belfast's Crumlin Road?"
The following June, the SDLP man, Senator Paddy Wilson, and
his friend, Irene Andrews, were found stabbed to death. Senator
Wilson was firmly opposed to violence and, unlike most Ulster
politicians, did not carry a gun; his body had thirty knife
wounds. Reponsibility for this deed was claimed by a group of
Protestant "paramilitaries" calling themselves the Ulster Freedom Fighters. One twenty-year-old Protestant girl (who talked
some time ago to the Canadian journalist Kevin Doyle) had
been married for roughly twelve hours to a young Catholic
laborer when she became a widow. Her husband was abducted
from their flat in the Shankill Road area. His body was found in
a country ditch a few days later. He had been castrated, tor-
tured, and murdered with a shotgun blast to the back of the
head.

MARIE'S AUNTS called on the parish priest next morning. Marie's
parents, still furious, intended to go along, but were talked out
of it by the aunts; Marie was grateful for this. She herself went
to the church and prayed that it would all come out right. She
prayed that Father Molony would understand. The priest called
at the Boyle home a few days later. He talked to her father and

mother first. Then he spoke to her alone. He wasn't cross, as
she had expected. He asked about Matthew. He told Marie she
wasn't doing anything wrong. At this, Marie began to sob. She
hadn't cried in front of her parents; she wasn't going to let
them think she would give in. But now Father Molony said it
was all right if she and Matthew went on keeping company, but
not to rush things, and if they decided finally that they wanted
to get married, to come back and see him; he would instruct
Matthew and give them the necessary forms.

Marie could hardly believe it. Her prayers had been answered. She couldn't wait to tell Matthew. Her parents were
suddenly calmed down, and though, when Marie thought about
it later, she decided that Father Molony had convinced them
that being obstructive would merely drive her and Matthew
together—that the best policy would be to let it drift along
and perhaps come to a natural end—this didn't affect her
spirits.

Her euphoria in fact lasted five days. The following Saturday
Matthew took her to dinner at a hotel as a celebration, and
Marie wore new shoes her aunts had bought for her before they
went home. On Sunday, her mother said to her on the way
home from mass, "Next time he calls for you, he's not to come
to the door. We don't really like this."

Marie's balloon burst. Obviously her mother and father
couldn't keep up an attitude so contrary to their feelings. It
was, Marie thought sadly, back to square one. And after that,
the strain in the Boyle house was great. Matthew was rarely
mentioned. Marie would tell her parents when she was going
out and when she would be back, and she would watch from
her bedroom window for Matthew's car in the street. He was forbidden to come to the door or to call her on the telephone.
Fiona and Lesley, his sisters, rang Marie if he was going to be
late.

For a while Marie's brothers and sisters treated her like an
outcast. They hid her lipstick and hairbrush, and locked themselves in the bathroom when she wanted it to get ready to go
out. Her father no longer talked to her unless he absolutely

had to, and then he was bitterly cold. Her mother was more up and down—sometimes friendly in a woman-to-woman way, sometimes very upset. Marie was often the scapegoat in any domestic trouble, and would be told, "It's all your fault." Neither Marie nor her mother was in good health; both felt nervous and depressed. When her mother flared up, she would go on at Marie: Marie was losing her faith; mixed marriages were doomed to failure; Father Molony didn't have Marie's welfare at heart; Marie would be dominated by this Protestant boy the way generations of Northern Ireland Catholics had been downtrodden by Protestants. Marie proposed that Matthew come and talk with her mother, but she refused. On one occasion Marie's mother asked her where she was thinking of getting married, and Marie named the local Catholic church; she had never thought of getting married anywhere else. Her mother said, "Oh, no, you're not. If you marry him, you can clear off away from here to do it. And don't think your father or I will come to the wedding or help you in any way."

Matthew much of the time thought he understood the Boyles' point of view, their fears and anxieties. He and Marie talked about it, sitting in his car or in a café. They thought part of the trouble was that her parents' concern for their family was overwhelming; her mother and father had no outside interests except the church. They were totally wrapped up in the family's security on earth and salvation in heaven. Not that Matthew's uncle and aunt had been particularly pleased to hear that Marie was a Catholic; they too were worried about the peril from terrorists the pair might be placing themselves in. But they told Matthew that what mattered most was whether Marie would make him a good wife. Matthew has still not told his grandparents about Marie, he is so worried about his grandfather's inevitably stout Orange reaction. He has also not discussed the matter with his own vicar, whose daughter ran away last year with a British Catholic soldier; he thinks the conversation might be embarrassing. Marie took him to see Father Molony, who was friendly enough but treated Matthew like someone from a distant, backward planet. The priest assumed that Matthew was agreeable to having children of the marriage baptized and brought up as Catholics, and in fact Matthew was, though a bit taken aback to find his acceptance taken for granted. Marie was told she would have to make a promise about this. Once they decided to get married, a dispensation would have to be sought from the bishop so that the marriage might be a lawful union in the eyes of the Catholic church.

Although Matthew takes his own religion seriously, he gives the impression of thinking that the external forms of worship are essentially a feminine perquisite. Perhaps, too, he is prepared to surrender some of his own rights to her because of her softness and femininity—elements in the Irish matriarchal tradition. For her part, Marie doesn't share her parents' feeling of being a member of an oppressed minority. And neither Marie nor Matthew feels very deeply involved in "the Irish Problem," though it envelops them. Matthew says, a trifle helplessly, "We're not causing it. It's the politics of the place. We don't want anything to do with it." Yet the politics of the place are inescapable, and as Matthew is aware, the resulting violence, whether seen as extraordinary or normal, is present and hideous—sometimes haphazard, sometimes well-aimed. In St. John's ambulance corps courses, Matthew has learned how fine the line is between life and death. Once, on a tour of a hospital, he saw bodies, or what purported to be bodies, in plastic bags, each marked with a person's name. Like almost everyone in Ulster, Matthew and Marie know those who have been touched by calamity—by death or awful injury—in the last few years. Like most people, they wonder if it will ever end.

One small grumble of theirs is not having a secure place to which they can go simply to be with each other. Matthew says, "Usually, you'd be able to go to the girl's house just to sit and have tea or watch television, but we can't." He takes Marie to his aunt and uncle's house once in a while, but other members of the Ferguson family are liable to drop in, and Marie doesn't feel at ease there. They are forced to stick to their routine of company social events and films and dances, now and then for a fling driving in Matthew's Datsun to a country hotel fifty miles away for a steak dinner. They have good times. Matthew loves fishing, and Marie loves him enough to have spent several wet afternoons hanging about on riverbanks while Matthew angled for chub or pike. Marie likes music, and Matthew has let himself be taken along to several opera performances. Marie didn't get far with bridge, but together they won the mixed doubles in a firm table-tennis championship. If they seem old-fashioned, it is because they are like a good number of their Ulster contemporaries; the idea of living together before marriage doesn't appeal to them.

Last year, when they were beginning to wonder how they would ever manage to get married, a colleague at work told Marie about a small association she had heard of, devoted to the problems of mixed marriage in Northern Ireland. This group, Matthew found out, was having a weekend conference at a place called Corrymeela, near Ballycastle—a little town on the northeast coast, sixty miles north of Belfast. There were difficulties—how and when to tell Marie's parents, another Boyle family row to be faced—but Matthew and Marie decided that the opportunity to meet others who had been in their predicament would be worth all the trouble.

CORRYMEELA—Gaelic for "hill of harmony"—is half a dozen white buildings set on a grassy hillside that slopes steeply down to the impressive, rocky Antrim coast. Despite the broad bulk of Rathlin Island, a mile offshore, grey seas roll in from the northwest, and on a January day the spot brings to mind such uncomfortable early Christian outposts in the north as Iona and Lindisfarne. Corrymeela was built as a holiday hiking center, but since 1965 it has been in the hands of an ecumenical group formed by Ray Davey, then Presbyterian chaplain at Queen's University, and used to bring together people involved in the Ulster conflict. Politicians, clerics, and paramilitaries have met there. Ghetto families have vacationed there, and during some periods children from particularly violence-ridden streets of the city have been evacuated to the place. At Corrymeela, close relatives of people murdered by gunmen of the two sides have met one another. Corrymeela has a small Belfast office, which functions as a mail drop and contact point for several groups working to reconcile the warring parties, who for safety reasons don't wish to publicize the names, addresses, and telephone numbers of their members. It was through this office that Matthew got in touch with the Northern Ireland Mixed Marriage Association. NIMMA, as it is called by the twenty-odd Ulster couples who belong to it, was founded four years ago by a few people who had run into family and ecclesiastical difficulties because husband and wife were of different religions and who thought others might benefit from their experience.

Matthew and Marie got to Corrymeela on a Friday evening in time for tea, the evening meal. A blizzard had been blowing all day, but despite snowdrifts and icy roads, seven couples had turned up. In the dining room there were no fixed seating arrangements, but a list was drawn up for doing the chores; twice during the weekend Matthew and Marie (who were given separate bedrooms) took their turn helping to set the tables and to wash the dishes. At tea, Peggy Brennan, a twenty-six-year-old physiotherapist who is NIMMA's secretary, introduced them to some of the other couples, and sitting with Matthew and Marie, gave them a rundown on NIMMA activities.

Membership involved being willing to shell out a pound or two when there was no money left in the kitty to pay for mimeographing and posting the quarterly (or thereabouts) newsletter. The newsletter and releases about conferences such as this didn't identify any of the members by name, since being linked openly with an organization like NIMMA not only could be dangerous but could blight one's career. No one involved in a mixed marriage in Northern Ireland will talk about it in public unless assured of anonymity, and NIMMA couples have declined to appear on radio and television programs, though they have happily helped with scripts. But they have in numerous cases provided direct, personal help: finding a home in England for a mixed couple who found it too perilous to stay in Ulster; finding a friendly priest and church for a couple who had received no help from the parish priest of the Catholic partner; and frequently talking to engaged or interested couples, like Matthew and Marie, whose parents and relatives were up in arms. Peggy Brennan has met several young people who were simply glad to be able to talk to someone who had been in the same boat. One Protestant boy had slept in his car the night he asked a Catholic girl to marry him; he didn't dare go in and face his father and mother. One Catholic girl began to feel that everyone in the street could see into her heart and know that she was going out with a Protestant. But Peggy has also talked one young mixed couple out of the idea of getting married; she felt they were mostly interested in annoying their parents.

Most of NIMMA's members, reflecting the nature of things in Northern Ireland, take religion seriously. They are keen to know what their churches are doing, or not doing, to come to grips with the problems of marriage between Catholic and Protestant—or indeed across any other religious divide, though so far no Jewish or Muslim partners have presented themselves. The official Catholic position was restated early this century in a papal decree of Pius X, usually referred to as *Ne Temere* (1907): mixed marriages were forbidden, unless the church gave special permission for them in order to avoid "a graver evil"—presumably marriage outside the church; Catholics could in any event be excommunicated if they failed to marry according to the rites of the Catholic church, and any such marriage would be null and void. (This was given bitter prominence in Belfast in 1910 when a Catholic named Alexander McGinn, who was alleged to have been prompted by his priest, left his Protestant wife and removed their children, claiming that he was not married to her.) The Catholic Code of Canon Law, dating from 1918, demanded strict written guarantees that in any mixed marriage the children would be baptized and educated as Catholics, the non-Catholic would not attempt to convert the Catholic, and the Catholic would "strive with prudence" to convert the non-Catholic. These conditions were somewhat modified in a decree of the Holy Congregation for the Doctrine of the Faith, *Matrimonii Sacra-*

mentum (1966), and in a letter from Pope Paul VI, *Motu Proprio Matrimonia Mixta* (1970), after which the promises not to try to convert and to try to convert were dropped and the non-Catholic's pledge to bring up the children as Catholics was eliminated. The conditions were modified, that is, except where the bishops chose to maintain them.

In Ireland, the printed application for dispensation to marry a non-Catholic is still usually given to the Catholic for signature. The person signing attests to a declaration to remain steadfast in the Catholic faith and to a promise "to do everything possible to ensure that all the children born of [the] marriage will be baptized and brought up in the knowledge and practice of the Catholic religion." The priest concerned records his opinion of the non-Catholic party's reaction to an explanation of all this, and completes the sentence "I think the likelihood of the children being baptized and brought up as Catholics is very good/good/slight." The form is then sent to the bishop, who makes up his mind whether or not to allow the marriage. Although in principle Catholics are now allowed to get married in other churches if a priest is present, in Ireland in practice they find they are pushed into getting married in a Catholic church.

Half a dozen churchmen were at Corrymeela for one part or other of the weekend. They were a Methodist minister and a Church of Ireland vicar from central Belfast; a local Methodist minister; the Reverend Jack Weir, moderator of the Presbyterian church in Northern Ireland; the Church of Ireland Archbishop of Armagh and Primate of All-Ireland, the Most Reverend George Simms; and Father Adrian Hastings, formerly a Catholic missionary in Africa and now a lecturer in religious studies at Aberdeen University, Scotland, who was there for the entire weekend to speak and to lead discussions. Through contacts with Spanish missionaries, Father Hastings learned of Portuguese army massacres in Tete province in Mozambique, and in 1973 he brought this to the attention of the London *Times* and thereby of the world. His most recent contribution to that paper was a letter to the editor, printed a few days

before the NIMMA meeting, suggesting that criticism made
by the Catholic Bishop of Ardagh and Clonmacnoise about a
vacuum in British government policy toward Ulster owed something to the Bishop's unease with the Northern Ireland peace
movement, which had been having some success in bringing the
two communities together. Father Hastings wrote to the
Times: "Human society has its perennial mechanisms for rec-
onciling divided groups, the chief of these being the common
education of the young and marriage across the divide. The
logic of the peace movement is to encourage shared education
and mixed marriages; the current discipline of the Catholic
bishops of Ireland is to oppose them."

Archbishop Simms talked after tea. People sat in the lounge
in a stretched-out oval of chairs—NIMMA couples, Corrymeela
staff, a few local people, and Matthew and Marie, whose el-
bows were touching, and who looked as if they would like to be
holding hands. The northerly gale rattled the windows and the
archbishop—a wiry, grey-haired man—gave the impression of
having to speak a little more loudly than he normally did. He
talked about the joint Anglican–Roman Catholic commission
on mixed marriage, set up by the Pope and the Archbishop
of Canterbury, on which he had served. After six meetings in
various countries over eight years, the commission had recommended that mixed marriages take place before ministers of
the church of either partner; that the Catholic be told of his
obligation in the eyes of his church to bring up the children
as Catholics, but that no promise be demanded; and that there
be joint pastoral care by the ministers of the two partners. The
archbishop said, "When two persons meet and want to marry,
it is their own affair. But two churches are also meeting, two
doctrines are encountering one another, two authorities are to
be reckoned with, two societies and two cultures. And yet marriage is about unity. We want the unity of the marriage to be
preserved and developed. We don't want it to be threatened,
damaged, torn apart."

All this was fine—or so those who spoke in the ensuing discussion, which was accompanied by coffee and biscuits, seemed

to agree. It was what they hoped an intelligent leading ecclesiastic would say. But on the ground, in Northern Ireland—"the end of the line," as one person put it—did it help? Peggy Brennan said, "Many mixed-marriage couples feel that the churches are playing a high drama that the couples are just pawns in." Rules and regulations may be slowly modified, but many still have an irksome and often a divisive effect. The Catholic church formerly provided an extremely threadbare ceremony for mixed marriages, which it insisted take place within it, and though it now allows a nuptial mass to take place at the wedding, the non-Catholic partner is not allowed to receive communion, while the Catholic partner may—an act of separation at the moment of intended unity. The churches seem to foster their own differences for their own purposes, whether by ecclesiastical nit-picking or condemning the truth of the other side.

Anyone cooler toward religion than the people at Corrymeela might have felt that the churches were fortunate, in this age of the secularization of practically everything, to have members who took their religion so seriously that they wanted to get married in church, to worship and bring up their children as practicing Christians. The very language used by the churches —whether stern ("dispensation," "discipline," or "church authority") or mild ("inter-church," "inter-communion," and "spiritual welfare")—might put off those not involved in religion. Thus, the dilemma of the churches at once mirrors and sustains the dilemma of Ireland. Churchmen on both sides are the inheritors of church traditions, of their own revolutions, reformations, and partitions; of distinctions about orders and sacraments that they take with desperate seriousness. (One Church of Ireland vicar visiting Corrymeela refused on theological grounds to take part in a communion service at which a Methodist officiated; but he participated the next day, when a Catholic priest was in charge.)

As his letter to the *Times* indicated, Father Adrian Hastings is a forward-looking priest, but much of the originality of what he had to say when he talked on Saturday seemed to lie in a tense awareness of the relation between what ought to be and what could be. A tall, slightly gawky man in his early forties, he remarked that all human societies had marriage. In our Western society, however, marriage had become "personalized," its social implications reduced, and we exalted the nuclear family, living in its own little box, and often watching another little box. Yet through marriage one acquired new relatives—aunts, uncles, cousins, and so on. Marriage could have political consequences, in the way that in the past, through alliances of royal families, it had had for nations. In many African tribes, marriage was still seen as a link between two lineage groups. Marriage could be a way of making peace—it could have been for the Montagues and the Capulets. What began as a personal choice of two individuals had wider consequences, such as grandchildren for grandparents (two couples who themselves might otherwise never have met), and relatives who might provide support of one sort or other—lend you money, help you find a job or a house, or simply have you in their house for a chat. If one lost this—if one was "without family"—life was impoverished and possibly more stressful. And as for Northern Ireland, where tribal and ecclesial loyalties had coalesced and marriage outside one's own church was condemned, Father Hastings thought it should be noted that "where there exist two communities living side by side, people are given only three possible courses of action: domination by one group or the other; social mixing between the two communities, which must result in intermarriage; or war." He believed that the churches in Northern Ireland had to choose where they would take their stand.

ON SATURDAY, there was a thaw. The wind had dropped and the sun shone, and in the afternoon Matthew and Marie walked along the shore to Ballycastle. A military patrol of men from the part-time Ulster Defence Regiment was searching cars on the road leading into the town, which had the slightly forlorn feeling of a seaside place in winter. But a cheerful coal fire was burning in the hearth of the saloon bar of the Antrim Arms,

Ballycastle's best hotel, where Matthew and Marie found several other couples from Corrymeela comfortably ensconced. Quite a number of those who have met through NIMMA have become good friends, who see each other for dinner or visit on weekends. They are perhaps a little special in the eyes of prior acquaintances who have married partners of their own religion. Marie and Matthew were soon at home in this company, and Marie was admitting that—supposing she and Matthew finally got married—the wedding itself worried her a lot. Clearly she thought of it as the biggest thing in a girl's life, and she didn't want to be robbed of it, of the white gown and the bridesmaids in a church among family and friends. But what if none of her family showed up? What if they did turn up and had a flaming row with Matthew's family?

NIMMA members have plenty of experience in this area. Dave Mills, an engineer, said that none of his family had come to his wedding—which relieved him, because his mother had threatened to turn up and scream at him in the midst of it. Peggy Brennan said you just couldn't tell—sometimes parents got over their hostility as the ceremony approached; they wanted to get involved in the preparations. Sometimes they find the reality doesn't match their dreadful anticipations. Relatives meet relatives from the "other side" and say with an embarrassed smile, "I didn't think I was going to like this." Some Catholic parents, finding a priest on hand at a joint ceremony, are appeased, since they can say, "Father so-and-so was there, so it was all right." Patrick Brennan, Peggy's husband, who is a teacher, said that his bachelor Uncle Joe had met Peggy's Aunt Martha, a widow, at his and Peggy's wedding reception, been smitten by her, and had pestered her for weeks afterwards to go out with him. Sometimes it takes a year or so for the parents to come round. One formerly vitriolic Protestant grandmother now babysits regularly for her Catholic daughter-in-law's children. One father, a Church of Ireland vicar who a few years back denounced his son's marriage to a Catholic girl on doctrinal grounds, has modified his stand: among his best friends now is a Catholic priest.

But for most Northern Irelanders the exceptions don't prove the rule. The fact that one Catholic turns out not to have horns doesn't mean, in Protestant eyes, that other Catholics aren't closely related to the devil. (The traditional suspicion was neatly expressed in a Catholic mother's remark to her son about his girlfriend: "She seems a very nice wee girlie. Are you sure she's a Protestant?") Moreover, just because someone from the other side proves to be a reasonable and friendly human being doesn't create a feeling that you can talk about anything in front of them. Some areas of comment are taboo. One family had decided their new Catholic son-in-law was a decent fellow, but had to restrain their usual sectarian remarks when he was present; for instance, during the television news a nudge or wink might be called for if it looked as if someone were about to blame a crime on the IRA—"Remember, Paddy's here."

Some parents never come round. Patrick Brennan's mother hasn't, four years after his marriage to Protestant Peggy. If he calls the house and his mother picks up the phone, she silently hands it to her husband or one of the children. In numerous cases the bitterness goes terribly deep, and is cherished and even paraded, like the pains of Irish history. Letters go unanswered, or are returned unopened. Possibly because family pride is so strong in Ulster and the moment when children break away from their families is in any event fraught with tension, the additional element of religious difference in the outsider who is carrying off one's son or daughter creates hurts that are not soon fixed and gulfs that are often unbridgeable.

One couple in the Antrim Arms bar, Seamus and Angie Kennedy, told Matthew and Marie what they had gone through to get a Catholic dispensation for marriage. Angie's Protestant family had emigrated to Massachusetts in 1956, when she was nine. Her father runs a small machine shop in a town I will call Conway, not far from Springfield. Angie grew up in Conway but came back to Northern Ireland every other summer to stay with relatives, and in 1971, with a degree in Spanish from the University of Massachusetts and a year's remedial teaching work in Boston behind her, she returned to be a teacher in the

Shankill. (Although many North American political leaders, including five U.S. Presidents, have come from Ulster stock,
Protestant Northern Irishmen emigrate with reluctance and
few nowadays for once and for all. Their love of country is
fierce. Angie's father plans to move back to Ulster when he
retires, if the Troubles have died down. Angie talks with a
strong Ulster accent, with no indication of her long American
childhood.) Angie met Seamus, a social worker in Belfast, one
Saturday in a pub in a country town where she was on a summer
training course. At first, though attracted to each other, they
thought there was no future in getting involved. But Seamus
convinced himself and Angie that the Catholic church was
making progress. He bought various pamphlets on marriage
from the Catholic Truth Society's bookshop in Belfast. Vatican
II and *Motu Proprio* encouraged him. "I read Bishop Philbin's
pamphlet on authority and conscience, to learn about the man
who would be saying yes or no to our dispensation," Seamus
told Matthew and Marie. "The bishop writes in it to the effect
that authority should not be authoritarian. I was sure that we
were going to be okay."

Seamus's young local parish priest helped them complete the
application form for a dispensation, on which they had to
specify the date of the marriage and the church where they
wanted it to take place. Angie said, while Seamus made a
trip to the bar for a round of drinks, "We were a bit simple.
Though I'm not a Unitarian I'd sometimes been to their services
in Belfast. The Unitarians said we could get married in their
church, and so we put that down, and the date, May 1973."

The form was then sent to the bishop of Down and Connor,
Dr. William Philbin, a scholar of Greek and Irish literature.
He refused to give permission for the marriage. The priest,
sympathetic to Seamus and Angie, telephoned the bishop to
restate their case and was told that too many mixed marriages
were taking place; there was a danger of the Catholic laity
being scandalized. The priest then tried to see the bishop in
person, but was not granted an interview. Seamus decided to
write to Bishop Philbin, humbly asking for advice about getting married to Angie. Two weeks later he had a reply saying

that what he wanted was "not in accordance with the laws of
the Church in this country. Please be guided by your parish
priest." The priest, as it happened, was moved to a less con-
genial parish later that year. "He was lucky it wasn't Rathlin
Island," said Seamus.

"We felt very much alone just then," said Angie, and Marie
looked at Matthew, as if someone were speaking her words for
her. "There was no NIMMA then. We didn't know whom to
ask for advice." Angie had been sure of the dispensation. The
dresses for her and the bridesmaids had been made. A deposit
had been paid to the hotel where they were going to have the
reception. One of Angie's aunts, well known as a vehement
anti-Catholic, had as a peace gesture offered to bake the wedding cake. Angie had to tell her and thus arouse her old feelings.
Angie lost her deposit on the reception. She told Seamus hotly
that if the wedding wasn't fixed by April it was all off. Seamus's
mother now decided that the bishop must have good reasons,
and therefore, she said, *she* wasn't coming to the wedding, when
and if it took place. Seamus was shocked by the bishop's refusal; he couldn't understand how the church could claim to
be the repository of truth and act like that.

It began to look as if they would have to get married elsewhere. They made a weekend trip to Dublin by bus to see a
liberal priest, who offered to help them if they wanted to get
married in the Irish Republic. They heard from Angie's father,
who suggested that they have the wedding in America. Suddenly this seemed the best thing to do. In April they filled up
a second form asking for permission to marry and put down
for the date and place of marriage, August, Conway, Massachusetts. Then they waited. Weeks went by. No word from
Bishop Philbin. Seamus's priest didn't hear. Seamus didn't
hear. In June, Angie wrote to her father saying that it might all
be off—no dispensation. Her father went to tell the Conway
Catholic priest, who had agreed to take part in a joint service
in Conway Congregational Church. The priest said he had
received the dispensation direct from Bishop Philbin in May,
assumed the bishop had told Seamus's parish priest, and had
been waiting for Angie's parents to confirm the arrangements.

Angie said: "My blood still boils when I think about it. The high-handedness! The bishop didn't have the courtesy to tell us."

Seamus felt the bishop acted hypocritically, giving permission for the marriage to take place in the United States but not in Northern Ireland. Seamus said, "If it was wrong here, it was wrong anywhere."

They gave a party for their Belfast friends before they left, and were married in Conway Congregational Church in August. The priest and the minister—who work together on various community projects—shared the service. One of Seamus's brothers was best man and a cousin of Angie's was the bridesmaid; they alone of the two sets of families and relatives in Ulster could afford to make the trip. Seamus and Angie saw Niagara Falls, the Appalachian Trail, and Washington, D.C. But Angie is still upset that she didn't have her May wedding in the Unitarian church in the city she considers to be her home.

"You're right," said Marie. "It isn't fair."

IN MOST PLACES, the effect of such happenings could serve to turn a couple away from religion. Even in Northern Ireland, some people are known to have had no more to do with churches after encounters of this kind. But the clergy are not alone in being obstinate; many lay people appear determined not to leave their religion in the hands of the clergy. Seamus has found that though he goes to church less, he worries about religion more. Matthew said that until he met Marie he had been unquestioning about the Church of Ireland. Now he had questions and wanted answers. Angie goes more frequently to the Unitarian services than she did before marriage, and though from time to time she still says that "the Catholic church is a horrible institution"—at which Seamus, knowing her reasons, nods glumly—she also admits that not all bishops act as Bishop Philbin did in regard to them.

Bishop Philbin is considered to be a "hard case." So is Bishop Cornelius Lucey, in Cork, in the Irish Republic. And so are many Presbyterian ministers, who are terrified of the

Catholic menace. There are also many well-meaning clerics on both sides who declare that time will heal, but don't attempt to speed up the healing process; good relations between the churches are fine but best if they don't lead to intermarriage. The Catholic orders are considered by many people to be advanced in social and political matters—the Dominican nuns of Aquinas Hall, Belfast, have a reputation for helping in communal activities across the religious divide—but the hierarchy has not encouraged any Jesuits or Benedictines to settle in Northern Ireland. However, two recent episcopal appointments —Bishop Edward Daly, of Derry, and Bishop Francis Brooks, of Dronmore—are taken as hopeful signs. Bishop Daly talks in person to engaged mixed couples, encourages his priests to take part in joint marriage services with Protestant ministers, and has declared that if one partner takes religion more seriously than the other, the wedding should be held in that person's church, whatever the denomination.

Father Michael Hurley, director of the Irish School of Ecumenics in Dublin, says, looking at the whole of Ireland, that mixed marriage is "probably the single biggest divisive issue in Irish life." He has organized interchurch conferences on the subject, which were not attended by any Catholic bishops, but at one of which Garret Fitzgerald, then the Irish Foreign Minister, who is the son of a Presbyterian mother and Catholic father, received communion from a Protestant clergyman. Some hitherto diehard Protestant ministers are beginning to realize that they need an informed and educated laity, which their churches have rarely had. (Some perhaps bear in mind the words of a Protestant lecturer at Queen's to a Unionist party meeting a few years ago: "What the party has to fear is not being outbred by Catholics. It is being outbred by reasonable men.") One of Bishop Philbin's parish priests, Father Desmond Wilson, resigned from his post in 1975 and set up as a free-lance, supported by local people in Ballymurphy, Belfast. Among the reasons he gave for resigning was the Catholic church's failure in Northern Ireland to provide a lead for its flock in regard to integrated education and mixed marriage.

Father Wilson proposed a new form of words to replace the present "promise." Both partners should be asked, he thought, "to use their best efforts of wisdom and grace in order to make sure that their children will have the benefit of worship and knowledge of God."

Children create moments at which mixed couples must make new decisions. The "promise" looms larger when the first child is born: is the baby to be baptized a Catholic? The very certificate of baptism may give the impression the child belongs to one religion only; one parent may have a great feeling of loss. In Ireland in the nineteenth century some mixed couples followed the practice—sometimes called the Galway convention—of raising boys in the father's religion, girls in the mother's. One NIMMA couple have christened their four children alternately, the first Catholic, the second Protestant, and so on; if, having acquired a religious identity, the children later want to change, then that will be fine, the parents say.

Education forces further problems on a mixed family. If they have been successfully lying low until this point, decisions about schools bring them into the open. Unless they can afford private schools, or have children bright enough to win scholarships at grammar schools like the Belfast Royal Academy, most people have to choose between state and Catholic schools. Seamus says, "If the government encouraged an experiment in mixed education, we feel we'd have to support it." As it is, despite the strictures of some of their clergy, a small number of Catholic parents are said to be sending their children to state schools. The children may have to put up with occasional taunts of "Mick" or "Fenian," but—as Seamus and Matthew remember —fights between boys from Catholic and Protestant secondary schools have always been frequent, a necessary rite if the boys met when going to and from their separate establishments. The chances of fights would be reduced—or at least placed on a nonreligious basis—if the schools were not segregated.

Together with the usual pains and pleasures of married life, mixed couples have some intensified ups and downs. The marriage may bring out prejudices the partners didn't know they

had. Some find they had better not talk about anything to do
with religion; a few split up for that reason. In a book entitled
The Northern Ireland Problem, two Quakers, Denis P. Barritt
and Professor Charles F. Carter, write that the churches in
Ulster are wise to discourage mixed Protestant-Catholic marriages, "for the tensions existing in a mixed marriage frequently
disrupt family life, and are an important source of social
problems."

NIMMA members don't see it that way. They believe that
the heart-searching and opposition beforehand create a marriage
(if it takes place after all) that is in most respects stronger
than usual. The determination needed, particularly in Ulster,
to see a romance through to the altar is a determination val-
uable in seeing a marriage through. There are pleasures to be
got from doing something that various people condemn as
disastrous or impossible. Perhaps, too, couples who get involved
in such situations are those who by their nature want to break
out of the closed family/religious/tribal network of their own
kind, in order to find diversity and fresh blood. Marie, eldest
of seven, was intrigued by the fact that Matthew was one of
three, and an orphan. Furthermore, for those who go on taking
their religion seriously, new facets of the problem are forever
popping up—how grace is to be said at meals; what sort of
family prayers there should be; which church one is to go to
on Sunday, and whether one goes alone or with one's partner?—
and successfully tackling them can provide a sense of achievement. One person at Corrymeela said, "A mixed marriage is a
down-to-earth form of 'power sharing'—something Ulster politicians have yet to work out."

A mixed marriage is also a sacrament, a sign. On Sunday
morning at Corrymeela everyone attended a well-mixed service.
Father Hastings celebrated a simple mass, interspersed in Protestant fashion with hymns, and was assisted by a young Methodist minister. A kitchen table served for an altar. Matthew and
Marie walked up together in the long line to take communion:
the wine in a chalice held by the minister; the communion
bread brown wholemeal baked at Corrymeela and broken into

small fragments, which Father Hastings placed in each communicant's hands. In the afternoon, after lunch had been cleared away, those who had come to Corrymeela for the weekend said goodbye to one another. Matthew was going to leave Marie near her house in Bangor before going on to his aunt and uncle's house in Newtownards Road. Peggy Brennan told them to keep in touch. As Matthew's car started up, Angie Kennedy waved goodbye and Seamus called out the customary Northern Ireland farewell, "Safe home!"

FOR A SHORT WHILE after their trip to Corrymeela, Marie and Matthew felt more confident. They now knew people who had had difficulties similar to their own, and could call on them for help and advice. They had encountered a few churchmen who were aware of the problems caused by their institutions and were working to minimize them. Marie had liked being in a place where she hadn't felt she was hiding something; it had been pleasant to be somewhere with Matthew for a few days, to be unexceptional, even to do dishes together.

And yet after a week they began to wonder. Were they any closer to knowing what to do? Did it help much to be told that they, and couples like them, were helping to draw the churches together and to produce a common Christian mind when Marie's parents still wouldn't let Matthew into the house? Marie can't help feeling a little envy of a Catholic girl she knows at the firm who is marrying a Catholic boy; the girl gets engagement presents and talks about shopping for her trousseau, while Marie feels she must keep quiet about her friendship with Matthew. "You don't want too many people to know," Marie says. "You don't have the usual kind of happiness." As for when they will get married, Matthew says, "We're biding our time." They were going to get formally engaged on Marie's birthday, just after Christmas, but didn't. They don't want to feel they are being rushed into doing things by outside pressure. They want to make the right decisions.

Sometimes they think they might be better off going abroad to get married, and perhaps they would if, like Angie, they had family living abroad—and if Marie's parents hadn't told them to clear off for the wedding. They resent being told to leave their own country. It is hard for an outsider to imagine as he stands in one of those dour Belfast streets, where you can look west and see Black and Divis mountains looming over the city and turn to the east and see the dark cranes of the shipyards where the *Titanic* was built, that native Catholic and native Protestant alike feel a passionate attachment to Ulster. Matthew knows there are good reasons for them not only to get married abroad but to work abroad for a while, perhaps for a company in a developing country: it would get them away from their families and enable them to save for a down payment on a house in a good, safe area when they got back. Possibly if everyone in Northern Ireland lay low outside Belfast, the violence might end, or possibly suburbanization and secularization have their own cost in coldness and apathy. Matthew, in any event, is afraid his family would miss him abroad, and he suspects that he and Marie would not fit in in another country—that they wouldn't be outgoing enough to make friends and enjoy it. This is their home, in spite of everything. "We're not going to be like our parents," Marie says crossly. "We have our own future." But they look older than their years. Some who know them have the impression that they are wedded to their present state of courting: going out together several times a week but living in separate, well-established homes, from which they will find it hard to break away.

Chapter Four

ACTS OF UNION

– 1977 –

IN THE TRAIN—the late-afternoon express going north from Dublin—the poet Seamus Heaney sits making corrections to the script of a lecture he is to deliver tonight in Belfast. Outside, along the coast, sudden dark showers alternate with moments of radiance; wide curving strands, small stone-break-watered harbors packed with fishing boats; headlands; hedged fields; wet gorse- and furze-filled hedges. Heaney now and then puts a page marker in one of the books he means to quote from, by himself or another of the present thriving generation of Irish poets or by James Joyce, from whose *Portrait of the Artist as a Young Man* Heaney could, if necessary, recite long passages by heart. Heaney is thirty-eight. He wears a suit of fine light-brown Irish tweed. Curly brown hair surrounds a face in which all the features are amiably big except for the intense slits of eyes. He has made this journey many times, particularly in the last five years since moving his home from Northern to Southern Ireland, but his neglect now of the passing landscape stems from absorption in his task, improving the lecture. It is to be about the dual, often competing traditions of those who find themselves born in Ireland, speaking English. He feels the excitement he always feels going back north to an intensity that doesn't seem to exist in Dublin, returning to face an audience aware of particular furies and rivalries, passions and distinctions. There is almost a need to reassemble himself before he speaks. He ponders questions that may well be asked by people who will see him not only as possibly the finest poet in Britain and Ireland but as the son of a Catholic farmer and cattle dealer in County Derry.

Heaney grew up in a thatched farmhouse not far from the northwest corner of Lough Neagh—just about halfway between Belfast and Derry city. The place was called Mossbawn. *Moss* was a local word for bog, itself an Irish word meaning soft and —he was later to discover—one of the few borrowings the English language has made from Irish. The nearby bog was (in his words) "a wide low apron of swamp on the west bank of the River Bann, where hoards of flints and fishbones have been found. The bog was rushy and treacherous, no place for children. They said you shouldn't go near the mossholes because 'there was no bottom in them.'" He was the oldest of nine children; one small brother, aged four, died in a road accident. An unmarried aunt, Mary, was one of the household. The family moved from Mossbawn when Heaney was fourteen, and though the new farm was not distant, the effect was to seal off his childhood, almost hermetically.

At Mossbawn he learned to milk cows and mow with a scythe. He breathed the odors of turf and warm milk, the smell of cattle on his father's clothes. His voice was implanted with what he calls "the sound of English as it is spoken in the back of the throat in south Derry." He remembers his mother reciting rhymes that were part of her schooling—Latin roots with their English meanings, lists of suffixes and affixes, bits of Wordsworth. A cousin of his father's used to chant ballads of the 1798 rising. Young Heaney heard regular patterns of words in the house: the Catholic catechism and litanies; the BBC weather forecast naming Rockall, Malin, Shetland, Faroes, Dogger, Finistère. He went to primary school at the village of Anahorish; the school was run by a Catholic priest but, exceptionally for Ulster, was also attended by some Protestant children. So there were songs of division, Loyalist and Nationalist, as one side taunted the other:

> Up the long ladder and down the short rope
> To hell with King Billy and God bless the Pope.

Walking to school he sometimes met herdsmen or road workers. One, leaning on his spade one day, said to the boy, "Aye, the pen's easily handled. It's a lot lighter than the spade."

Although it was a while before he became conscious of the fact that he could dig with his pen, he was thrust fast up the academic ladder. The bright country boy did well in examinations—he won a scholarship to St. Columb's, a Catholic boarding school in Derry, and another scholarship to Queen's University, Belfast, where he got a first-class honors degree in English. The escape route from a farming life led naturally to teaching: he taught first in a Belfast secondary school, then a teacher-training college; then in the English department at Queen's. He met his wife, Marie—who also became a teacher—a year after graduating from Queen's. Two of his brothers and a sister are teachers.

THE TRAIN CROSSES the river Boyne at Drogheda; inland, a mile or two, the riverside fields where William III's army defeated that of James II and kept Ireland for over two more centuries as part of a Protestant United Kingdom; and a few more miles inland, the Neolithic passage graves near Newgrange—the matter of Ireland, a poet's inheritance. Heaney, looking back, borrows from Patrick Kavanagh, the Irish poet he much admires, the remark that he dabbled in verses and found they were his life. He discovered at school that some poems gave him a sort of aural gooseflesh. He was packed with the classics, English literature, and Irish history. The dabbling began at college,

with his admiration for Gerard Manley Hopkins, Dylan
Thomas, and Kavanagh fairly conspicuous. His doubts and Latin
learning were expressed in the nom de plume *Incertus* that he
attached to a few poems submitted to and mostly rejected by
college literary magazines. In his memory of the time he and
a few like-minded friends "stood or hung or sleepwalked between notions of writing that we had gleaned from English
courses and the living reality of writers from our own place
whom we did not know, in person or in print." Then, at
twenty-three, the odors of Mossbawn began to rise again, and
he discovered ground of his own. The first poem making this
clear was called "Digging." In its last lines, he put the words of
the road worker to use: "Between my finger and my thumb /
The squat pen rests. / I'll dig with it." Writing this poem produced a new sensation—"having experienced the excitement
and release of it once, I was doomed to look for it again and
again."

For would-be writers hanging around Queen's in Belfast in
the mid-1960s, there were some providential elements to set
against what seems to many the original sin of being born
in Ulster. Heaney was buoyed up not only by his own talent
but by talented friends—fellow poets including James Simmons,
Michael Longley, Derek Mahon, to name some of a number
of Northern Irish writers who appeared at this time. There was
also the presence of the British lecturer Philip Hobsbaum and
his wife, Hannah, who held at their flat Monday-night sessions
where young poets could read their work, face the criticism
of their peers, and feel supported by being members of a
chosen group. Heaney has written in a recent issue of *The
Honest Ulsterman* (a lively bimonthly that stems from the
same period):

When Hobsbaum arrived in Belfast, he moved disparate elements
into a single action. He emanated energy, generosity, belief in the
community, trust in the parochial, the inept, the unprinted. He was
impatient, dogmatic, relentlessly literary; yet he was patient with
those he trusted, unpredictably susceptible to a wide variety of
poems and personalities and urgent that the social and political

exacerbations of our place should irrupt and disrupt the decorums of literature.

As they did. And when in 1969 Northern Ireland began to fill the front pages and TV screens, possibly one good thing commentators could say about the benighted place was that poetry was blossoming at the same time as sectarian terrorism. The renewed Troubles kept some people from going out; instead, they stayed at home and read books. Moreover, Ulster writers were able to feel they had something their colleagues in England lacked—a sense of touching the pulse of the people, of being in contact (as Heaney has written) with a field of force, and thus being aware, when they wrote, that they were telling not just their own secrets but those of the community. Heaney says, "I was lucky in several ways. The kind of reception my poems and then my first book got drove me on. And what happened in the North made the thing more urgent and more public. It stretched the gift. It stretched everybody."

He and his wife and soon two small children lived in a three-bedroom house on a Belfast housing estate. He wrote at Christmas 1971: "We live in the sick light of TV screens, with a pane of selfishness between ourselves and suffering." Yet he went on civil-rights marches, and like others in the city, faced army searchers and inquisitions. *"What's your name?"* "Heaney." *"Over there!"* A frisking. A pop as the flashbulb lit a photo. On one occasion he was marched to a police barracks with his three-year-old son because his car road license was out of date. Like many he was often scared by vigilante patrols and always worried for his family's sake. There was the constant unease and the momentary nightmare. One evening he appeared on a television discussion and the next day his mother-in-law, who was visiting, answered the Heaney telephone and heard a voice threatening Heaney's life. How do you confront the problem of being a poet in such times?

Tonight, in Belfast, someone may well ask this, or a similar question. He has had to face it many times in the past eight years, posed by strangers, colleagues, or himself. How do you *say* something about the Irish "situation"? And/or, aren't you living in an ivory tower in Southern Ireland? The first two lines of "Digging" are: "Between my finger and my thumb / The squat pen rests; snug as a gun." But apart from that, direct reflection of contemporary violence was singularly lacking from his first two books of poetry; the pen was digging, not firing. He was forced to make statements in prose about why he wasn't making statements in verse. "You have to be true to your own sensibility, for the faking of feelings is a sin against the imagination. Poetry is out of the quarrel with ourselves and the quarrel with others is rhetoric. It would wrench the rhythms of my writing procedures to start squaring up to contemporary events with more will than ways to deal with them." Now, in the humbling presence of other people's deaths and injuries, he says, "Political talk seems sullying."

And yet contemporary events have inevitably worked their way into Heaney's imagination, into the mind and feelings of a man already stretched between his education and his family background, between his acquired knowledge and his ancestral pieties. He began to find in and beyond the sensuous matter of childhood a subject that gave him both scope and a myth— bogland. Bogs had a "strange, assuaging effect" on him. As a child at Mossbawn he had been told butter would keep fresh for years if stored under the peat. He remembered that, while he was at school, the skeleton of an elk had been taken out of a nearby bog. "So I began to get an idea of a bog as the memory of the landscape or as a landscape that remembered everything that happened in and to it. In the National Museum in Dublin you realize that a great proportion of the most cherished material heritage of Ireland was found in a bog."

Moreover, in 1969, the year the Troubles recommenced, Heaney read *The Bog People*, a book by the Danish archeologist P. V. Glob about preserved bodies found in Jutland bogs— bodies, perhaps, of people sacrificed in early Iron Age times to the earth goddess. Glob's book provided evidence of the preserving power of bogs. With photographs of bodies and severed heads, in appearance so terrifyingly new, it told of the persistence of the past into the present, and of the pull of the earth. The photographs of these victims, Heaney said later, blended in his mind "with photographs of atrocities, past and present, in the long rites of Irish political and religious struggles." In the Iron Age of Northern Europe were parallels for Ireland now. There was "a society where girls' heads were shaved for adultery . . . a religion centering on the territory, on a goddess of the ground and of the land and associated with sacrifice. In many ways the fury of Irish republicanism is associated with a religion like this, with a female goddess who has appeared in various guises. She appears as Caithleen ni Houlihan in Yeats's plays; she appears as Mother Ireland. . . . I think the republican ethos is a feminine religion in a way."

By way of Glob and bogland, Heaney (till then the poet of a vivid but personal landscape) began to find an answer to the question of what images and symbols might be adequate to the Irish predicament; now he could offer what Yeats called "befitting emblems of adversity."

OUT TO THE WEST a grey cloud clashes with the sun; two incredible rainbows arch up and over. The train rocks on a bumpy stretch of roadbed, and Heaney carefully annuls several lines of his talk with a felt-tip, then writes new words in. Fame accumulates now, a rising dune of awards and prizes and critical praise. His bust is sculpted; his portrait painted for the Ulster Museum; a caricature accompanies a parody of his work in a witty guide to the British literary intelligentsia. Articles appear about his poetry in serious monthlies. "Some people are going to start comparing him with Yeats," says one critic, at once making and bowing out of the comparison. Heaney admires Yeats but doesn't appear overwhelmed by him, as so many of the great man's successors have been. He appreciates but won't emulate Yeats's oratory. He takes issue with Yeats's remark that the artistic intellect is forced to choose between perfection of the life and of the work. He thinks life and work must be intertwined, a continuum.

So: where to live? An academic year as a writer-in-residence in California wasn't just an escape. He had a chance to see that racial/tribal/ethnic rivalry wasn't only an Anglo-Irish problem. He enjoyed being there, but thought the amount of "psychic elbow room" in America might make an artist a bit strident, unless he had a firm grip on a myth of his own. Back in Ireland, he wanted to take his myth and put it at the center of his own life as a poet. Belfast didn't strike him as the ideal place to bring up children. In July of 1972 he and his family moved to a cottage (owned by a woman in Toronto who offered the use of it to them), a gate lodge of Glanmore Castle, formerly the Synge estate, in County Wicklow in the Irish Republic. The move was news, headlined in one Eire newspaper: ULSTER POET MOVES SOUTH. In Belfast, Ian Paisley's sheet, *The Protestant Telegraph*, gave him a half-page send-off, called him "the well-known Papist propagandist," and mentioned the address of the house he was leaving, perhaps in case someone might feel inclined to go and hurl something at it.

For the nearly five years he spent in the Wicklow countryside he didn't teach. There was plenty of broadcasting work in Dublin, and a demand for readings and reviews. In the South, an artist's income from his art is not taxed. Marie had a teaching job, and after she and the children had gone off to school there was quiet in the house; he could stare out of the window into fields and hedges. He got down to ditch level again and recovered more of his Mossbawn childhood. He felt he had done the right thing by moving there and yet felt like an exile, "an inner émigré," and sometimes missed the engagement of life in Belfast. In the end, poems were the best answers he could make to why he was there, and poems came.

At Glanmore, Heaney began work on a modern version of a long medieval Irish poem usually called *The Frenzy of Sweeney*, which he calls *Sweeney Astray*. Sweeney is an Irish king—in other words, a warlord—in County Antrim, who is cursed by a local saint and, with the ground cut out from under him, goes flying round the countryside nesting in trees and hiding in ditches. For a green-fingered poet Sweeney is a splendid mouthpiece, as Heaney realizes: "a man who lives in intimacy with the animal and vegetable world; a tongue almost of the land itself, a voice that utters its bleakness and beauty." Sweeney "speaks some of the most beautiful verses about the Irish landscape that are ever likely to be written"— for example, the piece in praise of the trees where he nests:

> The bushy leafy oak tree
> entangles the tall light.
> The forking shoots of hazel
> have nests of clustered nuts.
>
> The alder is my darling
> all thornless in the gap
> some milk of human kindness
> coursing in its sap.
>
> The blackthorn is a jaggy creel
> stippled with dark sloes;
> green watercress is thatch on wells
> where the drinking blackbird goes.
>
> Sweetest of the leafy cliques
> the vetches strew the pathway;
> the oyster grass is my delight
> and the wild strawberry.
>
> Ever-generous apple trees
> rain big showers when shaken.
> Scarlet berries clot like blood
> on mountain rowan.
>
> Briars insinuate themselves,
> arch a stickle back,
> draw blood, and curl up innocent
> to sneak the next attack.
>
> The yew tree in each churchyard
> wraps night in its dark hood.
> Ivy is a shadowy
> genius of the wood.

Holly rears its windbreak,
a door in winter's face;
life-blood on a spear shaft
darkens the grain of ash.

Birch tree, smooth and blessed,
delicious to the breeze,
high twigs plait and crown it
the queen of trees.

The aspen pales
and whispers, hesitates:
a thousand frightened scuts
race in its leaves.

But what disturbs me most
is the dangerous swing
of an oak rod, always
testing its thong.

Sweeney is sundered by dualities, too. His saga arises "from a culture that precedes the Norman and English invasions of Ulster"; it is "a work that allows two mythologies a home in its story. So in one way Sweeney represents a fallen establishment east of the Bann, tormented by hindsight; and yet in another way, he is a genius of places and cultures associated with west of the Bann. His story is like a prism that can refract different psychologies and break the hard light of opposing minds into a beautiful elegaic spectrum." The poem ends:

I ask a blessing, by Sweeney's grave.
His memory flutters in my breast.
His soul roosts in the tree of love.
His body's tucked in its clay nest.

THE TRAIN HALTS at Newry, near the head of Carlingford, one of the loughs with Viking names. Customs officials walk through the train, inspecting a few suitcases and drawing attention to the fact that for railway purposes this is the border with Ulster; here one leaves one part of Ireland for another. The sun is gleaming off wet rails and windows. Heaney is brooding over the last page of his lecture typescript. He lives now in south Dublin in a big Edwardian semi-detached house near the shore, not far from Yeats's birthplace in Sandymount. A desire to better Marie's and the children's lives—better house, better schools—led him to move in from Wicklow. He has taken a job as head of the English department of Carysfort College, a Catholic teacher-training college five minutes' drive from his house. Despite money worries caused by the big mortgage, he has turned down offers of higher-paid posts at higher-powered groves of academe, possibly with greater tensions and responsibilities. At Carysfort he teaches two full days and two half days a week—something he does well, and willingly, giving something of himself and yet not being drained. He also runs a fortnightly books program on Irish television. He is a member of the Irish Arts Council and attends monthly committee meetings. He is in demand for poetry readings and lectures and appearances at arts festivals, not just in Ireland and Britain, but in Switzerland, Holland, the United States. Although he says no to many, in one recent month he read his poems in Cambridge, England; went to an arts festival on Inishbofin island, off the Galway coast; and made a week's tour of Ulster with two Belfast friends, the poet Michael Longley and the folksinger David Hammond, performing in village halls and schools. Heaney's performance on these occasions is in no way theatrical, but soft-voiced, the words dragging the audience in. He feels that he is writing for a few dozen people with whom he has a silent and creative exchange.

Most holidays he goes back for a day or so to the Derry farm and walks round the fields with his father, talking as sons and fathers will, not of poetry or ambition but of cars, insurance, leaky roofs, the other children. He is not a handyman: hammers, nails, government forms resist him. He spends a good deal of time with his two sons and small daughter, occasionally takes them to mass or reads poems to them. When away from home he often writes love poems to his wife Marie. He reads only a few books a year that seem to matter to him—recently some of the Russian masters, who seem to him less composed than the English. He is, friends say, generous with himself and his time—offers to teach for colleagues who are unwell—and Marie tries to protect him from distractions. He writes in an attic room with a south-facing window giving him a slice of Dublin bay, where the Vikings landed, and a chunk of the Wicklow Mountains. On the floor by his desk lies an old copper knapsack sprayer, used for spreading blight killer on potato fields.

On the making of poetry, Heaney talks with evocative precision, nicely matched to his audience. A poem—he said in one broadcast to schools—is "alive in an animal, mineral, and vegetable way. It comes out of a creature, out of a man's mind and feelings, and it lives and is clothed in the substance of words. When a word is used in a poem it not only belongs to the English language, it belongs to the poet also. . . . The words are built together to make a home for his feelings, they house the truth he has to tell." While to the Royal Society for Literature he has spoken of his pleasure in finding in Sir Philip Sidney's *Apologie for Poetrie* the statement, "Among the Romans a Poet was called *Vates*, which is as much as a Diviner." Divining, Heaney remarks, is "a gift for being in touch with what is there, hidden and real, a gift for mediating between the latent resource and the community that wants it current and released." So a water diviner "resembles the poet in his function of making contact with what lies hidden, and in his ability to make palpable what was sensed or raised." Heaney comes on things in a similar way, "by that somnambulist process of search and surrender that is perhaps the one big pleasure of poetry that the reader of it misses."

Yet for all his insights into the craft, he realizes that it doesn't do to become too self-conscious about it. "A poem always has elements of accident about it, which can be made the subject of inquest afterwards, but there is always a risk in conducting your own inquest: you might begin to believe the coroner in yourself rather than put your trust in the man in you who is

capable of accident." And again: "I like the paraphrasable ex-
tensions of a poem to be as protean as possible, and yet I like
its elements to be as firm as possible." Or: "You are confirmed
by the visitation of the last poem and threatened by the elu-
siveness of the next one, and the best moments are those when
your mind seems to implode and words and images rush of
their own accord into the vortex."

Heaney is fond of words like *watermark, bedding, hard-core,
sleepwalking, hinterland, thickets*—words of digging and divining. A word like *Anahorish*—the name of the place where
he first went to school—gives him a chance to explore the
business of being Irish in Ulster. The poet's way is made clear
even in nonverse pieces, as in one (from a group called *Sta-
tions*) where he writes: "Flanders. It sounded heavy as an old
tarpaulin being dragged off a wet load." He says of Patrick
Kavanagh's poem "The Great Hunger" that "its elements are
water and earth rather than fire and air," and being the sort of
man who is enthusiastic about what is close to himself, could
well be talking of his own work. His own books of poetry
have come at roughly three-year intervals, the results of many
drafts on unlined foolscap, first in pen, then typed and re-
typed, relentlessly pruned and filled in and often discarded. A
poem is generally ambushed by hard work, but once in a while
he has a visitation. In May 1969, in Belfast, he wrote twenty-
two poems in one week; a number of these survived and appeared in his third book, *Wintering Out*.

Heaney the scholar is sometimes evident in the poems but
not obtrusive; there are references for those who catch them to
poets as far apart as Ovid and Osip Mandelstam, to Norse or
Elizabethan history. He is prepared to think of a poem as more
than just "a verbal contraption"—Auden's term, which Heaney
suggests is the remark of an artist keeping a few tricks up his
sleeve. For Heaney the enterprise of poetry is both minefield
and dance floor; it is a place where you must move carefully,
an arena where you are called on to perform. Poetry—more
dualities—is at once a love act "between masculine will, skill,
and intelligence and feminine clusters of image, word, and

emotion," *and* an expression of fearfulness. He felt while writing the poem "The Tolland Man" a sense that "unless I was deeply in earnest about what I was saying, I was simply invoking dangers for myself." The poet is a "double agent." His technique is not only his "way with words" but his "stance towards experience." Technique is the ability to bring together life and work, the result of "the creative effort to bring the meaning of one's experience within the jurisdiction of words."

Just what goes into that effort is best shown in one of his poems. "Act of Union" appeared in his 1975 collection, *North*, as a poem of twenty-eight lines divided into two fourteen-line sections. Two years before, a version twice that length—four sonnets—had been published in the British weekly *The Listener* under the title "A New Life." Before that, he had done a draft of the poem in free verse. It is a poem about the birth of a child, and also an allegory about Ireland (the woman), England (the man), and Ulster (the child). In *The Listener* version it was more of a love poem for Marie. In its present state it is less so—words with erotic overtones have been cut, and the sensuous optimism has been modified. In "A New Life" the last two lines run: "His fury cradled, us two hand in glove, / The triangle of forces solved in love." Whereas "Act of Union" ends: "No treaty / I foresee will salve completely your tracked / And stretchmarked body, the big pain / That leaves you raw, like opened ground, again." Heaney says, "I thought the resolution of 'A New Life' was too hopeful, the resonance too complacent. There were confused things in it, and some things a bit opportunistic, like the reflection on Casement's diaries. I still like the melody of 'A New Life' but came to think it was too dandified. Perhaps there was a darker mood I wanted to express. I think the brutality of the times gets into the shorter, less cajoling version. Perhaps I became puritanical about the consolations I thought art itself should offer."

THE TRAIN RUNS ON, west of the Mourne Mountains, past stone-walled Ulster meadows. The lecture is ready. He has put a slip of paper in *A Portrait of the Artist as a Young Man* so that he can quickly find Stephen Dedalus's thoughts after Stephen's conversation with the college dean about the object the dean calls an oil funnel and Stephen calls a tundish.

The language in which we are speaking is his before it is mine. How different are the words *home*, *Christ*, *ale*, *master*, on his lips and on mine! I cannot speak or write these words without unrest of spirit. His language, so familiar and so foreign, will always be for me an acquired speech. I have not made or accepted its words. My voice holds them at bay. My soul frets in the shadow of his language.

Heaney walks to the bar car. Powers whisky (Cork) or Bushmills (Ulster)? Both excellent. He orders a Bushmills and coincidentally finds himself in conversation with a young man in a black bomber jacket, a vicious scar on the back of one hand, who wants to talk about poetry. Being a poet is a profession in Ireland. Writers are presences, in life and afterwards, with territories earmarked, handed on. Yeats country, Joyce country; parts of the city belonging to Wilde or Beckett. Patrick Kavanagh's widow is recognized as she enters a shop in Baggot Street. There is almost a ghetto comfort, the security of the small, known world, to be set against the distintegration of European culture as posited in literature courses. And tonight someone will ask, "Mr. Heaney, don't you think the contribution of Irish letters to world literature is somewhat overvalued?" Ah. Well. He himself distrusts the English iambic pentameter. He is interested in the virtues of the parochial as opposed to the provincial. He has had good luck. But he needs to keep ahead of the scholars and camp followers. He is at a point where he must do as he bloody well likes. But he fears hubris. He knows he must keep his ear to his own ground.

He is now entering what, with a slightly self-mocking smile at the Mailer-ish term, he calls round two. He is at work on a batch of poems, about which he has ambitions of at least two kinds: on the one hand, "When the poem seems to stop, to start again and go on from there—striving for a single breath"; and on the other, not to respond too directly to the compulsions of the times. After the British ambassador to Ireland was assassinated last year, Heaney wrote a poem, "Triptych"; but in the latest version direct references to the killing have been removed.

Each of his poems is in its way an attempt at union, incorporating what to his girl students at Carysfort, talking of Wordsworth, he calls the physical elements and the dream vision; combining the national language which is Irish and the mother tongue which is English; making the declaration *non serviam* to the oppressive demands of the Irish past and yet seeking out a native mode; joining the verbal energies with their sense and felicities to the energies of time and place. . . Dualities, arguments, conflicting pieties. Through all this he reverts to ground or bog level. He is, like Sweeney, a tongue of the land. He too would break the hard light of opposing minds into a spectrum. His poems acquire their force from cogent images of his own life, as in the lines he wrote for his aunt Mary Heaney, recalled cooking in the kitchen at Mossbawn:

> And here is love
> like a tinsmith's scoop
> sunk past its gleam
> in the meal-bin.

The train comes into Belfast. Heaney lifts his black bag, which looks like a doctor's, full of books, his lecture, poems. A poet —he knows—cannot have a direct answer for the problems of the time. Tonight, when it is put to him, he will say that a "solution" lies in "changing the structures of feeling." Many feel that his work contributes toward that end.

Chapter Five

THE STONY GROUND

– 1978 –

STARDATE 3197 IN A distant galaxy. And on a raw late-autumn evening in 1978, Captain Kirk and the crew of the starship *Enterprise* are on the television screens of possibly half the 2,400 houses that form the Creggan housing estate—which is set on a 400-foot-high hill overlooking the city of Londonderry, in Northern Ireland—as tea is made, coal is put on the fire, homework is done, shirts are ironed, and (in thirty or so houses) food parcels are packed to be taken up to the Maze prison by bus next morning. Greeny-yellow streetlights flicker on over the narrow roads, and children who have been swinging round lamp posts or playing in gutted phone boxes run indoors for sausages and chips, bread and marge. Outside the Sinn Féin advice center on Central Drive a gaunt-cheeked youth of sixteen sets up a homemade ladder and climbs to collect the green, white, and orange tricolor that hangs from a broom pole over the doorway. An army patrol goes by, the four soldiers in camouflaged battle dress staggered on either side of the road, self-loading rifles at the ready. The corporal yells over to the tubercular-looking youth, "You're a bit late tonight, aren't you?" and they head off at a sudden tangent across the long-awaited twin football pitches, still a sea of mud, and down Rathkeele Way, scattering a pack of dogs, before taking a short-cut through an overgrown back garden.

In the shiny gym at the Parochial Centre, Charley Nash, the British lightweight champion, is training for his bout two days hence at the Grosvenor House in London. In the adjacent hall they are readying chairs and cards for tonight's bingo, a game that many in the Creggan believe to have been a personal invention of Bishop Daly of Derry. At St. Mary's Church, across the road, four priests are preparing to hear confession. John McChrystal, a city councilor and member of the Irish Independent party, who has a son in the Maze for handling explosives and a daughter married to a British soldier, walks down Bligh's Lane on his way to a community association meeting; he looks out over the cemetery where the Protestant and Catholic dead of Derry lie in the same ground and across the dip of the Bogside to the old walled city itself—a rocky, much-blasted acropolis beside the River Foyle. He sees across the dark river the now almost totally Protestant area of the Waterside, where he was born, and still ventures. Along the road an ice cream van pulls up. A brief recorded blur of loud music—just identifiable as Bing Crosby's favorite, "The Bells of St. Mary's"—rises with the damp mist and plumes of coal smoke through the street light, toward the stars. Seen from on high, the dimly lit terraced houses of the Creggan appear to have been crawling for a long time up the steep slope and to have halted now near the summit, forming an encampment, a rath, or a hill fort, in which an encircled tribe might stand for the last time.

A STRANGE PLACE to have built a public housing estate. Gerrymandering is given as one reason the then Protestant-dominated city council began the Creggan development here in 1946—extending the mostly Catholic west ward of the city so that the Catholics (a majority of the city population) couldn't affect the vote in the other wards. *Creggan* means stony ground, but the site, carved out of hillside bog resting on blue clay, promised damp and exposure to rain and wind. Derry is one of the wettest places in the British Isles. The hill meant for many a daily long climb. But for those who moved into it over the next few years, the Creggan was better than tumbledown nineteenth-century cottages in the Bogside, or huts in the ex–U.S. forces base at Springtown Camp, some way from the city. The Creggan houses were mostly three-bedroom units, terraced, with a living room and kitchen downstairs; a combined bathroom-toilet; fireplaces downstairs but no other heating arrangements; somewhat slung together (an apprentice bricklayer working on them got ten shillings and sixpence a week; the "large fines" aggregate used in many of the houses attracts the damp). A council estate: grey, off-white, or pale-green stucco and pebbledash; steel-framed windows. But no worse (in fact, maybe better) than similar developments in, say, Deptford or Newcastle—places, admittedly, that have never felt the same unrest or excited the same expectations as the Creggan.

An optimistically named Green Walk and the pedestrian Bligh's Lane crisscross the estate, but most roads fail to provide their houses with the splendid view of the Foyle and the city. Many of the plates for street names—a large number of which are of Donegal origin—are missing. There are fewer cars parked outside houses than one would see in an English council estate, and a good number of those here are damaged, awaiting do-it-yourself repair. As on estates elsewhere, amenities are sparse: no big stores; a few scruffy play areas; one stark pub, the Telstar. A desperate-looking doctors' office but no health clinic; no business offices; no professional families. A forlorn parade of shops, nameless and without advertisement, slumps along a section of Central Drive. Some shops when in fact open appear to be closed. Their doors are of steel plate and their windows doubly protected by wire screens and thick wooden shutters. Above the shops, the windows of the flats have been filled in with concrete blocks: they were too well placed for snipers. The bleak effect of these buildings is matched, across Central Drive,

by what looks like a large concrete incinerator, its roof edged
with an overhanging rim of barbed wire—the windowless community hall. Curious to think that this rundown by-product of
Fabian thought, the welfare state, and neo-garden city planning
should be one of the last havens of the IRA.

Creggan graffiti:

IRA

STUFF THE JUBILEE

POLITICAL STATUS FOR BILLY PAGE

BRITS OUT, PEACE IN

SMASH H-BLOCK

PROVOS RULE

KILL INFORMERS

WE STILL LOVE THE PROVISIONALS

PEOPLE IN THE CREGGAN complain of impositions but also
acknowledge various forms of dependency. There has clearly
been involuntary peonage but also obedience to the authority of
the republican tradition. They put up with an unjust status quo
for too long, and it finally blew up. So while the romantic and
resentful blame England, the knowledgeable also blame the
land and the atmosphere and their mothers and the church.
Ulster is the part of Ireland closest to Britain. Ulster is also the
most Irish part of Ireland, where the Irish past survives tangibly
in ancient tools, prehistoric crops (like flax), and old ways of
speech. The legendary hero Cuchulain was from Ulster. In
Derry, "the place of the oaks," Columba founded his religious
community in 545 A.D. before he went to Iona. Here the
O'Neills, chiefs of Ulster, rebelled against the English in the
sixteenth century. And in Derry, in 1609, the London guilds
and livery companies, prompted by the English government,
established London's first new town—which was also, unlike

Stevenage and Harlow, a bastide town, the last so built in Europe, its fortified walls meant for the control of this part of Ulster. Ever since, they have been a symbol for those physically or psychologically inside them of holding out against the surrounding kerns and bog people; and for those outside them, a symbol of alien domination. Many in the Creggan who grew up in the Brandywell and Bogside hold among their earliest memories the annual burning on the city walls of an effigy of Governor Lundy (regarded as a traitor by the Protestants), while in the Catholic houses below they heaped turf and rubbish on their fires so that odiferous smoke blew into Protestant faces. Orange drums beat their tattoo into young Catholic hearts, and most grew up knowing that parts of town were out of bounds for "their side." Sides have been firmly drawn, roles long taken, as for a drama (which is in fact life.)

Around Derry the 1922 border sweeps in an arc of roughly three-miles radius. It cuts off the city from much of its natural Donegal hinterland and reduces its natural trade. Yet despite the border, until the more severe checkpoints of recent times a number of Derry professional people managed to live in the South and work in the city; one says, "I used to light a cigarette at home in the Republic, get in the car, and stub out the cigarette as I went into the office." Many Creggan people have families and friends in Donegal; those with transportation can spend Sundays on a Donegal beach or hillside. They feel, inevitably, somewhat split.

The Creggan itself had a period of conscious identity in the early 1970s. This arose out of the renewed Troubles, which came in the wake of the civil-rights marches and housing action movement of 1968–69. Universal franchise in local elections and public-housing allocations fair to Catholics were achieved, but—belated reform preceding a sort of revolution—there followed riots, petrol bombs, and barricades. There was a brief moment when the British Army, taking over as a security force from the Royal Ulster Constabulary, was popular, and shortly thereafter, as searches proceeded and internment was introduced (August 1971), when it was not. For a short while, however, in the Creggan and Bogside, Free Derry existed. The writ of Westminster and Stormont ceased to run; barricades interrupted the bus routes; the Derry files of the Northern Ireland Housing Executive were burned in a Creggan bonfire; the policing of streets was taken over by residents' committees who fined speeding motorists and tidied the athletic ground; and Radio Free Derry broadcast from a house in the Creggan's Cromore Gardens. After Bloody Sunday, on January 30, 1972, when thirteen people were killed by army bullets in an unequal confrontation between men of the 1st Parachute Battalion and demonstrators against internment, fury united the Creggan. The IRA had more recruits than it could handle.

Yet this Creggan solidarity was a negative thing: it was propped up by the surrounding army, by CS gas, rubber bullets, and resentment. The continued assassinations and constant bombings in downtown Derry, as the IRA blasted away shop after shop, were more than most people could bear. The brittle charisma of the Irish "volunteers" cracked as the Provos and the Officials began to feud. And the IRA murder of Ranger William Best—a nineteen-year-old from Rathkeele Gardens who had joined the British Army and ill-advisedly come home on leave to see his mother—gave most Creggan mothers second thoughts. By the time the army moved back in, crushing the barricades on July 31, 1972, the rift in the Catholic community was already deep. Since then it has been like living through a slowly waning war, with the added demoralizing trouble for most people in the Creggan of not wholeheartedly supporting either side.

DERRY: ROUGHLY 75,000 people. The Creggan: estimates vary, but the estate's population, which perhaps peaked at 19,000, is now thought to be somewhere between 11,000 and 13,000. Derry not long ago had one of the highest birth rates in the world. Now, though average age is rising and family size falling, the Creggan is still one of the most productive places in these isles. When schools close in the afternoon the streets buzz with children; gardens, houses, and footpaths are suddenly full of

them. Older children are out pushing infants in prams. In some
streets parents with only seven children are thought to have a
small family. In Rathkeele Way, where at one point there were
more than three hundred "wains" (or pre-teenage children)
among fifty-two families, one woman had eighteen (six died in
infancy), another has fourteen, many have eight, twelve, ten
. . . Doors are always opening and shutting. Voices, calls, questions. Pathways are worn in the highly figured carpets between
front door and kitchen around the battered living-room suites.
In winter the little ones with coughs and colds are kept on the
sofas, wrapped up, near the fire. One large family in Rathkeele
Way gets through twelve to sixteen pints of milk a day, brought
by two milkmen. Half-hundredweight sacks of potatoes go in
half a week. It is hard to get into bedrooms because of bunk
beds and double beds and—without built-in cupboards or space
for wardrobes—piles of clothes and shoes.

What are the effects of growing up at such density? No bed
to call your own (the younger ones not only shift around but
are carried, while asleep, from one bed to another). First come,
first served in the toilet, and then bangs on the door: "Who's
in there? Hurry up, will you!" One youngster says, "You stay
in as long as you can get away with it—though it's a terror if
it's in use and you're trying to get to school." Hard to remember,
when you've grown up, that there was anything unusual about
these conditions, like sometimes having to sit—for lack of room
in the kitchen—on the back doorstep or the stairs to eat your
dinner; learning to do your homework in the midst of pande-
monium. Perhaps learning, too, to keep your own counsel, to
amuse yourself and be by yourself in the midst of a crowd, or
just get out of the house for a bit of air and hang around with
friends. ("I had no idea he was mixed up with them," a mother
says, "until the army came and showed us the gun.") And yet
everyone mucks in: daughters help their mothers in the kitchen;
sons and daughters contribute much of their wage packets if
they go to work. And when they say there's no privacy, they
don't mean from one another, but rather that the front door of
the next house faces directly into theirs across a shared entry,

or that when you're eating your breakfast cornflakes you may see a British soldier smiling in at you, nose pressed against the kitchen window.

In each sitting room stands a cabinet for the family treasures: precious cups; a silver spoon; china figurines; photos of children. In one or two such troves is to be found what looks like a stick of hard fudge about four inches long, flat-ended, and surprisingly heavy—a so-called rubber bullet (which is made of plastic). Rarely does a room lack a colored print of the Sacred Heart. And though the Creggan does have its better streets—generally the earliest built, nearest the city, with neat hedges and flower-packed gardens—there are others, such as Creggan Heights and Melmore Gardens, that give the six social workers who look after the Creggan much of their business. In the poorer houses some rooms have an overpowering smell of bodies, of stale clothes, and sometimes of pee. Just about everybody smokes in the Creggan; ashtrays are full of butts. It is a place where it is still an act of hospitality to offer a pack or actually toss cigarettes round the room on the assumption that everyone smokes. Fingertips are yellow-brown with nicotine, and clouds of smoke eddy round the television screen.

Some people in the Creggan say, "We've never been better off." But if no one is starving, a girl like Moira P., with a husband in the Kesh and four small children, is living on £18.45 a week supplementary benefit after deductions for rent arrears. Several windows in her house are broken; several rooms are barely furnished. In the living room a row of cushions lines the skirting board where a sofa might be, and the television is broken. Quite a lot of Creggan people do without lampshades so that forty-watt bulbs give a better light. Unemployment in Derry is roughly 15 percent, but in some streets of the Creggan 40 percent of the men and boys are out of work. Does overpopulation lead to underemployment? Or does having nothing to do lead to more babies? There is, one feels, either an anachronistic peasant precaution or an archaic recklessness in having all those children when you can get neither a big enough house nor a secure job—a trust that the Lord, who (the church says) enjoins marriage for procreation, will provide; and the Lord, via the Department of Health and Social Security, just about does. And yet one Creggan mother says proudly, "I love the noise and bustle of children. I got involved in the first tenants' association for the children's sake. They were never a bother. When they were little, I used to line them up on the couch and tell them 'Snow White' so that I could scrub the floor."

In any event, complaints about poor housing and no jobs don't lead to any widespread movement to clear out. Some go. Most come back. Leaving Derry is the most difficult thing a Derry man or woman can do, and Creggan folk are no exception. Saint Columba in exile about 563 wrote that he would swap all Scotland for a hut in Derry. Some women in the Creggan who have been GI brides or have been married to Japanese seamen have come back, often dragging their husbands with them, otherwise without—home is more important. Men have returned from jobs abroad to be unemployed in Derry. Last winter a killer whale got stranded above the anti-terrorist booms in the River Foyle, and the people of Derry fretted about it, knowing how it must have felt, alone, away from its proper home. Creggan men have in the past often gone to Britain for jobs, but now, with unemployment there too, they feel they might as well be on the dole at home as on the dole away from it. One eighteen-year-old boy from a Republican family, studying at the technical college, says, "I'd spend the rest of my life in the Creggan if there was a house to move into." A hundred and fifty Creggan families were interviewed by a London sociologist; only one family said that the Creggan wasn't the best place in the world. Perhaps this fierce attachment to one's place is a product of deprivation in other things. Éamonn Deane, secretary of the North West Centre for Learning and Development in Derry, says, "If you're born into a situation where failure is hanging over you all the time, to preserve your sanity and self-respect you build up a myth that where you are is the best place—Derry is the best; the Creggan is the best. If you faced the reality you'd go mad."

Deane himself came back to Derry after a year in Canada because, he felt, "There was so much unfinished business." It is commonly agreed that Derry is an uncommon place; it has a

claim on you, if only to live there. There is a sense of isolation—
London is on the other side of the moon and Belfast is
somewhere else—but it is also a village with a close consciousness of kin. After marriage, women are often still referred to
by their family names. Brendan Johnson, a social worker who
grew up in the Creggan, says, "It's a place where everyone
knows everyone. You can start talking to a man and he'll be
telling you at once about your grandparents or how he knew
your Uncle Jimmy." There is a local accent (the name Nash,
for instance, is pronounced *Nish*), and the British hardly understand you. "Abowty!" they say in greeting, or simply "Yes!"
as a hullo.

The pride of place has now and then welled forth in music,
from the "Londonderry Air," or "Danny Boy," through the
hymns written by Mrs. C. F. Alexander, including "All Things
Bright and Beautiful," to the songs of Phil Coulter, a native
son who wrote "Puppet on a String" and "The Town I Love."
No one is surprised to hear that Derry is known worldwide,
though not for the happiest of reasons now; that the Creggan is
famous, like the Bogside, in Germany and Japan, with Dutch
cameramen and French photographers prowling through it in
the footsteps of American political scientists (and everyone
knows what British television reporter Bernard Falk looks like).
Like the Shankill and the Falls, it has become dignified with
the definite article, a small place enlarged by recent history.
Even the most chauvinistic Cregganites feel bound now and
then to deflate their own reputation. Councilor John McChrystal says, of the recent Troubles, "Compared with the Lebanon
or Cyprus or Rhodesia, this was nothing." And a Rathkeele
Way mother says, "This place is like a holiday camp compared
to the Ardoyne."

ANOTHER CAUSE OF the isolation that people feel in a place like
the Creggan is the sense they have of not possessing alterna-
tives that other places offer. They are deprived of the feeling
that they can do something about their predicament—whether
it's painting the outside of the house or hiring a lawyer to get
a son out of jail. The lack of confidence sets in early on. At

eleven plus, a number of children begin to suspect they are uneducable; at sixteen, many are told they are unemployable. Then it's the dole, or the brew, as they call it here: hanging around on Creggan street corners; wearing a rut between home and the social security office in Asylum Road; losing impetus. "When you're on the brew you can never find time for anything," says a Creggan man, "except maybe watching TV or throwing stones at soldiers."

For Creggan children there is a brief golden age before they reach eleven. The Troubles don't seem to have bothered these children as much as one might expect. At St. John's Primary School at the foot of the Creggan, Hugh Kelly, the headmaster, is proud of his immaculate modern buildings full of apparently cheerful and attentive children. Kelly, who has taught in other parts of Ulster and the United States, says, "As far as I can tell, the Troubles have affected our small children no more than World War II affected us, as kids, when Derry was occupied by half the navies in the world. Children have to be adjustable. If they have a good family structure behind them, there's not much to worry about. However, we have social problems here which affect the children—many broken homes; a high rate of alcoholism among men; and a lot of drug-taking by women. So we try and make the school a home. And I believe that our children are better behaved than those in some other Northern Ireland towns. They're generally brighter than those I once taught in a privileged area of Philadelphia."

Kelly points out to visitors the now-painted-over marks of stray bullets in several walls and ceilings. On one occasion a Provo gunman entered the school, rifle in hand, intending to go up on the roof and shoot at an army post that was then across the way. Kelly talked him out of it, and out of the school. After the IRA set off a bomb at Aldershot that killed a number of civilians, a British soldier went berserk in the army post. He fired several shots at the nearest Irishman, who happened to be Hugh Kelly sitting in his office. The shots missed. Kelly says, with a survivor's forebearance, "It was a natural thing for him to do."

While the Creggan was on its own during the no-go period, attendance at its secondary schools was higher than ever: over 90 percent at St. Joseph's Boys' School. After that, attendance slipped—and one excuse was that house searches by the army had kept everyone up all night. The boys frequently rioted against the soldiers at dinner break outside school; if the riots threatened to spill into the schoolyard, teachers went out and with whistles halted the trouble. In those days "Up the Provos" was not only painted on walls outside but scribbled in the margins of exercise books. Kevin McCallion, a Creggan-bred teacher at St. Joseph's, says that the history of the Russian Revolution used to prompt analogies—a boy would point out similarities between, say, Bloody Sunday and the 1905 march to appeal to the Tsar. Now such comparisons are no longer made, at least overtly, and the doodles in exercise books are more likely to be "Manchester United for the Cup." But one boy who was blinded by a rubber bullet is still at St. Joseph's, working for his A-levels, a living proof of all that happened.

At St. Cecilia's, a Creggan girls' secondary school, teachers at the height of the Troubles felt that the students found it to be an oasis, a sanctuary. Inside it the girls could escape from the constant concerns of outside—where in fact two St. Cecilia girls were shot dead, caught in cross fire. The pressures on the girls now spring less from the effects of the Troubles than from family circumstances. A girl may miss school because her mother is at work and she is needed to look after younger children, or has to go to visit father or brothers in prison. A teacher at St. Cecilia's says she is constantly amazed at how absolutely normal the girls are. Disciplinary problems are rarer than in the past—possibly because, with a falling birth rate, the ratio of teachers to students is higher; and teacher turnover is smaller too.

And yet some teachers acknowledge that their profession has had a responsibility, for good or ill, in the teaching of Irish history—and for that matter, in the inculcation of a violent stance toward life. The strap is still often used in the local boys' schools. In the late sixties, class-conscious teachers and priests

at St. Columbs—the Derry Catholic grammar school to which
the brighter Creggan boys go—used to refer to Creggan pupils
as "slags"; the Creggan was "Cannibal Island." Éamonn Deane
attended a teachers' conference at which a Christian Brothers
monk, well known for throwing desks at his pupils, denounced
boys for stone-throwing. Graduates of St. Columbs vie at re-
calling scenes of the church militant that would seem to match
Amnesty International's recent report on RUC mistreatment
of prisoners. Éamonn McCann writes in his memoir *War and
an Irish Town* of various bizarre punishments at St. Columbs
and adds: "Not all techniques were quite so sophisticated.
Father F. might simply knock a boy unconscious and tell two
of his class-mates to 'cart him outside. I'm not having him
here, lying about in my class-room.' " There were, as Kevin
McCallion remembers, other teachers too who made their
point—like Frank Macauley, also an editorial writer for the
Derry Journal. Most history textbooks were British. When Mr.
Macauley came across a sentence that began, for example,
"Our armies, while attacking the French . . ." he would say,
"Right, boys, strike out 'our' and write in the word 'British.' "
   Much Irish nationalism is learned in the home. Naturally,
like Irish football for the boys and Irish dancing for the girls.
Passionately, with talk of Cromwell; the Easter Rising; the
blood flowing down O'Connell Street; the British prison ships
in Belfast harbor; and Padhraic Pearse's words, "There are
things more horrible than bloodshed, and slavery is one of
them." In a number of Creggan houses when "God Save the
Queen" came over the radio there was a rush to be first to
switch it off. One Creggan father said recently, "Perhaps we
shouldn't have been surprised when we found one day that our
children were putting into practice all that we'd been talking
about so long."
   For some children who came of age in the Creggan there was
an education in resentment and frustration: hearing explosions
in the night; waking to army searches of their homes; aware
suddenly that their parents were powerless—mum and dad
couldn't do *anything* for them. Soldiers are all sorts—tactful

and arrogant, cool or scared—but naturally the less polite moments of searches tend to stick in the memory, and affect one's
subsequent behavior. A Creggan mother of eleven children
recalls how, when the army came to lift her son, a soldier gave
her wild abuse about the size of her family. She had just baked
for Halloween eleven apple tarts with the initials of each child
on them, and the soldiers told her they had caught her son with
a gun in a car. While she had hysterics (she cried for a month),
the house was searched. During a full search the family is told
to bring all its valuables into one room and stay there, so
there can be no accusation of theft. The soldiers take off the
light switches, tap the walls, go through letters, and look in
the box of Rice Krispies. Sick children may be got from bed
and fetched downstairs. The mother of eleven says, "Once the
British Army comes in your house, it's not your home any
more." Now her youngest, a little girl, hides when she sees
soldiers. However, during a follow-up army check on the house,
Brendan, the smallest boy, came downstairs with his boots
untied on the way to school, and the major stooped and tied
up his boots for him.

John McChrystal says, "There's hardly a lad on this estate
between fourteen and twenty who hasn't been hauled up to the
army camp at the top of the hill and gone through an ordeal
there that left him burning with fury." Cregganites swap tales
(whose basic accuracy may on occasion, from constant retelling,
acquire a certain tallness) of army behavior: one hears of young
Catholics being picked up by the Special Air Service troops and
threatened with being dropped off in a tough Loyalist area; of
how, when the army get you in the back of a Land-Rover, they
often forcefully put the boot in; and how, when up at Piggery
Ridge for questioning, you get a knuckle in the back of the head
which slams your head against the wall. One fourteen-year-old
boy, whom Éamonn Deane knows, encountered an army patrol
in Brooke Park as he headed down into Derry. He ran—who
knows why?—but he ducked into the library and the patrol
came in after him. Cornered, he threw books at them. He was
charged with IRA membership and sent up to Crumlin Road
jail, Belfast. A year and a half later the case came up, and the

charge was dismissed. A year and a half in jail and then dismissed! The lad himself, Deane said, didn't feel embittered. He said that if he had been let out they would have got him for something else.

One can begin to see how—whether or not such a lad belongs to the IRA—he might be moved in that direction. Adolescent pride produces a natural enough reaction to being put upon and searched. There is a desire to be an equal among one's friends; a desire to be a man in one's own mind; perhaps even a desire to prove to one's mother that one is a man—one has balls at last. And these factors are probably more to the fore than the Easter Rising when a patrol hauls you up short and stretches you out against a wall and questions are fired at you that swiftly take away any residual manners. The lad asking the questions, wearing the uniform, isn't much different from you; only he has the right to carry a self-loading rifle and you don't.

Thus a soldiery came to be an army of occupation; they were a red flag to a bull, a dare and a challenge to Creggan youth. Outside the schools and the shops on Central Drive the lads hurled stones at the troops who had sometimes thumped them about, and the army fired back CS gas and rubber bullets. (Stone-throwing is a local skill: one Creggan seven-year-old, a crack shot with a stone, has put several soldiers in hospital, and is now "in care.") Many Creggan parents felt, as John McChrystal did, that their children had a case: that, disapprove of violence though one might, the army was abusing the kids and their parents couldn't protect them and therefore their rebellion was justified. There was in a way nothing political about it, at least at first—just a grudge that had to be worked off. Though soon enough bombs were being placed in Derry shops and offices by youngsters who found themselves serving an older cause.

Of course, the fact that perhaps a third of Creggan youth over sixteen have no jobs perpetuates the furies—and there are twice as many unemployed boys as girls in Derry, where shirt factories and shops absorb female labor. At sixteen begins a desperate search for work or training, asking everyone you know—the milkman, priests, bartenders. And finding a job doesn't mean you can keep it. BSR Electric moved into a factory next to the Creggan and then after two years went back to England, leaving many redundant. Young Damian Moore worked at the bus depot until he was eighteen and was then laid off, he believes, because he would have had to be paid a man's full wages. Eamonn Deane believes that youth unemployment in Derry reflects deficiencies in education and the way young people are viewed as problems—which they then often become. At some government training centers they learn how to build a wall, which is then knocked down. Trade unions won't let trainees do useful work—for example, they have to burn furniture they've just made rather than let it be sold. Deane says, "This is not only a destruction of resources but of what's in people's heads."

Deane is associated with a group that is trying something different with a youth workshop in the once-derelict Foyle College building in Derry, helped by a grant from the Northern Ireland Department of Manpower Services, which has put £250,000 of European Economic Community cash into youth employment projects this past year (1978). The workshop's purpose is described by its director Colm Cavanagh as "not to keep youths off the streets or to keep them from becoming republicans but to enable them to become aware of themselves and their potential." Seventy-five youngsters aged between sixteen and nineteen turn up there daily. Twenty-eight of them are from the Creggan, mostly boys but with a few girls too who come down the hill each morning in an old minibus to work at welding, woodwork, fabrics, painting, plastering, toy-making, bricklaying, repairing the old building, and studying local and family history. They each get a training allowance of £19.50 a week and can stay a year. (There is a long waiting list to join the workshop.) The crafts learned may help them find jobs or may simply give them a sense of their own worth, and this may, among other things, teach them how to cope with being unemployed. A study group is now trying to identify skills in the Creggan so that the right jobs can be encouraged in the area. And in the meantime the Creggan lads feel like sailors voyaging over a flat-earth sea, toward an edge over which they may drop into nothing. It gives them a nervousness, perhaps compounding the already slightly manic adolescent force that can erupt at any moment—as in attending a football match (if only they had a team to follow), or in throwing stones, or in merely dumping one of their number in a water barrel to celebrate his birthday. And they are rightly wary. Is society about to kick them hard for something, they aren't sure what, in which case should they get in a few kicks first?

THE CREGGAN as a deprived area has a number of groups wanting to be of help. (The "deprivation" is mostly in terms of jobs and housing and hope, but is perhaps easier to picture in the shape of a Creggan boy who has been shown how to grow runner beans and doesn't realize they can be eaten.) There are social workers; the church; the tenants' association; the Sinn Féin advice center on Central Drive; and the community association resource center in a Portakabin next to the community hall, where several young community workers try to deal with problems about taxes, benefits, criminal injury compensation, blocked drains, and housing allocations. They also try to get people to help themselves, but realize that even the most independent need help with bureaucratic rigmarole. Supplementary benefits, for example, are a source of even greater confusion in Northern Ireland than in Britain. There are problems because in Northern Ireland rent arrears—higher than average in the Creggan—can be deducted from social security benefits, and a service charge of fifty pence a week deducted, too. People may be aggrieved because a broken window has been left unfixed or because in the course of repairs a perfectly good front door was removed and an inferior door installed. Some of these problems loom large, and have to be talked about not just for themselves but because a family may have even greater problems it can't discuss.

However, some problems do exist in their own right. The Housing Executive considers nearly 10 percent of Creggan housing to be "unfit," and is currently reroofing and rewiring the earliest houses built there. Creggan residents are awaiting with interest an inquiry into recent allegations that money appropriated by the Housing Executive for modernization has "disappeared." Two hundred and fifty Creggan houses are occupied by squatters, and though eviction notices can't be enforced, some squatters end up paying a "use and occupation charge," much like a rent but giving those who pay it none of a tenant's rights.

Housing has been a Derry problem for so long that it has produced its own genre of humor. For example: A small boy is playing in a Derry street, chanting as he bounces a ball, "The Protestants have all the houses, the Protestants have all the houses, the Protestants—"

He is interrupted by a priest who stops and says, "That's not quite right, my child—and never forget, Our Lord Jesus was born in a stable."

The priest walks on and hears the ball begin to bounce again and the boy start chanting, "Our Lord was born in a stable because the Protestants have all the houses . . ."

Since 1968 housing has ceased to be much of a sectarian issue in Derry, but it remains a concern in the Creggan, where some houses are vastly overcrowded. Feuds occur over who gets which house. There used to be forty or so Protestant families on the estate, but during the Troubles, although there was little overt intimidation and the local clergy told them to sit tight, most moved away. There are now said to be two or three Protestant families living in what has become a de facto Catholic ghetto, but they don't proclaim their difference. Some social workers believe there are more people living in the Creggan than official estimates suggest, with several families doubling up in one house. (A three-bedroom Creggan house costs between £6.50 and £8.20 a week in rent and rates.) There is also a waiting list of roughly a hundred and forty for Creggan houses— formed in part from young people who grew up in the Creggan and want to live close to their parents, or people who want to be transferred from farther-out estates; in the Creggan you can get home from work for lunch.

THERE ARE FREEDOMS as well as deprivations in the Creggan: freedom, for one thing, to talk and talk and talk about the injustices of the past as if they still existed (the rancor still exists); freedom, moreover, from many of the normal restrictions of authority and civil law. Only recently have the police, the Royal Ulster Constabulary, been seen again in the Creggan, generally delivering summonses with an army squad to give them cover. (A month or so ago the RUC delivered to a Creggan man a summons for driving the wrong way up a one-way street in Belfast; he lives on a one-way street, and the RUC, delivering the summons, drove up it the wrong way. In any Catholic area the RUC has the problem of being considered an almost totally Protestant and traditionally anti-Catholic force; and its attempts to recruit Catholics so that it can get over this are thwarted by Catholic fears of what would happen to them in IRA hands if they joined the RUC.)

But there was never much ordinary crime in the Creggan, and it may be almost an aspect of normality that more break-ins are being reported, and blamed by many on ex-IRA men. A hand-lettered sign, in orange and green chalk, has been put up over the doorway of the frequently robbed Creggan Post Office in Central Drive:

Derry Brigade Irish Republican Army
We unreservedly condemn all raids on this P.O. and the inconvenience caused to people in this area. Actions of this type do not further Irish Freedom.

The Provos are also known for meting out their own "punishments" by kneecapping, head-shaving, and execution to offenders against their code: most recently two young women involved in a robbery had their hair sheared off and paint poured over them. Cregganites claim, however, that there is more petty crime—such as car thefts and meters being "done" —on the Protestant Waterside. Car crashes in the Creggan in the past few years have often met with RUC advice (if no one has been hurt) to "sort it out yourselves." A recommended way of getting rid of a car abandoned outside your house is to call the army and suggest there is a bomb under it. No one pays much attention to planning restrictions: several "mobile shops" are parked, seemingly forever, in front gardens, and in one house a small general store operates in a front parlor, no doubt fulfilling a local need. The city bus service runs downtown and back every twenty minutes, but there are also unlicensed cabs or "people's taxis," which charge the same tenpence fare per passenger and head down into the city when they have a carload.

Although flying the Irish tricolor is illegal in the North, it hangs—except when stolen by army souvenir hunters—outside the Sinn Féin center on Central Drive. Provisional Sinn Féin claims a certain apartness from its military wing, but the distinction remains obscure; the Provos with greater clarity explain their division from the Marxist Official IRA, which is now said to have mostly faded into the Irish Republican Socialist Party, perhaps lessening the Hatfield-versus-McCoy type of feuding that went on between them. The paramilitary leaders of both sects are well-known names in the Creggan, though well-wishers suggest it is better not to print them.

The chairman of Derry Provisional Sinn Féin, Johnny Johnson, is available to visitors most afternoons in the Central Drive office (a squat for which the Housing Executive refuses to accept rent)—two dilapidated rooms with peeling wallpaper, bare concrete floors, and an old couch with torn cushions. The filing cabinets are empty, the result (Johnson says) of army raids; he and several colleagues were held last August for three days at a police station in Belfast. ("Not a hand was laid on us—and the grub was respectable enough.") An army patrol drops in every day or so and exchanges badinage: "I thought you were on leave then . . ." "When are you getting some new posters?" On both sides the eyes, over smiling mouths, are cold. Johnson —who is in his late thirties, with a modified Zapata mustache and longish hair—enjoys explaining Sinn Féin's proposals for an independent Ireland of thirty-two counties, divided into four provinces under a federal government. "You have to have a political answer when the violence is gone," he says. "Otherwise it's all been wasted." Moreover, "you can't bomb a million Protestants and then have a free Ireland." The Protestants would continue to be in a majority in the northern province. As for the present Eire government, they are "the pro-Brits in Dublin," and as bad as Roy Mason, the British Secretary of State for Northern Ireland. Still, Johnson believes that the Brits themselves, the colonial masters, will eventually recognize the solution that comes from the barrel of a gun. It is now the Last Phase of the Struggle. But Sinn Féin acknowledges its minority position. "We're the last straw," Johnson says, "for the really desperate. We're down to the hard core, the most determined of the youth and the old."

It is hard to judge the size of the Republican hard core in the Creggan—one in twenty may be a reasonable guess. A determinedly Republican woman, with a son in Long Kesh, judges her own neighborhood and finds it wanting. "I think we're still at war. But the majority just want to live in peace." Old friends are nervous about letting their children play with hers in case, corrupted by her ideas, they end in prison, though occasionally one such friend will ask her for advice, saying "My son's just been lifted for doing a car—nothing to do with the Provos, mind you." She thinks her neighbors are more interested in TV shows like *Opportunity Knocks*, bingo, and the Wednesday-night dances at the Parochial Centre. "The only way we're going to get rid of the British is by doing away with the TVs, the sex, and the football," she says.

Certainly IRA violence has cost it support—not just assassinations or kneecapping, but the fact that a man's car is taken and left wrecked next morning; such an act may lose the IRA more friends than a maiming or bombing. Tales of protection money being paid by pubs and shops contribute to a Mafia-like image rather than that of a national resistance. Even within families there are differences of attitude: one brother, "lifted" out of crowded Creggan life into jail, doesn't necessarily create emulation among his kin—though they may not condemn him, either; he is simply doing things his own way. As for their feelings for Britain, an elderly former British soldier who has returned his medals talks sharply of present-day British soldiers, who according to him have no morals, manners, or discipline. Other younger Cregganites take the Queen's shilling and go off to serve in Germany. In the broad, war-weary middle, plagues

are called for on both houses. A youngster working at the resource center talks of "the cowboys on both sides." People are
probably more anti–British Army than they are pro-Provo.
There are said to be many more ex-IRA men than IRA men in
the Creggan.

Similarly, despite the ubiquitous graffiti, not many support
the campaign for political status for IRA prisoners. The conditions in H-Block at the Maze Prison, where 330 IRA men—
70 of them convicted murderers—are "on the blanket," refusing
to wear prison clothes or clean out their cells, are generally regarded as self-imposed. A woman like Mary Nelis is exceptional
—a mother of ten and a staunch Republican made all the more
so by having a son in the Kesh. She takes part in protests all
over Europe for political status.

Once a month Mrs. Nelis is among the little crowd of people
waiting quietly at 8:00 A.M. on Central Drive for a city bus
chartered by the Sinn Féin Prisoners' Defence Fund. Each
Wednesday and Saturday it stops there for its first batch of
passengers; it calls at two points in the Creggan and one in the
Bogside. The ride to Crumlin Road or the Maze takes two or
three hours each way, and the fare is a modest fifty pence. You
would think it was a load of people going downtown except for
the fact that most have bags and cardboard boxes full of provisions, books, and cigarettes. Husbands and wives are on the
way to visit their sons; brothers and sisters go, too; young
wives have babies on their laps. Some are going, anxiously, for
the first time; some for the umpteenth. The newcomers tend
to sit in silence, but the veterans chat with each other, read the
morning's *Sun*, and hand a Beano to the kids. The bus is soon
full of cigarette smoke. At the other end there is a good deal
of hanging around, a search, a ride in a prison bus, and then a
half-hour visit. When Mary Nelis saw her son Dennis recently
she found him confused; he couldn't get the words out and
didn't seem to understand what she was saying.

THE CREGGAN'S SITE, unkindly in some respects, is in one way
handy: anybody dying there is close to the city cemetery, which
sprawls over the windy flank of the hill, just below the lowest

Creggan streets, with a fine view of the river and Derry city. Protestants and Catholics have been buried here in the past alongside one another and those with obviously British names. Here lie O'Connells and Davidsons and Carrutherses. Here took place some stiff fighting in recent years. And here, now, in the southwest corner is a zone of green turf reserved for those who have died with perhaps bomb or gun in hand, their graves marked by a white flagpole for flying the Irish flag on anniversaries and by a granite group memorial. Such names as Coyle, McCool, Carlin, and Lafferty. The most recent is Dennis Heaney, June 10, 1978. The memorial—"Erected by the Officers and Volunteers of the Derry Brigade in honour of their comrades who made the supreme sacrifice that their country could be free"—is surmounted by a carved grey stone figure of the emblematic Irish hero Cuchulain, based on the memorial to the Easter Rising at the general post office, Dublin. A dying warrior, shield and short sword in hand, bound it seems to a tree trunk; and on his shoulders a phoenix-like bird, flapping its wings.

It is possible to have many thoughts on this spot: about the dark goddess who has demanded the tribute of such deaths; or about what sort of wacky empire or occupying power it is that allows a terrorist organization to set up such a monument, advertising its deeds. Johnny Johnson says that the last bastion of Irish independence is going to be in Derry. But one suspects that even in the presently, variously beleaguered Creggan there are glimmerings of a future in which much of this may seem old hat: a future in which EEC farm prices might make for such prosperity in Ireland that few down there want anything to do with the boyos up here, and perhaps in which even Ulster manufacturers and farmers see a readier and more profitable way to world markets via Dublin rather than Westminster. Cuchulain himself looks like an American Indian, and prompts thoughts on the end of a noble race.

We had fed the heart on fantasies. Yet a doctor who serves many Creggan patients says, "It's easier to treat unreal fears than real ones." He notices that many Creggan people feel they should be given immediate help if they are in trouble, and that ordinary difficulties tend to create complaints faster than elsewhere. People here still expect doctors to make house calls, even in the middle of the night. There is much hysteria: "Come quickly, Doctor, a man has been shot!" though the doctor may then find a houseful of excited people and a man not badly hurt but perhaps bruised by the butt of a gun. In a crisis the person in shock may not want Valium, but everyone around him does. He thinks many Creggan women are dependent on tranquilizers, but can't tell if it is worse than in other U.K. council estates. (One Creggan woman says of another woman, nine of whose eleven children have been arrested at one time or other, "She eats Valium like candy.") There is a lot of bronchitis and arthritis, and more lung cancer than before. People seem to have low resistance—colds spread fast—perhaps because of poor diets. With the onset of the Troubles the rate of admission to mental hospitals went down; now it seems to be going up again. In the Creggan (as elsewhere in Ulster), when the homicide rate rises, the suicide rate falls, and vice versa. Now there are an increasing number of suicides. Several young people recently killed themselves by jumping off Craigavon Bridge across the Foyle, while in the Creggan last September five teenagers got worked up and slashed themselves, though not mortally.

There are obvious dangers in taking such signs and saying "Things are getting better." For one thing, someone may immediately plant a bomb and blow off a few innocent limbs to prove that it isn't so. For another, there is much that remains abnormal—army checks and searches; the need for proof of one's identity; barbed wire preventing access to the historic city walls of Derry; an unease one feels in certain places, a sensation of being watched; and a knowledge or expertise one could only have acquired in Northern Ireland in the last few years, like getting *out* of a car if you come under fire so that flying pieces of car metal don't hit you as well as bullets.

Yet despite the mid-November IRA bombings, which reminded Derry and other Ulster towns of the terrorists' presence and capabilities, people in the Creggan note what may be aspects of returning "normality," such as an increase in vandalism—slingshots are in; a building at St. Cecilia's was recently flooded, and a cat decapitated. A local headmaster surprised his staff not long ago by asking, at assembly, for prayers for those in authority. In drawings by primary-school children there are fewer pictures of soldiers shooting over walls. (A few years back, one child's nativity scene showed an army helicopter instead of a star over Bethlehem.) Charley Nash, the boxer, repeats what he tells people he meets on tour: "It's as peaceful here as anywhere in England." The man who once ran the Free Derry radio transmitter from his Creggan house, exhorting listeners to "Keep the murderers out! Make every stone and petrol bomb count!", is running a voluntary association for one-parent families.

If any good has come out of the Creggan experience, it may be the present commitment of many people there to community schemes, tenants' associations, mutual-aid groups, and the like. Many former political activists have turned to social work. (They don't necessarily regret or feel ashamed of having at the height of the troubles planted a bomb or two; they just wouldn't do the same thing now.) Some here believe that the new breed of nonpolitical community workers may effect more significant change than has been achieved by the much-trumpeted transfer of city council power from Protestant to Catholic politicians. Meanwhile, more Catholic women are using contraceptives or attending a church-approved family-planning clinic. People are going out more. In the past, Creggan women rarely got much beyond their own doorsteps and a gossip with the neighbors, but now it's bingo, dances, the charismatic, among other things. For parents, of course, the worry of waiting for children to return home at night is multiplied here. "You never sleep till you hear the last of them coming in," says John McChrystal. Teenage girls are interested in discos, hairstyles, and part-time jobs, while their male counterparts wonder if the new Derry City football team will ever get off the ground. At St. John's primary school they did a project on the Norman Conquest recently, and for the staging of the Battle of Hastings more children wanted to be English than Normans. Frank Macauley is clearly still up against it.

FOR THE ARMY, "normality" is best achieved by not going on about it. Senior officers quietly hope it is being "eased back" in Ulster, in Derry (as even they call it), and the Creggan. The army has the advantage of freshness. The locals may be tired out, but the soldiers come in from West Germany or Britain on a four-month tour of constant duty. Yet the soldiers have possibly the disadvantage of first impressions, of conclusions jumped to, and of seeing it as a problem on just one level: get rid of the gunmen—therefore convince the people of the place that they must give up the gunmen. The army, one feels, doesn't always appreciate the compost of history, geography, and social conditions that nurtures the unrest and resentment. And the necessary empathy often isn't there. Even highly trained officers who have been well-briefed on the background to the Troubles think of the people in the Creggan as "Paddies." And naturally the natives think of these khaki-uniformed peace-keepers as "Brits," and can't help flinching when they hear an English accent.

At the top of the Creggan hill is an army camp, known from its swine-breeding days as the Piggeries—as local Republicans are delighted to tell you. The army had a battalion here and now has a company. Patrols of the Creggan and neighboring areas take place at irregular times, on foot or by Land-Rover, and the soldiers keep an eye open for packages in cars; new cars; people walking together who don't usually walk together; people who are in a certain spot daily and then are somewhere else— police work of a sort. The patrols are smaller than before, and house searches less frequent. (The locals say that army intelligence is much improved.) The army attempts to be as unobtrusive as possible, but four men with self-loading rifles walking down a street in combat gear are not inconspicuous.

The army realizes that for some their presence seems to legitimize the Provos, as the sight of British soldiery bolsters

THE STONY GROUND 165

the arguments of those who say, "We are at war." But they also believe that if they weren't here, the Creggan would become an arsenal. The army claims to know who the top IRA men are but are frustrated by lack of evidence—the bosses keep themselves clean. Many downtown checkpoints have been removed in recent months, but they remain on various roads leading into town. Liaison groups with army and local representatives try to deal with aggravations arising from searches. The soldiers on searches get to know certain families, and come into a house asking "Where's Billy? Where's Michael? Where's Joe?" A few families are abusive, some are civil enough, and in one or two there are cups of tea. The best ambassador is a thoughtful and cheerful corporal leading a search patrol. For the power and responsibility are great, and a foul-mouthed or bad-tempered NCO can put things quickly back to O'Connell Street or the Boyne.

In the past year only one round has been fired in the Creggan, and that was apparently unpremeditated—a "cowboy shoot." However, two petrol bombs were hurled at the Piggeries camp last summer by heroes who hid behind a group of eight- to twelve-year-olds throwing stones. A booby trap was found during the autumn in a back garden in Creggan Heights. Detonated up at the camp, it blew tiles off roofs two hundred yards away. (If it had gone off where it was placed, it would have demolished half a house and any children playing in the next-door gardens.) During the summer there was a spate of bomb hoaxes as the lads—for "a bit of a crack"—let off fireworks to keep the army busy. The army is aware that things are not yet normal ("If they were, we'd be having tea and buns with one another") but does find itself these days looking for lost children, sorting out a family fight that erupts into the street, and tracking down robbers. They know that bombs can go off at any time or that a sniper bullet without warning can kill; as indeed one did in downtown Derry last September.

ON SATURDAY AFTERNOON many of the people from the Creggan are down in Derry, shopping, browsing, chatting, meeting friends, or in the case of the youth, hanging around in case something happens. The women are there to stock up on groceries cheaper than those they can get on the estate; those without cars, the majority, catch a bus or a cheap cab home. To the blitzed and frazzled heart of the city these shoppers lend a momentary bustle. The doors of Littlewood's and Well-worth's and the other big shops in Waterloo Place swing back and forth. Raincoats flap and shopping bags twist in the wintry squalls. To one side of Wellworth's the lads wait, propped against boarded-up shop fronts or against the metal screens over windows, wearing almost a uniform of boots, denim jackets, and trousers that are too short. In the middle of Water-loo Place, backs to the municipal loo, stand a line of Provisional Sinn Féin supporters—among them a number of Creggan faces —with placards that are being blown back and forth by the wind, protesting against conditions in H-Block and the presence in Ireland of British troops. One of their number is making a speech. A grey RUC Land-Rover followed by an army foot patrol passes tactfully behind the loo, rather than between the Sinn Féiners and the youths. The boys look at one another with barely conscious surmise: Is this it? Who is going to throw the first stone?

Apart from the riots that occurred in the Waterside and Bogside at the anniversary civil-rights marches in early October, the last rioting in Derry was in August 1978. Before then a regular Saturday-afternoon "crack" had been common enough, with stones and bottles thrown and occasionally a bus hijacked and burnt; an aggro against the army and authority, given greater substance if the fire brigade was got to turn out. On these weekly occasions the troops took shelter behind their riot shields, firing a plastic bullet now and then, tightly con-strained until the moment when a group would rush forward, batons whirling, to seize a small number of youths and hustle them away. By teatime the battle would have ceased. The lads went home to the Creggan and Bogside talking almost ad-miringly of the army snatch squad—"Y'see how they got Micky!"—clutching a plastic bullet for a souvenir and perhaps bearing a severe bruise from its impact. (At close range these bullets can and have been lethal, sometimes to innocent by-standers, but at long range they make a sort of skid mark on the flesh, which then feels very sore. Most Derry people try to put a safe distance between themselves and such confrontations; car owners feel an immediate urge to get their vehicles out of the way of flying stones.) Although most of the youths now feel that a Saturday-afternoon crack may not be worth a six-month sentence, the riots perhaps had a cathartic effect for the lads involved, a match of the day that did wonders for their self-esteem, and from which they would go home hoping to see themselves on the regional TV news, as in an instant replay.

On this Saturday, the shoppers come and go, paying little attention to the Sinn Féin speaker, Barney McFadden, a solid-looking man of late middle age, wearing a flat tweed cap and a blue parka. He speaks into a microphone (the amplifier, powered by a car battery, sits on a nearby municipal bench), ". . . while here in the six counties is the biggest concentration camp in Europe . . ." From the bemused smiles or distant looks of the shoppers, one gets the impression that this is a set speech, which they have heard before and don't really take in any more. And yet it wouldn't seem like Saturday afternoon in Derry if Barney McFadden weren't here, blasting the Brits: ". . . Callaghan, Newman, Mason, all guilty of torture and murder . . ." Indeed, if Barney weren't here, something would be terribly wrong.

He is followed by Johnny Johnson. People waiting for buses have bought their small children ice creams as a Saturday treat. Some of the Creggan girls have encountered one another and are showing off records or makeup they have bought. Johnny Johnson is shouting, pitching in, ". . . and the girls of Ireland are raped in Armagh jail!" Some small boys are climbing the scaffolding round the new Ulster bank building, and three dogs snuffle past as Johnson slangs the shoppers, the apathetic Irish as well as the malignant Brits: "Each one of *you* keeps those men in the Kesh . . ."

At the end there's no applause. A little later a single bottle flies from the pavement into the road and smashes, but no one pays any attention. Nothing happens.

SUNDAY MORNING. Holy pictures, crucifixes, statuettes of the Blessed Virgin, mass cards, and other religious paraphernalia abound in Creggan houses, but attitudes toward the church vary. One mother of thirteen who has a son inside and has been deserted by her husband says, "I'm a great believer in prayer." One Republican mother of eight says, "I go to mass and I believe in God, but I don't need the local clergy. They're all behind the peace people, the do-gooders. They refuse to come to grips with the problem, which is alien rule." A local community worker says, "The church took away some of our responsibility. A priest would walk into a room with pink wall-paper and say, 'That's lovely green wallpaper,' and no one would tell him different." A Sinn Féin supporter says, "Even if we beat the British, we'll never beat the church; people do what the priests tell them." Some who have grown up in the Creggan talk of the dependencies here, on Britannia's dole and Rome's religion and—perhaps first and foremost—on their mothers, primal centers of the home, bearing children, bring-ing them up, cleaning, cooking, granting or withholding sex, even working part-time, and of course making sure their brood go off to church to learn of sins venial and mortal and the possibilities of hellfire—the faith.

And even if, as some believe, the church has less influence than it did, it still dominates the Creggan's social life through the Parochial Centre, with its gym and hall; and the most con-spicuous structure on the estate is St. Mary's Church. Here the Creggan's rites of passage occur. Here take place baptisms, first communions, marriages, and funerals. This is where on February 2, 1972, the funeral service was held for the thirteen —six from the Creggan—who were killed on Bloody Sunday. Here four priests, who live in a comfortable residence behind the church, take turns saying mass (three masses each weekday and six on Sundays) and hearing nightly confessions in old-style confessionals or—the new style—private rooms. The church is a gaunt concrete-beam and granite-block building, painted a chilly grey-green. Father James Doherty, the youthful, go-ahead administrator of the parish, wants to alter the pre–Vatican II layout in order to bring the priest into the congregation and the congregation around the priest. The church seats 1,500 people and is crammed at the Sunday-morning masses.

At the 10 A.M. mass, which Father Doherty is celebrating, the congregation is mostly women and children. The junior choir is giving its inaugural performance at a mass. Several dogs have got in and are wandering around, as in Dutch churches in the seventeenth century. A few babies are burbling or crying. Today's gospel is Saint Matthew 18, verses 21–35, the parable of the talents. How often should I forgive the man who injures me? Seven times? No, seventy times seven, said Jesus. Father Doherty preaches on this theme, the game of resentment: a feud is between families; between nations it is a war; a new game is needed called forgiveness—a tough game to learn, but it is the only game which everyone wins.

The mass is in English now, and the priest celebrates it facing the people. For the creed the congregation rises; they pray that "we may heal the wounds that mutual intolerance has inflicted upon us." Lord hear us. There is a chance for private prayer for the departed, the sick, for a better house or the means to pay the savage fuel bills. The Lord's Prayer is said, and then the congregation is encouraged to offer one another a sign of peace. Some, mostly those up front, exchange hand clasps. At communion there is a rush for the altar rail; half the congregation goes up, and Father Doherty needs the help of the other priests to lay the hosts upon the outstretched tongues. A prayer for peace is said by all, robustly, and in the calm that follows there are announcements: This is the twenty-ninth Sunday of the year; at the preceding Sunday the collection amounted to £770. Father Doherty speaks the last words: "This mass is ended. Go in peace."

Chapter Six

IRISH MILES

– 1979 –

THE SHANNON and the Bann are longer. The Lagan and the Liffey are better known and debouch in Belfast and Dublin, respectively. The Moyle and the Lee, the southern Blackwater and the Barrow have their admirers. But the Boyne, which is neither large nor swift-flowing, is pre-eminent among what Louis MacNeice called the fermenting rivers of Ireland in that it runs not merely through the mild countryside of County Meath but through the visible evidence of several millennia of Irish history. The river's name derives from Boann, one of the chief goddesses of pre-Christian Ireland. Like the Jordan, the Boyne is a holy river, figuring as such in Irish mythology and Ulster sectarian polemics. It rises twenty miles or so west of Dublin and for seventy miles takes a semi-circular course, roughly north, northeast, then east, to reach the Irish Sea at Drogheda, a town halfway between Dublin and the Northern Ireland border. It flows out of the green midlands of Ireland through some of the richest farmland in the country, and consequently from the first has attracted invaders, settlers, and colonists who have left along its banks reminders of their existence. The river springs from a source, near the tiny village of Carbury, known as Trinity Well—whose waters, like those of most of the three thousand holy wells of Ireland, are said to have special powers. Soon enlarged by small tributaries and the overflow from the great Bog of Allen, the Boyne heads north under the aqueduct of the disused Royal Canal and the Galway-Dublin railway. The first town it reaches in an as yet uneventful passage is Trim.

It was at Trim that Seamus Heaney and I began a late-June walk along the Boyne. Heaney, Irish poet and teacher, had just assessed the year's work of his students at a teacher-training college in Dublin, and his wife, Marie, examining a winter's growth in the poet's girth, believed a few days' walking would do him good. He had a lecture on Wordsworth and Yeats to deliver at University College, Dublin, at eleven-thirty on Wednesday morning, and then could get away. A teaching colleague of Heaney's offered to drive us to Trim [the two daily buses from Dublin left inconveniently in the early morning and evening], and we accepted, though this meant abbreviating the post-lecture, pre-prandial gins and tonic at U.C.D.—a session that might well have continued at Hartigan's or O'Dwyer's or wherever the Dublin midday is stretched into the afternoon by words and booze, and at which our expedition, for the moment barely hinted at as "Oh, just a stroll, in the Boyne valley . . .", might have come to be not only delayed but regarded as something significant and symbolic and perhaps not altogether welcome in those competitive purlieus —an Irish poet, originally out of the North, and an English prose writer fraternally reconnoitering the sacred waters of the Boyne!

John O'Doherty's Honda got us swiftly away from these hazards. We ate sandwiches en route, and setting foot in Trim at two-thirty, made at once for a shoe shop so that Heaney could buy some boots. I was wearing a pair of leather L. L. Bean fisherman shoes, well broken in. I recommended (re-

membering their breaking-in) that Heaney buy footwear that
could be worn comfortably at once, and with this rather than
looks or durability in mind, he purchased a pair of rather
rakish off-white boots with "Dr. Marten's" stamped prominently
on their sides, as if they were ships needing names. They would
look all right, he thought, after he had stepped in a few cowpats. At the sweetshop next door we bought ice creams to give
us impetus, bade farewell to O'Doherty (who was carrying
Heaney's old shoes back to Dublin), and set off through Trim.
It was trying to rain. I wondered whether Sterne's Corporal
Trim in *Tristram Shandy* hailed from hereabouts or whether
it was simply as an authority on Ireland that Sterne invoked
him when he had him say, "The whole country was like a
puddle." Heaney said—bearing in mind the therapeutic reasons
for this exercise—that he had to get out of Trim before he could
get into it.

Trim *is* trim. A small market town, which won the Irish
Tourist Board's Tidy Town competition in 1972–74, with little
shops whose names are often lettered in a snaky Gaelic display
script, the place has the air of a country town of fifty years ago.
Tractors trundled up the main street, and people looked at us
with interest, knowing we were strangers. Many of the buildings were of grey stone under grey slate roofs that glistened in
the light drizzle. It was wet enough to make me put up my
umbrella. I had on my back a green nylon knapsack, while
Heaney carried his gear in a single-strap canvas book bag, at first
over one shoulder and then, when this proved uncomfortable,
with the strap bandolier style across his chest, holding the bag
in mid-back. Seeing a tourist information office, we went in and
asked the colleen in charge for details of hotels and inns in
Navan, our objective by nightfall, and for directions on how to
find Trim Castle and the riverbank along which we hoped to
walk to Navan. The Navan hostelries were named and noted.
The castle and the river were, sure enough, just around the
corner. We purchased a little guide to the town. But the riverbank walk—that was obviously a question the girl hadn't been
asked before. It was, she thought, "difficult." Would we let her
know how we made out?

Trim's glories are its ruins. It has two ruined abbeys, a ruined friary, and ruined town walls and gates. Large sections of the walls were demolished by the Big Wind, which did damage all over Ireland in the early nineteenth century. The present cathedral is a reduced but still splendid edifice called St. Patrick's. There is also, outside the walls, a turn-of-this-century St. Patrick's Church whose marble altars were made by Pearse Brothers of Dublin—one being the father of Padhraic Pearse, leader of the Easter Rising of 1916. In the grounds of this church in August 1978 a young English army lieutenant was shot and seriously wounded while posing for wedding photos with his bride, a local girl, who had been working as a nurse in London. He had done several tours of duty in the North. The Provisional IRA, who claimed responsibility for the deed, are thought to have a number of "volunteers" living in the neighborhood of Trim, carrying on the tradition of fanatic and militant opposition to both "invaders" and recognized government that in former times caused those in power to build structures like Trim Castle.

The castle is Trim's principal ruin, the largest medieval fortification in Ireland—and several thousand castles or tower houses were built in the country between 1150 and 1600. It stands in a field sloping down to the Boyne, which runs shallowly through the middle of town. Faced by another ruin in another field on the far bank, the castle has been much worked upon by time, gravity, various military ventures, and the Big Wind, which disassembled a large section of the curtain wall (Cromwell's men, besieging the castle in mid-seventeenth century, brought down a smaller section). A green sward skirts the remains of the great stone keep, built in two stages by Walter de Lacy and the Crusader Geoffrey de Geneville in 1220–25. On the grass sat a dozen cows, their recumbent attitude furnishing indubitable proof, Heaney and I agreed, that my umbrella was a good thing to have along. In an excavated area southwest of the keep are believed to be foundations of the first keep, built by Hugh de Lacy in 1174—an act recorded in an account of the Anglo-Norman invasion of Ireland called "The Song of Dermot and the Earl":

Then Hugh de Lacy
Fortified a house at Trim
And threw a fosse around it
And enclosed it with a herisson.
Within the house he placed then
Brave knights of great worth.

The Anglo-Normans were brought to Ireland in a manner
similar to that in which the Angles and the Saxons were
originally brought to Britain. They were invited first of all as
allies by Dermot MacMurrough of Leinster, who was fighting
Rory O'Connor of Connaught for the high kingship. The
Anglo-Normans (who were French-speaking) soon took over
much of the country, under the overlordship of King Henry II
of England, and were soon feuding among themselves, like the
Irish kings, and in sore need of their castles.

Famous visitors to Trim Castle at different stages of its
development and devastation have included King John, who
came with a suitable army to visit his Irish barons; King Richard
II, who was here, fighting his Irish wars, when his rival Henry
Bolingbroke staged a coup d'etat in England; and Henry V, who
stayed here as a child of eight. Across the river, in what was
by turns an old abbey, a house, a private school, and then a
house again, lived in 1718 Esther Johnson, Swift's friend Stella.
Arthur Wellesley, later Duke of Wellington, went as a child to
the school; he was afterwards member of Parliament for Trim
and as Prime Minister steered through the 1829 Act of Catholic Emancipation, which gave Catholics the right to sit in Parliament—which the Irish, since the Act of Union of 1800,
shared with the English at Westminster.

JUST AFTER THREE, Heaney and I sallied forth from the castle
precincts and set off eastwards. The rain was holding off. We
took one backward look at the castle against the grey sky and
strode forward in the direction of the riverbank, where a solitary figure stood—a young man, as we saw at closer range, with
a surveyor's tripod. We asked him about walking conditions

between here and Navan. He looked doubtful. There were lots
of ditches and streams coming in to join the river, he thought.
It might be better beyond Navan, where he had heard there
was a towpath to Slane next to the abandoned riverside canal.
As for his tripod, which we inquired about, he was surveying
for a new road bridge that would bypass Trim. The Board
of Works, he said, had recently been dredging the Boyne
along here, getting much silt out of the riverbed and exposing
shelves of stone, which stir up the water and add oxygen to it,
for the benefit of fishes (and fishermen).

The path was blocked by a fence, a garden, and a large
PRIVATE sign, so we made a detour across a field and up the
road, which ran parallel to the river. Just before a bridge at a
place marked on the map Newtown Trim, we paused at a gate
in a stone wall. The Echo Gate, the Trim guidebook calls it.
From it there was a view across a field and the Boyne to a
ruined monastery on the far bank. Newtown Trim was a medieval suburb, it seems, and is now just ruins. Heaney leaned
over the gate and called out across to the monastery, "Go
home!"—and the echo came, *"Go home!"* "Good gate!" called
Heaney; a second or so later came the hollow reply, *"Good
gate."* "Cistercians . . . Trappists . . . silence!" shouted Heaney,
getting into the swing of it. *". . . silence,"* replied the echo.

I judged that to be a good exit line and walked on toward
the bridge, Heaney following, reluctant to leave this poet's
plaything. At the bridge, a fine piece of medieval masonry, a
few people were fishing while their children played on an adjacent ruin, the Crutched, or Crossed, Friary, so named after
the friars or knights of Saint John of Jerusalem, who formed a
medical corps for crusading armies, wore a red cross on their
uniforms, and after the Crusades set up a hospital here. For
half a mile beyond this pile of stones, Heaney and I succeeded
in following the riverbank. In the river there were occasional
natural weirs—stone ledges, outcrops of rock, and little islands,
among which the silver-green Boyne waters tumbled. We passed
a woman fishing from the bank. She had long red-gold hair,
and didn't turn her head as we walked behind her, swishing

through the grass, tall nettles, and flopping poppies. I was thinking that this was a fine symbol of woman's emancipation—spending the afternoon fishing—and looked at Heaney, whose narrow slits of eyes seemed inturned. I wondered what he was thinking. Boann, perhaps. She ought to be here.

For a while, the sun almost came out. The yellow-lit grey clouds scudded before the southwest wind, which was at our backs. We made our way along the edge of a meadow which a farmer was mowing with a tractor, and clambered down into a gully, where a small brook rushed in to join the Boyne. The Knightsbrook River, said my Irish ordnance survey map of the County of Meath. The Knightsbrook runs down through Laracor, two miles away, where Swift had a living and made his base from 1700 to 1710. The brook at first seemed impassable, but Heaney spotted a place with far-spaced steppingstones, meant perhaps for Brobdingnagian strides; but we made it over. His Dr. Marten's were beginning to look less new.

Heaney was brought up on a Derry farm; his father farmed and dealt in cattle. Heaney learned as a child how to mow, scythe, and milk cows. Now, at forty, in tweeds and with a big-featured face, he looks more like a farmer than a scholar-poet. ("Jaws puff round and solid as a turnip" are his own accurate words, in a poem called "Ancestral Photographs.") I am a generation further away from the land: my grandfather had a dairy and fields rented for his herd, on the Isle of Wight, but insisted that my father—who wanted to be a farmer—enter a bank. When Heaney and I matched the names of plants and wild flowers we could see, he came out well ahead. There were irises and forget-me-nots, mint and gorse, cow parsley and celandine; big oxeye daisies; meadowsweet and charlock; ragwort, herb Robert, yellow flag, and marsh valerian. Lovely words! Heaney told me some local names, such as *borr*, which is what in Ulster they call the elder trees, thick along the riverbanks here, the white flowers on them looking, he thought, like full plates of meal. Vetch in Ireland is robin-run-the-hedge. I thought the sound the river made was running, running. And now we began to feel warm. It was still three miles to Bective,

the next settlement. In Dublin the pubs and bars are by law
closed in mid-afternoon, the so-called holy hour. Heaney wondered if there were a holy hour in Bective.

We were now forced by wire and brambles and a deep,
unbridged ditch to leave the river again, ascending a steep and
overgrown bank and making our way along a thick hedge to the
narrow road to Bective. And along here after half a mile or so
of road work we came to a pump—a large iron pump, with a
purposeful-looking curved handle, standing in a little concrete
area at the roadside. We took turns at pumping and holding
our mouths under the gushing spout—the water cool, with the
definite stony taste of well water. Both Heaney and I were
hung over. The previous evening had begun with a reading by
the Irish poet John Montague at U.C.D., had continued with
drinks at U.C.D., then at a bar, and finally at a bardic session
at the Heaneys', fueled by wine and whiskey, that went on
until 2:30 A.M. Montague and Augustine Martin, a U.C.D.
professor, rivaled each other for an hour with a duel of spon-
taneous chanting—making up a poetic dialogue of invocation,
description, and abuse as they went along. This was followed
by recitation, all present taking turns to speak their favorite
poems of Yeats and Patrick Kavanagh, plus any other verses
that came, fully or partly remembered, to their lips. The authors
had to be guessed. I quoted now to Heaney, as the water
splashed over his cheek, two lines from one of several poems of
his that have pumps in them:

> The helmeted pump in the yard
> heated its iron,
> water honeyed
> in the slung bucket . . .

We passed several small houses on this stretch. In the front
garden of one cottage a man was up a stepladder, cutting roses
from a trellis. Everyone we had passed (save the woman on
the riverbank) had given us a nod or hello, and this man was

no exception. Heaney called out as we ambled by, "It's keeping up." The gardening man replied, "Oh, yes, you have it at your backs."

"We do, that," said Heaney.

"Are you going fishing?"

"No," said Heaney, "we're tormenting ourselves by walking."

"Oh, the fish are great in the river."

"Salmon?"

"No, the trout."

I had the feeling that we were upholding a tradition that the Irish, strange for such a tradition-bound people, were letting slip—that is, tramping: our possessions on our backs, a few things in our pockets, our heads in the air, and the country at our feet. Patrick Kavanagh, a country cobbler's son who became a farmer and then a poet, once went off tramping during a quiet spell on the farm. He set off in March with five pounds in his pocket and stayed two months on the road, getting back home in time to sow turnips, and cured of wanderlust.

As we came into Bective we looked out over fields and slowly rising ground to the east and saw—two miles away—the hill of Tara, dwelling place of the Dark Age kings of Ireland, a yellow-green ridge crested with a long clump of trees. But Bective itself at that moment interested us more, half a dozen houses at a road junction a few hundred yards from a bridge across the Boyne, and a general store, the left half selling groceries and the right half housing a bar, which was open. Here we shed our packs; here we sat down on bar stools and drank a pint and a half apiece—I of Smithwick's bitter, and Heaney of Guinness stout. Three other customers were in the bar, all agriculturally clothed—one to my left by himself, a taciturn fellow who grunted uninformatively in reply to what I hoped was a friendly remark designed to open a conversation that might leave me wiser in local knowledge, particularly about which bank of the river to choose between here and Navan. On Heaney's right the other two drinkers were talking quietly together, using occasional words (Heaney reported) like "redolence" and "sensibility." More farmer-poets? While we were there, Heaney used the phone to call a Navan hotel. Success! The Russell Arms would reserve some rooms for us. What was more, they served dinner until eleven P.M. Navan, by the river's bent-elbow route, was another seven miles. We ought to be there long before eleven.

It was, according to my watch, six P.M. I looked at my watch because the electric clock over the bar, which had said a quarter past eleven when we came in, now said twenty to eleven. The second hand, moving anti-clockwise, confirmed the fact—time in the Bective bar, if not throughout the Boyne valley, was moving backwards. We grabbed our things and set off quickly before we found ourselves even further back in the past than we had imagined ourselves to be. We traversed the bridge to the north bank (which looked like it would be best to Navan) and headed across a field stretching before the lovely ruins of a twelfth-century abbey: a lichen- and ivy-covered tower; loop-holes, battlements, lancet arches, and the remains of a cloister. The Cistercian monks—obviously monks militant—possessed 245 acres hereabouts, together with a mill and a fish weir on the river, and the right of their abbot to sit as a spiritual peer in Parliament. As we walked along the meadow edge, dragonflies darted out of the rushes along the river; at our approach, ducks took off from the sliding river surface; and the blue-green reeds bent forward, dipping their heads constantly in the stream.

After the open meadow we came to a narrow bank on which thick woods impinged. The river wound into the distance of trees and fields and plantations, with the glimpse of a great house—Balsoon House, said the map—on the far bank. The map worried us by drawing our attention to the Clady River, a tributary due to spill into the Boyne at any moment now. Anything called a river might take some crossing. However, when reached, the Clady proved no more of a hindrance than the Knightsbrook had been. A series of stones, not very evenly spaced, allowed us to hop over. Then the bank widened. There was gravel underfoot, and for a while the sense of an old river-bank road. Swallows swooping. I said, "If only they flew more slowly so that one could see *how* they flew so fast"—a disjointed thought that Heaney fielded neatly, replying to me with Yeats's words, "I meditate upon a swallow's flight . . ." Meditation was the only way of setting about it.

We brooded also upon derelict ancestral houses and their overgrown demesnes. We passed a long-disused stone slip in which a boat presumably had once been moored; hard by was a tumbledown boathouse. Clouds of midges betokened a fine day on the morrow (though it seemed a little soon after the recumbent cows to draw attention to this). Heaney spotted among the elder, alder, ash, and hickory growing along here a clump of bamboo, and cut himself a six-foot pole which, he said, he'd always wanted as a boy for a fishing rod. His acute countryman's eye also served me well along here. I was a pace or two in advance of him, and was just about to step into some thick brush overgrowing the path when he grabbed my shoulder and said urgently, "Look out there!" Prodding with his bamboo pole, Heaney pushed aside the brush and long grass to reveal a crevasse a foot or so wide into which I had been just about to walk, and perhaps plunge—since no bottom was visible—into the Irish netherworld.

A little after seven-thirty, we reached a high stone bridge spanning the river, which here ran through a slight gorge. We decided to climb here and strike north to reach a road. Despite the initial suppleness of his Dr. Marten's, Heaney had a blister forming. Navan seemed distant and the evening well advanced, although, thanks to the northern summer twilight, it wouldn't be dark for another two hours. Irish miles had a separate legal existence until 1826 (when they were abolished); one Irish mile was approximately 1.27 British miles. They still feel longer. Perhaps this is so because one consults the Irish ordnance survey maps as if they were British maps, with the same scale, whereas the scale of the Irish is half an inch to a mile, rather than one inch as was until recently most common in England. (Maps there are metric now.) Consequently, what looks like an hour's walk is in fact two hours'. Moreover, when country walking there are no paths as straight as the routes on which crows fly. One respects crops by walking the long way round the edge

of fields. One follows meandering riverbanks and curving con-
tour lines. And now, getting up the embankment of the bridge
took some zigzag climbing, effectively doubling the distance.

On the bridge, we walked out into the middle and sat for a
few minutes looking up and downstream before bidding a temporary farewell to the Boyne. A grassy track ran across the
bridge, which had once (we conjectured) carried a railway. Its
course ran northwards in a cutting which had become—as Irish
land when left to its own devices often does—a sort of bog.
Heaney, despite his blister, was in good spirits, possibly affected by the boggy ground underfoot. He has written a number of poems that have to do with bogs and with their preserving power, whether of food or implements or bodies that
sink in them; and bogs have become for him a way of getting
at and expressing in poetry the tenacious quality of Irish history
and much that has happened in it, and that keeps resurfacing,
looking much as it did when it first went under. When the
ground got too wet, we walked along one edge of the cutting.
We noticed that the gateposts to a field were made of old
railway sleepers. Rabbits scattered into the banks. After a mile
or so with small farms on either side we met a road. Under it,
through a bridge, ran the former railway line, and there on the
far side of the brick arch was the former railway station, spic
and span, looking as if—save for the missing tracks—the 7:30
P.M. to Navan was about to come steaming in.

Perhaps I went a bit astray at this point. I said we must obviously turn right on the road to get to Navan. Heaney said
clearly we should go left. The station (in retrospect to be seen
as having been done up as a house) disoriented me and gave
me the feeling of being in another time and in an unexpected
landscape. "Going astray" is not uncommon in Ireland. The
phenomenon affects the natives, too. Some tell of getting into
the middle of a well-known field and wandering around for an
hour, maybe, not being able to find the way out. Patrick
Kavanagh and his mother went astray once, while coming home
in an ass-cart from a visit to friends. All evening, in the rain,
they drove around a skein of wet roads near Inniskeen, getting
nowhere. "Everything seemed strange," Kavanagh wrote in

his book *The Green Fool.* "The folk we saw were not ordinary mortals." Finally they decided to let the ass choose its own direction, and this worked. When they reached home, other traditional solutions to the predicament were proposed, such as turning one's coat inside out. One listener said, "Paddy, ye were with the Wee Fellas."

"Only for the ass we'd never escape," Kavanagh replied.

"Indeed you would not," the listener supported, "sure the ass is a blessed animal."

After some dithering and discussion on the roadside, we agreed to adopt Heaney's route; it turned out to be the right one. We went left, as he had proposed, and soon met the Navan road. Possibly the railway station had been a figment. Perhaps I had been with the Wee Fellas. There were, however, nearly four miles still to go. The sky was darkening as the sun set and grey clouds came in from the west. After a mile along the lonely road the rain began to fall. Umbrella up, coat collars up, we walked along, Heaney limping from his blister. We sang "It's a long way to Tipperary," and Kavanagh's "Raglan Road," to the tune of "The Dawning of the Day," which Heaney's wife, Marie, sings in a way to bring the moisture to your eyes. It wasn't long before the decision was taken with one, barely spoken accord: time to try and hitch a ride into Navan.

Cars were infrequent on that road, but the goddess of the river was looking after journeymen that night—the second car stopped. Its driver was a friendly Australian who dropped us right outside the Russell Arms Hotel in Navan. There the lady behind the reception desk—perhaps unused to guests who arrived with knapsacks and bamboo staffs, looking touched with the Meath greenery—asked to be paid in advance. But neither Heaney nor I reacted huffily to this suggestion. Hot baths and food and drink were in our minds. We paid up.

The Russell Arms: staircases going this way and that; the feeling of being in two or three large Victorian houses knocked together in a period of expansion, and now, that moment passed, in old age propping one another up. In the bathroom I used, there were no lightbulbs in the fixtures and no plug in the bath. Fortunately daylight of a feeble sort persisted. I used the small plug from the sink and added my face flannel to stem the ebb from the tub. In my bedroom one out of three lights worked. However, on the ground floor all was well set up and jovial. The bar was full of early arrivals for a meeting of the local association of Tipperary Men—exiles, it appeared, from that fair county, all of a hundred miles from Navan. Heaney arrived, still hobbling, but otherwise restored by hot water. We drank apéritifs of Bushmill's whiskey, from the North, and dined off sirloin from the South. We toasted the Boyne with several carafes of red Spanish plonk. Meanwhile the river was running a hundred yards away, unseen, past the backs of the houses of Navan, which resolutely look the other way.

We talked about the words "the Boyne." Where Heaney grew up and went to school in Northern Ireland, they were loaded with significance. For Northern Protestants the Boyne connotes the battle in 1690 at which the troops of William III beat those of James II and thus kept all of Ireland firmly under British hegemony for the following two hundred and thirty years. In much of Ulster, to mention the Boyne is to reassert Protestant superiority. We swapped references that we recalled from ballads and folk songs—among others, "The Boyne Water" and "The Green Grassy Slopes of the Boyne," both of which celebrate Orange patriotism and William's victory. A huge and now unreadable nineteenth-century novel by J. Mangin is called *The Boyne Water*. And the river's name occurs as symbol or metaphor in modern Irish poetry as often as blackbirds do in medieval Irish lyrics. The Boyne figures in the specifically Irish section of Louis MacNeice's long poem, *Autumn Journal*, in which the poet (born in Belfast) evokes the yearly celebrations in Ulster on the anniversary of the Battle of the Boyne—"the voodoo of the Orange bands / Drawing an iron net through darkest Ulster." That section of the poem begins with a memorable, ironic passage:

> Nightmare leaves fatigue.
> We envy men of action

Who sleep and wake, murder and intrigue
  Without being doubtful, without being haunted.
And I envy the intransigence of my own
  Countrymen who shoot to kill and never
See the victim's face become their own
  Or find his motive sabotage their motives.

But he wrote those lines in 1939–40, and it would be harder
now, since the renewed Troubles and many deaths of the past
ten years caused by terrorists, to use the word "envy" in that
way—even though a sardonic tone comes through.

Tramping also leaves fatigue. Heaney and I retired before the
bar called for last orders. I slept profoundly, and failed to hear
the boisterous departure of the Tipperary Men, which Heaney
next day reported as taking place at sometime after two. He
might have recalled a line of his own: "Drunk again, full as the
Boyne."

NEXT MORNING Tara was our objective. We had bacon and eggs
—the pleasure of no bill to pay—and lighter loads, for we left
most of our gear at the Russell Arms reception desk. We walked
up to the main square, a junction of four roads in the center
of Navan, where we intended to catch the 9:20 Dublin bus as
far as Tara, seven miles south. Since we also intended to carry
on walking after lunch along the next section of the Boyne,
from Navan to Slane, we had decided that auxiliary transportation was permissible on this side jaunt. A number of people
were already at the bus stop, but we had fifteen minutes in
hand to try and find Heaney something easier on his back than
his present bag—he was impressed by the lightweight, unstiff-
ened nylon backpack I had bought for $4.95 in a Mystic, Con-
necticut, sporting-goods store some years ago.

Navan still had a saddler's shop, a hundred yards from the
bus stop, whose dusty front window disclosed rugged brown
suitcases, harnesses, and khaki knapsacks, none looking less
than ten years old. The venerable saddler took one of the knapsacks out of the window, shook the cobwebs off it, and

strapped it on Heaney's back. "Ah, it's a wonderful fit, sur," he said. The price for this piece of Old World craftsmanship, an antique that had never been used, was, he added, merely a fiver. "You'll take four pounds fifty," said Heaney, astutely keeping any interrogative note out of his voice and staring intently at the knapsack's rusty metal grommets. "Oh, it'll do you well, just right for tramping," said the saddler, as if he hadn't heard Heaney's remark. But he gave Heaney fifty pence change for the five-pound note. The saddler's wife appeared in the back door to witness what might have been their first sale of the year—or perhaps it was just the historic sight in Navan of two tramping men.

At the bus stop we joined the would-be passengers—for the most part elderly men, middle-aged women, and a pair of girls with most beautiful complexions. For entertainment while waiting, we had the spectacle of three demolition men at work on the Malocca Café across the square. It was a strangely two-dimensional sight. The three workers, wearing woolen caps rather than hard hats, were standing on the façade wall, all of nine inches thick, above the second-story windows. There was no scaffolding. The roof was already gone, and the men, carefully wielding their pickaxes, were demolishing the wall half-a-dozen bricks at a time beneath their own feet. We waited for one of them to miss or lose his balance, but none of them did, at least by the time the bus came in.

The Dublin road first follows the Boyne south, upstream. Then, the river bending away westward towards Bective, the road climbs the slopes of Tara. The driver stopped the bus for us to get out at a junction with a side lane, and we walked up this, still climbing. The lane was narrowed and heavy with hedges. The air was moist—not quite raining, not even drizzling; simply wet. One could see how things grew so well in Ireland, but one wondered how they ever ripened. From a nearby field came the sweet smell of new-cut hay. Heaney said that his friend Michael Longley, a poet, had told him the Vikings used to coast along the land until they smelled hay and then, knowing that there must be habitations, would buckle on their swords and come ashore. I said I thought the east wind was the Viking's wind, which filled their square sails on the voyage westward from Scandinavia—though no doubt they then coasted with the southwesterlies, which carried the hay smells, first raiding in Ireland and then settling to found such cities (trading posts at first) as Dublin, Wexford, Waterford, Cork, and Limerick.

Tara is a long hilltop; a windbreak of trees around the eighteenth-century church and attached graveyard; and an extensive meadow full of ridges, barrows, mounds, and earthworks. *Tara* means a place with a wide view, and the hill rising three hundred feet or so above the general level of the rich countryside allows one to see over much of the center of Ireland—yellow fields, green hedges, black copses, and blue distant hills. Grey processions of rain were marching along the Boyne valley. Some parts of the horizon were lost in mist or cloud, while others were sunlit. Crows were strutting and cawing in an adjacent field, while farther down the slope a man was driving sheep across a pasture. The mist, reaching us, turned to rain for a few minutes and then became mist again, through which the sun tried to break. The grass was long and wet, my boots not as waterproof as they once were. Heaney had the collar of his navy-blue raincoat turned up, tweed cap flat on his head, the empty Navan knapsack on his back.

We prowled around separately but occasionally converged on the same site: the so-called Mound of the Hostages; the two long ridges believed by some to be walls for a great Dark Ages banqueting hall; and the mound encircled by twin ditches known as the rath, or fort, of the Forradh. On top of this are three pieces of stonework within an iron-railed enclosure. One is a five-foot-high upright pillar called the Lia Fáil, a stone on which the early kings of Ireland were allegedly crowned, but known to local Irish speakers in the nineteenth century as the phallus of Fergus. Another is a Celtic-style cross, with an inscription in Irish, put up to honor thirty-seven insurgents who died during a skirmish in 1798 with government forces in the Tara vicinity. The third is a mawkish statue of Saint Patrick, bearded, with a bishop's mitre on his head, right hand raised in unctuous blessing and his gaze firmly averted from the erect Lia Fáil. "The triple deities," said Heaney, "though I suspect that in some ways the good saint here is a hybrid of the other two."

He sat down on a patch of dry gravel in the lee of Saint Pat, with his back to the plinth on which the saint stood. Saint Patrick was a Romano-Briton who is believed to have been carried off as a slave by Irish raiders at the age of sixteen, to have escaped after several years, to have studied in Gaul and been consecrated bishop, and then to have returned as one of the first Christian missionaries to Ireland in the mid-fifth century to preach the Gospel. Like many other invaders he made his way up the Boyne. At a hill overlooking Slane (which we hoped to reach that evening), Patrick (according to the earliest accounts, written roughly three hundred years after his mission) lit a great paschal bonfire on Easter Eve. On Tara, King Laoghaire saw the fire ten miles to the north and took it as a challenge to his authority; he is said to have driven over to Slane in his chariot to give the intruder a dressing-down, but was himself let down by his followers, who received the saint's blessing and became believers. Patrick went on to appoint three hundred bishops, attached to ruling families, to carry out the peaceful conversion of Ireland; as far as one knows, there were no martyrs. Almost all the churches in these parts are named after him.

And what about these kings? The Gaels from Gaul who conquered Ireland in the first centuries after Christ became an ascendancy class, providing perhaps several hundred ruling families. Ulster, behind its mountains and lakes, held out longest against the Gaels, the Ulstermen being led by Connor MacNessa, the Red Branch knights, and Cuchulain, the heroic Hound of Ulster. The Gaels provided perhaps 150 "kings" in a total population of less than 500,000. Professor J. C. Beckett, the Irish historian, believes that by the fifth century there were seven provincial kings lording it over the petty kings, and that by this time too the kings of Tara, one of the provinces, put in their claim to be *árd rí*, or high king. But the high king's authority was nominal, despite his making a circuit of the island and exacting hostages from the smaller kings. One can see why so many children with Irish parents are told (as I was by my Molony mother) that they are descended from an Irish king— in my case it was from Brian Boru, who fell at Clontarf outside Dublin in 1014, successfully defeating a Norse army. And the likelihood that these kings practiced polygamy would increase one's chances of being of royal Gaelic descent.

Tara was abandoned as a royal site about 700 A.D. The collection of legends that provide the names for the mounds and monuments date from four hundred years later; there are more names, in fact, than monuments. Some archeological work has been done, however, and excavation of the rath of the Synods (so called because of ecclesiastical meetings Saint Patrick and other missionaries are thought to have held there) has shown that dwellers on the site had some contact with the far-spread Roman world—a Roman seal, lock, and glass fragments have been found. Yet Ireland was never a part of that world (which is one reason the Dark Ages are so murky in Ireland); Irish ways were never tempered with Roman imperium or Roman law. And that there were kings on this spot seems supported by such finds as two gold torcs, now in the National Museum, Dublin. The kings apparently favored Neolithic burial mounds for their habitations: at Tara a Bronze Age passage grave (c. 2000 B.C.) has been found with pottery, bone pins, jet buttons, and a bronze awl of this date. Candy wrappers now decorate the ground at the grave's threshold.

When I returned to the rath of the Forradh after my reconnaissance, Heaney was still sheltering behind Saint Patrick, jotting words in a notebook. A small military observation plane swooped low and circled twice, apparently observing *us*. "They must think we're an SAS detachment," said Heaney, who looked like a character from *Odd Man Out*, while I, in safari jacket and green jungle hat, was clearly dressed for counter-insurgency operations. Tara remains a commanding height. But we were in any event overwhelmed at this point by a busload of children, who came surging noisily over the site, dashing up the mounds and down into the ditches, the places of palisades and homes and graves. They ran to the enclosure where Heaney sat and thronged round him. He was suddenly among schoolchildren, and found himself answering their questions, telling them about the place, as if he were the genius loci. Indeed, the children seemed affected by the spot, as were we. Heaney had used in his lecture the previous morning the term "cthonic forces," which I later got him to define for me as the energies welling up from a place. The forces were strong here, at least in this weather of mist, showers, and watery sun. Cormac and Laoghaire, Fergus and Queen Maeve; the old peoples who lived and died here; kings on hills.

Before leaving, we looked in the little graveyard, where among the Christian headstones is a *sile* or "sheila," as the word is pronounced: a grey rock face on which we could just discern in relief a female figure, knees spread wide as if making water on the ground—an image to avert evil or bring about fertility. In the Halls of Tara café on the road where the school buses parked, we had a twenty-pence pot of tea, nicely timed, as the heavens opened and rain tumbled down. Then, with long slices of blue sky overhead, we went back down the rain-fragrant lane to the main road. It was eleven-thirty, and the next bus came by after one. So we walked along with our thumbs out and after a while got a lift into Navan from a heating-appliance salesman, who had what Heaney later called "a touch of the volubilities." In the car he told us—learning he was in the company of writing men—that he "used to read books."

After lunch at the Russell Arms, I donned my backpack again. Heaney now had his fully loaded. The sun was still mostly out, and we went looking in Navan for the way to Slane along the river, misdirected at first by a local to the banks of the Blackwater, the river that joins the Boyne here. But we soon found some old stone steps beside a bridge spanning the Boyne, and these took us down to a path that ran between the southern bank of the river and a long-derelict canal running alongside it, in most places full of reeds, rushes, and nettles and looking even less navigable than the river it had been designed to supplant as an efficient waterway. Over it stood small stone bridges with low arches giving just enough room for barges to get through. At intervals were old locks, their gates and paddles collapsed and fallen-in. The canal was built between 1749 and 1800 to carry coal, grain, and other mill products between Navan and Drogheda, and most of its bridges and locks have inscribed on them the name of their designer, the engineer Richard Evans.

Our path between river and canal was at first graveled, then grassed, then overgrown. Heaney said, putting a travel writer's tone of authority into his voice, "At Navan the character of the river changes." This stretch of the Boyne gives the impression of having been worked over by an eighteenth-century landscape architect. The river is wider, with the Blackwater added to it. Great stands of trees are growing in effective places, funneling the eye up green fields that roll away from the river. There are appropriate ruins and occasional crags. We met one man hastening toward Navan, his breeches and jerkin giving him the look of a gamekeeper, and after him no one at all. The undergrowth, sometimes growing over the path, became forbiddingly luxuriant. Convolvulus grew larger, dock leaves were giant. We saw a kingfisher as it zipped between the reeds—"like blue voltage," said Heaney. The milestones that we passed, giving the distance to Slane (ten miles by my reckoning), appeared to be measuring the old Irish miles. The wind was from the north, but the sun produced a hint of summer heat. I kept a long stalk of grass in my mouth, sweet at first, bitter if one chewed it.

Heaney moved with a sort of shuffle—tweed jacket, khaki knapsack, bamboo staff. I walked at a faster pace and stopped now and then till he caught up, when he remarked about the advantages I had had of national service with a Light Infantry regiment in the British Army. Heaney, as an Ulster Catholic, has had experiences of the British Army there, of being frisked and interrogated, that have left him not wholly sympathetic to

Her Majesty's Forces, though he sees the difficulties of their peace-keeping role. In fact many Irishmen before and after Arthur Wellesley have made a career in those forces. In 1914, the recruiting teams did good business in the South, and it wasn't just the men of Ulster who died at the Somme; the Irish Nationalist MPs William Redmond and Tom Kettle were among 200,000 Catholic and possibly Republican Irish who fought for the British in the First World War. My grandfather Frederick Molony served in the Royal Engineers. His sister Bessie was a nurse on the Western Front in the Queen Alexandra's Nursing Corps. And his brother Tom died during the war in France from (his wife, Great-aunt Kitty, would always say) damp blankets.

Our histories are intertwined. The Boyne has relics of numerous ascendancies. Along here were more legacies of the French-speaking nobility who settled in the twelfth and thirteenth centuries in an area called the Pale. Beyond the Pale were what Shakespeare's Richard II called "the rough, rug-headed kerns," and even within it each lord built his house as a castle, fortified against the peasantry, rival lords, and the king. In this landscape the ruined castles had the air of follies, designed or deliberately ruined to fulfill an idea of the picturesque. Dunmoe Castle, which we passed near Milestone 4, was such a place. Said to have been built by a De Lacy, it last withstood siege during the Roundheads versus Cavaliers Civil War, was restored during the reign of James II, and burned more or less down in 1799. When Sir William Wilde, Oscar's father and a well-known Dublin eye surgeon and antiquarian, came past here in the 1840s, on a journey of research for a book about the Boyne and Blackwater, he was told by the peasantry that an underground passage led from the castle under the Boyne to the opposite bank. As we went by, the wind passing over the two castellated towers or through the high empty windows sounded as if someone were blowing over the top of a huge bottle. Between us and the castle, on the north bank, the river fell over a small cascade; the water slithered sideways as it went down. A little farther on we passed on our bank a ruined church, high on

a slope over the river, and then a more contemporary structure, a small corrugated steel shed, possibly for fishermen, on
the river's edge. It was nicely provided with no lock on the door
and several straight-backed chairs, on which we sat outside for
a while and watched the Boyne glide like a smooth moving
carpet over a weir. For such a calm and purposeful operation,
the resulting falling-water noise was surprisingly loud.

The temperature went up and down five degrees as the sun
went in and out; the path moved away from the river through
fields: cowpats; a pheasant; a herd of Jersey cattle; half-a-dozen
handsome horses. The next landmark, halfway to Slane, was
Stackallan Bridge, which like most Boyne river crossings has
nearby points of interest: here a wayside monumental cross; a
holy well dedicated to Saint Patrick; an ancient rath or fort with
earthen banks. We rashly assumed from the map that the path
now shifted, as the canal did, to the north bank; apparently the
towing horses would be loaded aboard the barges and then
barges, cargo, and horses poled across the river and into the
lock on the other bank. We therefore crossed the bridge.
Heaney, parched, went to get a drink of water at a nearby
house and brought back the information that it should be possible to reach Slane on this bank, but no promise of how easy
it would be.

In fact the path was soon densely overgrown. An unknown
plant, a cross between a mammoth dock and giant rhubarb, had
settled here in thick colonies, rising to five or six feet and
spreading out huge, salad-bowl leaves. It had to be beaten
aside. Over these plants we glimpsed a fine ruined mill on the
south bank, next to a splendid horseshoe-shaped weir. Then we
were within a few feet of the river itself but couldn't see it. A
short clearing gave us hope, but we were at once in jungle
again. My boots were soaking from the wet grass. Heaney and
I took turns in the van, bashing away at the plant life—not just
the triffid-like things but briars, thorns, and saplings. I broke off
one of the latter to use as a device for parting the way ahead.
We needed machetes. We needed more energy than we had.
We were being turned green by the Irish jungle. No one had

been this way for years, or at least several seasons.* We were wet from below and getting wet from above as rain fell, and haphazardly penetrated the forest. It was too thick for my umbrella to be of use unless we stood still. When we halted for this purpose for a few minutes, Heaney sat down to rest on an ivy-covered log, which—rotten—crumbled under him, leaving him on the ground; he stayed there.

"You look like Sweeney," I said; he took it as a compliment. Sweeney was an Irish petty king or warlord, the subject of the early medieval Irish poem called *The Frenzy of Sweeney*, which Heaney is slowly making a version of, called *Sweeney Astray*. Sweeney's problems begin when he is cursed by a local saint and finds himself flying round Ireland, nesting in hedges, tree-tops, and ditches—in the process, as what Heaney has called "a tongue of the land," speaking some of the most beautiful lines that have been written in description of the Irish land-scape. We needed some of the bewitched king's powers now to get up into the tops of the trees and zoom out of this. And indeed, when the last remaining suggestions of a path came to an end and the vegetation ahead looked impenetrable, we decided it was time to be flexible about our intention of walking "along the Boyne, to Slane." We fought our way up into the woods, dragged ourselves up the steep ascent, and found— blessed relief!—open fields! Heaney was suffering not only from yesterday's blister but also from an old thigh injury, acquired on the school football field, and, unable to get over barbed-wire fences, had to work his way under them. But we made it into and along the edge of the fields, and reached the parkland of old

---

* Or possibly since Sir William Wilde journeyed here in the 1840s, and in the fashion of the time eulogized the landscape, particularly the bank we were on, "where groves of noble beech trees and aged chestnuts fringe the heights, and an underwood of laurels, thorns and sweet-briars mantle upon the undulating surface of the shores beneath. . . . Here the river forms a number of sudden curves, each winding presenting us with a new picture more beautiful than its predecessor. The banks spring high and abrupt from the water's edge, so that in some places the massive trees, rising in piles of the most gorgeous foliage, appear toppling over us from their summits, and darken the deep smooth pools they overhang."

trees and rolling ground which is the demesne of Slane Castle, seat of the Earl of Mount Charles. *Demesne* is a fine word, from the French *domain,* and evocative of medieval estates. The present Earl had worked briefly for Faber and Faber, Heaney's London publishers, and we hoped that this (and the fact that Heaney had phoned from Navan to reserve dinner for us at the Slane Castle restaurant) would give us entrée if we encountered the Earl's gamekeepers before we reached the Navan-Slane road. Luck was with us here, however, and also on the road, where a fine fellow stopped and gave us a lift the last mile into Slane.

SLANE HAD 896 people in 1837 and 526 after the famine years in 1861; at the last count, in 1971, the population was 483. It is a well-planned eighteenth-century village with the unusual feature of four nearly identical Georgian houses built aslant the corners of the crossroads, where the Navan-Drogheda and Dublin-Derry roads intersect. It has two churches named after Saint Patrick and a hotel, the Conyngham Arms, which deserves more than the one Automobile Association star it displays. The rooms were clean and well-furnished; all lightbulbs and bath plugs were in place; the water was hot and the beer cellar-cool. Despite the fact that we looked, if anything, more shattered than the day before, Heaney and I were not asked to pay in advance for our rooms.

Slane was the home of Francis Ledwidge, the Irish poet, who was killed in Flanders in 1917. Ledwidge was a gentle, nature-observant writer, in tone and spirit close to the English poet Edward Thomas, who also died in the First World War. In Slane, Ledwidge is commemorated by a plaque on the bridge across the Boyne, which bears four lines from Ledwidge's "Lament for Thomas MacDonagh," a poet and friend of his, who was executed after the Easter Rising of 1916:

> He shall not hear the bittern cry
> In the wild sky, where he is lain,
> Nor voices of the sweeter birds
> Above the wailing of the rain.

And when Heaney and I were being driven to Slane Castle for dinner by Louis Cassidy, who is the local handyman and ferry-man-by-car of local people, he told us that Francis Ledwidge's brother Joe, now in his eighties, still lived in the village. Some people in Slane, said Mr. Cassidy, were still offended because a London publishing firm had given a party here some years ago to celebrate the publication of a biography of Francis Ledwidge, and had failed to invite a number of people (including Mr. Cassidy, we gathered) who felt they should have been invited. The long Irish memory strikes again.

In the twilight we drove a short way back up the Navan road and in through the arch of a gatehouse, along a drive past sta-bles, and down a slope to a cellar doorway of Slane Castle. The castle restaurant is one of the activities by which the present Earl of Mount Charles makes the place pay its way; other ac-tivities include renting the place to film companies for locations and throwing balls to which some guests come by helicopter. We were met at the door by Juliet, Countess of Mount Charles, who is in her twenties, petite and pretty; she nobly disguised her disappointment on finding out that when Heaney had said on the phone "around nine," he had been talking about dinner time, not the number of people who would be with him. We did our best to eat for those who hadn't come. Heaney had asparagus crêpes and I rainbow trout Provençal. There were bountiful dishes of *al dente* vegetables. The house red was a fine-bred claret, and Henry Mount Charles, the seventh Earl, who is twenty-nine years old, having seen his twenty or so other customers properly fed, joined us for the second bottle.

The Earl is a graduate of Harvard Business School, where he was known as Henry Slane; after working for Faber's, he was the Irish director of Sotheby's. Then his father, Marquess Conyngham, who owns land in England and had potential problems with capital transfer tax, asked Henry—as everyone in Slane calls him—if he would like to take over the castle and its thousand acres and make a go of it. This Henry and Juliet were now doing. They employ thirty men and women in the castle and farm. Slane has its own dairy cattle, fishing rights, and game birds. The independence of its present owners is enhanced by its own power plant—a private turbine producing electricity from the ceaseless Boyne. (This was installed by Henry's grandfather, who also made much money from a carpet works in Navan; the turbine has been stopped only once in forty years, for an overhaul in 1959.) Henry would have a seat in the British House of Lords when he succeeded his father, and he didn't disguise the fact that in running for profit this sort of establishment (which partly depended on the successful manipulation of the past, of associations, nostalgia, deference, and need for the unusual), a title—a "handle" as he called it—was very useful; though possibly the European Economic Community's Common Agricultural Policy's effect on farm prices counted for more.

After dinner, Henry gave us a tour of the interior. Slane Castle is mostly a product of the late eighteenth century. Henry's ancestors, the Conynghams, were a Scottish family who came to Donegal in 1611. Sir Albert Conyngham fought for King William at the Boyne in 1690. On James II's side fought Christopher Fleming, the twenty-second Lord Baron of Slane, whose family had held the estates from 1175 until they were confiscated in 1641 and sold to the Conynghams. Bits of the old Fleming castle are believed to have been incorporated in the Gothic Revival house which James Wyatt, the architect, designed here, with mock battlements and corner towers, and set on a rocky bastion overlooking a bend of the Boyne. Francis Johnston oversaw its completion. Capability Brown did the stables. Henry has a telephone switchboard and Telex machine in his ground-floor corner-tower office.

Of the many elegant rooms, that which serves as both library and ballroom is perhaps the finest—a round room, with crimson walls and white Gothic plaster tracery on the domed ceiling. It was especially built for a visit by King George IV in 1821, and would undoubtedly have appealed to the patron of the Brighton Pavilion. However, the main appeal for George IV at Slane was Lady Conyngham. One of the reasons that is traditionally given for the straightening of the Dublin-Slane

road—it is one of the straightest roads in Ireland—was George's
desire to get to Slane and Lady Conyngham as fast as possible. In fact, though well acquainted with her by 1815, George
is thought to have stayed at Slane Castle only twice, once before and once after he was crowned king. It was while dining at
Slane that George, in fine spirits, suggested sending Lord Tal-
bot, the Lord Lieutenant of Ireland, to look after England
while he, George, stayed where he was.

In the castle now are various prized mementos of these associations, and statues and pictures of the nobility England
and Ireland shared, for better and worse. There is a portrait of
the first Marquess Conyngham by Gilbert Stuart (George
when Prince Regent not only got Lady Conyngham's husband
this title but had him made Constable of Windsor Castle and
Steward of the Royal Household). And there is a full-length
life-sized portrait of a handsome officer, the Marquess of
Anglesey, also one of Henry's ancestors. It was at the Battle
of Waterloo, in 1815, as Henry reminded us, that Anglesey is
supposed to have said to the Duke of Wellington, just after a
cannonball whizzed by, "By God, sir, I've lost my leg!" And
Wellington is said to have replied, "By God, Harry, so you
have."

DAY THREE: a fine morning. Heaney had to be back in Dublin
that afternoon for a meeting and was catching the Dublin bus
at ten. He was, I suspected, pleased not to have to put his Dr.
Marten's to the test for another day. After an excellent breakfast at the Conyngham Arms we said goodbye. My boots had
been put to dry on the kitchen range at the hotel, and though
I went down to Slane bridge for a glimpse of the distant castle,
standing on "its swelling bank of greensward" (as Wilde described it), and of the woods overhanging the river which had
thwarted Heaney and myself the evening before, I decided to
keep my boots dry for the moment by forgoing any excursions
into the thick undergrowth between bridge and castle. I took
on faith that somewhere in the wet tangled shrubbery, under
yews and beeches, was the ancient ruin known as the Hermitage

of Saint Erc. Saint Erc, one of Saint Patrick's right-hand men and first bishop of Slane, is said to have often stood for hours at a time in the chill Boyne waters in order to cool his concupiscent desires. From the bridge, allegedly a favorite haunt of Mick Collier, last of the Irish highwaymen, there is also a spacious view downstream past Slane Mill toward the big bend of the river at Rossnaree. I returned to the village crossroads and marched forth on the Drogheda Road, spurning the temptations prompted by the Live and Let Live public house, and leaving over my left shoulder the hill on which Saint Patrick lit his paschal fire.

It was just gone eleven as I walked from Slane. It was fox-and-geese weather—the promise of the early morning already compromised by loose grey clouds scudding behind me, threatening showers. I was going to have to walk faster than Heaney and I had done to fit into this day all that I wanted, and I kept up a light-infantry pace for the first few miles, exercising the freedom of the road to whistle and sing, and swinging my umbrella at the trail, parallel with the ground. I turned right on the first minor road, which led toward the Boyne again and the great Neolithic burial mounds of Knowth, Newgrange, and Dowth. A vole ran across the road; at a farm gate stood a pair of milk churns awaiting collection. But despite the rural signs, there were also short stretches of ribbon development, as there seem to be on many country roads in the east of Ireland—development, admittedly, that often appeared to be proceeding by well-spaced fits and starts. A few new houses here stood empty in plots alongside unfinished houses or old, completed cottages that had for some reason long been abandoned. To whom do these derelict or unoccupied dwellings belong? Will the new houses ever be lived in? Are there sons and daughters in Liverpool or Boston who will one day come to glaze the boarded-up windows and paint the pebbledash? To keep a cow or a goat in one of these small hedged fields?

Heaney had given me the name of the archeologist, Professor George Eogan, who is in charge of the excavations at Knowth. At the top of a rise, opposite a farmhouse, I came to a high wire fence through which I could see the huge tumulus, parts of the covering turf peeled back, and black polythene protecting some of the excavated ground. I let myself in through a gate, and walking past a pile of spades and picks next to a fork-lift truck, found the prefabricated hut that was site headquarters. There I introduced myself to Dr. Eogan, a sharp-eyed but genial man in his fifties, who has been working on Knowth since 1962, digging during the summers with his students from U.C.D., and during term time sorting out the results back in the city. A postgraduate student, Aideen Ireland, gave me a tour of the excavations, starting at one side of the central mound, where we walked cautiously on the thin ridges of earth left between four-meter-square excavation pits, in which the diggers were working with tiny trowels and toothbrushes, finding, if they were lucky, minute pieces of bone or bead.

The mound itself is a megalithic tomb containing two passage graves. Some three hundred such graves are known in Ireland, and those in the three mounds that form a great cemetery on the Boyne are pre-eminent. They date, Miss Ireland told me, from 3000–2500 B.C. They are the works of a people about whom not much else is known, but who, on the basis of these tombs, could clearly gather their energies in a project that consumed much time and labor, who honored their dead, installing the cremated ashes in shallow basins of stone set in niches deep in the passage graves. The graves themselves were formed of huge stones. The mound covering those at Knowth extends over one and a half acres; it is some ninety meters in diameter and more than ten meters high. It is surrounded by a circle of large curbstones decorated with incised motifs—circles, U shapes, diamond shapes, spirals, zigzags and herringbones. The mound was carefully built in layers, thicker in the middle and sloping slightly downward toward the edges, presumably for better drainage.

We stood on top of the mound in the warm sun and cool breeze and looked out over the valley—to the flat-topped sister mound of Newgrange, a mile away; to the curving river and beyond to Tara; and to the Wicklow Mountains, visible beyond

Dublin twenty-five miles south. It was obviously a good site—
first time lucky, in a way, since these people were nomads and
hunters on the point of becoming farmers and herders, their
animals becoming domestic. And settling down seemed to involve giving a permanent dwelling place first of all to their
dead—levering tons of stone, slowly chipping away the magical
designs with hammers of flint. The early Irish were diggers and
navvies and artists. And after the cremations and burials, the
place itself was good for the living, then and thereafter, overlooking and controlling the fertile valley and the river with its
fish. In the Iron Age, people inhabited the mound itself, digging deep ditches round it and building stone walls on top. The
Celtic invaders made this cemetery their Olympus, the home of
their gods. The Vikings looted it and the Normans built a fort
on it. In 1699 the Welsh antiquarian Edward Lhuyd came to
the Boyne cemetery, the first of a line of inquisitive scientists
and excavators. In the eighteenth century the locals dug
here for handy road-building materials.

After thanking Miss Ireland and Dr. Eogan, I walked on
down the lane to Newgrange. At a junction I spurned the advice of the road sign, deciding, after a look at my map, that the
sign proposed a route better for cars and longer for me; and
after a few minutes doubt on the single-track road I'd chosen,
had the pleasure of seeing Newgrange appear again over the
high hedges, several fields distant. All along here the elder trees
were in flower and blackbirds were singing, as they presumably
have since Neolithic times, to movers of stone, monks, farmers,
warriors, and people walking down lanes.

I reached Newgrange at one P.M. Newgrange has been excavated and restored, and sits dramatically in the middle of a
wide field, green grass all round, an immense wall of small
white stones banked up on either side of the grave entrance,
and with half-a-dozen standing stones in front and one reclining
heavily incised stone as the grave threshold. Visitors are allowed to walk round and enter the passage grave. A party had
just left, but one of the guides, girl students, kindly led me
in. The huge stones forming the tunnel of the grave lean in-
wards, the roof stones press down. We squeezed along the pas-

sage and into the chamber, where the space expands out into
alcoves or niches and up to the corbeled dome. My guide, who
was about twenty, leaned back against a stone and gave me a
short speech: " . . . passage-grave makers, perhaps from Brit-
tany . . . shellfish eaters . . . some four thousand years ago . . .
burials . . . cremations . . . We don't know much about
them . . ." How pretty she is, I thought. Was this the age-old
conjunction of instincts, of sex and death? She told me that at
Newgrange on December 21, the day of the winter solstice, the
sun comes up over the eastern horizon and shoots a long shaft
of light through a slit in the roof over the grave entrance, and
down the passage, lighting up the chamber for precisely seven-
teen minutes. This and the arrangement of standing stones outside suggested that the builders had astronomical knowledge
and made calendar observations. She also pointed out the inci-
sions in some stones—the triple spiral motif, to be seen on several, was the subject of conjecture. I hazarded the idea that it
might symbolize Knowth/Newgrange/Dowth. That, she said,
was one of the conjectures.

Outside again: the breeze shaking the full-leaved trees along
the lane; sun gleaming off the white stone embankment of the
giant mound. I had neglected to bring any lunch. I lay on the
grass and read some notes I had made from Dr. Michael
Herity's treatise, *Irish Passage Graves*, in which, after much detailed scholarship, he lets loose:

The whole impression in the Boyne is of a township like medieval
Florence, sure of its economy, confidently undertaking the erection
of a great cathedral to ensure spiritual sustenance, at its head a
ruler of wisdom, strength and leadership. . . .

Dr. Herity believes that three hard-working communities lived
in this area, compact enough to have a common purpose, each
depending on the labors of some five hundred able workers to
build its tombs over roughly twenty years. He writes:

When death came, a great mausoleum was ready to house the dead,
the spirit of the supernatural watching from its walls, its elevated
site and the mass of its tumulus designed to awe the living. After

the cremation ceremonies the ashes of the dead, borne in pottery vessels ornamented with the same symbols as those on the tomb walls and accompanied only by the ornamental miniatures they had worn in life, were laid to rest in the house they had planned and built.

There is a line in Lewis Mumford's *City in History*: "The Egyptians loved life so much they even embraced death." I thought also of a poem Heaney has written, called "Funeral Rites," in which he imagines an immense funeral procession moving from Ulster to the Boyne, to—as he has said in a radio broadcast—"the megalithic burial chambers which were fabulous even in early Irish times. Then people thought of them as the burial places of heroes and semi-gods, but I think of them here as the solemn resting places for casualties, the innocent dead of the past few years."

I walked on, two miles to Dowth. This burial mound is unrestored, unexcavated since the nineteenth century, since when it has been a grassed-over crater. No one was about. I stood on the mound and watched the wind move like a demonstration of energy through the long grass. As at Knowth and Newgrange, there was a fine view of the river half a mile away. Newgrange was in sight to the west. Just to the east, next to a ruined mansion, stood the shell of a church, and in the surrounding churchyard, just scythed, a man out of Brueghel carrying hay on a pitchfork. As I walked back to the road, an elderly well-groomed lady came in, walking her dog, looking as if she did this every day.

I HAD FOUND a roadside pump just before Dowth. At it I filled my grumbling stomach with well water, and this kept me going through the next few miles of warm sun and winding road toward Oldbridge. In the course of the next forty-five minutes I was passed by two cars. I saw one man, a road worker, pruning a hedge with a billhook beside a bridge where the little River Mattock runs beneath the road to join the Boyne.

"Keeping fine," I said.

"Yes, not so bad today," said he.

When the Boyne came in sight again, at the junction of the lane I was on and the Slane-Drogheda road, it was spread-out and slow-moving. Fishermen were angling from the far bank. More ruined houses loomed through the trees. A mid-afternoon torpor overhung everything, but I kept going and at ten to three found myself at Oldbridge, where a narrow stone and iron bridge spans the river and another era of Irish history is immanent. And there, too, on a wide grass verge, a piece of ground over which hundreds of troops charged toward the river one July day in 1690, sat a gypsy caravan. It was prairie-schooner-shaped but small. The panels on either side of the back door were painted red, yellow, gold, and green, like illuminations in the *Book of Kells*. A subsidiary dwelling had been set up on the grass nearby, a sort of nomadic hut made of canvas stretched over wooden hoops; indeed, it looked like an upside-down coracle. The canvas was partly rolled back to reveal bedding inside: a mattress, several plump pillows, and an eiderdown embroidered or patchworked with a magnificence to match the painting of the caravan. There was something Oriental about these sparse but luxurious belongings. A goat, tethered to a stake a few yards away, was chomping grass. Several horses, seemingly the steeds of the caravan's owner, were in an adjacent field. An iron pot hung from a tripod over a campfire. And in the grass a man lay on his back holding a baby aloft; the baby was giggling; the man was uttering fond parental noises to make it laugh. I gave them a wave and a hail in greeting, and the man—after a serious look presumably to see that I wasn't an agent of council authority or the farmer who owned the field—nodded, smiled in return.

The tide reaches up the Boyne from the sea to this point. Walking onto the bridge, I concluded that the tide was out; this accounted for the present shallowness of the river. It would have been easy to ford, which was the reason William III chose it for one of his two river crossings on the morning of July 1, 1690, and the reason James II (who was with his staff on the slopes of Donore Hill to the south) had many of his troops on the other bank, guarding the crossing. (July 1 was the date of the Battle of the Boyne in the old-style Julian calendar. In the new-style Gregorian calendar adopted in the British Isles in January 1752, the date is July 12.) In any event, when William realized the ford at Oldbridge was well covered by the Jacobite forces, he cleverly sent a large detachment from his ample army (35,000; James had 25,000) off westwards to cross the river at Rossnaree, between Knowth and Newgrange. James thought this feint to his flank was the real thing, and diverted much of his Oldbridge force to meet them. William's plan of deception succeeded. The diverting and diverted parties sat and faced each other across a bog all morning, while William's main army came across the river at Oldbridge and met the rest of James's.

It was a European battle. William Prince of Orange, Stadt-holder of the United Provinces, had been offered the British throne by those who wished to preserve the Protestant succession and constitutional monarchy. Catholic James, deposed in England, with French support, was making his penultimate stand in Ireland. He had fighting for him Englishmen, Scots-men, Irishmen, Dutchmen, and Frenchmen. William had Dutch, Germans, Danes, Scots, English, Huguenot French, and even some Catholic Irish. To tell each other apart the Wil-liamites wore green sprigs in their headgear, the Jacobites wore white cockades—but this didn't prevent allies from now and then fighting one another.

Across the bridge there is thick undergrowth on either side, a tough place for a skirmish. It was, one participant recalled, "an excessive hot day." When William's Dutch Blue Guards forded the river, they held their muskets and powder above their heads; as they came up the bank the fifes and drums were playing "Lilliburlero." I sat down by a desolate gatehouse at the first bend in the road and changed my socks—an old soldier's trick for the restoration of tired feet, rubbing my bare toes in the grass, and airing them for five minutes before donning Mr. Bean's boots again. Road signs directed me toward the Jacobite camp, but after a mile or so of uphill plodding along tortuous lanes, I struck out across the fields to Donore Hill, whose sum-mit was crowned by a clump of trees and a small walled ceme-tery. Among the obstacles were barbed-wire fences, deep

ditches full of mud and nettles, thorn hedges, and fields full
of cows and possibly one or two bulls; but eventually I was
there, seated on the stone wall surrounding the graveyard—
3:50 P.M.

I had my jacket off for the first time on this walk. It was hot,
but not excessively so. I looked north down the long slope of
hillside on which the last stages of battle had taken place. To
the right, three miles or so away, I could see the buildings of
Drogheda, and beyond, for the first time, the sea. To the northeast, the mountains of Mourne. It was twenty miles from where
I sat to the North/South border, along which there are still ambushes, booby traps, sudden murders, and the working out of
old horrors. What is always impressive about battlefields is the
fertility of the fields, the felicity of the countryside. But here,
without much effort, I could imagine men in the ditches and
hedgerows, pikemen holding off cavalry, the confusion of
charges, retreats, and orders not getting through. Smoke—
bayonets—musketballs—and a good deal of dying and injury
less stoically received than Lord Anglesey's. The Jacobites lost
nearly a thousand men, and William some five hundred. (Even
so, seven thousand of William's men had died from disease
the previous winter.)

At Aughrim, a year later, the Catholic army met its final
defeat in Ireland, but this battle at the Boyne has always been
considered the real defeat. James retreated that night to Dublin
and took ship for France. And in the war of words that has
been so much of Irish history, the Boyne is immortal. Most
Irish schoolchildren were brought up to identify with one side
or the other; the account of the Boyne battle in most Irish history books, until very recently, discloses the cultural, religious,
and political bias of the book's author. No Catholic child was
ever named William. The Protestant king spent only a fortnight in Ireland, but he became for Northern Protestants the
symbol of the Irish-British union. King Billy is the affectionate
title they've given him, though at the time many of his supporters thought him cold and standoffish. He didn't speak English very well. And who knows if—as Ulster iconography insists—
he actually rode a white horse on that day of battle? Many in

the North, despite the ubiquitous slogan "Remember 1690" painted on walls and gables, have no clear idea of when the battle took place. Some believe it occurred in biblical times. There is the famous story of the visitor to the North who is puzzled by all the references to King Billy and the Boyne, and asks an old Ulsterman what it's all about. He is told, "Away with ye, man, and read yer Bible!"

Celebrations of the Boyne battle anniversary were first held in the North in 1797, as liberal Presbyterianism began to be supplanted by the Orange Order and by a "no surrender" attitude regarding the maintenance of a Protestant ascendancy. In 1914 that attitude was so entrenched that Protestant Ulster nearly revolted at the prospect of Home Rule for all of Ireland —a situation in which they feared they would be swamped by the Catholic majority. When it looked as if there might be a Unionist rising in March that year, British generals considered moving the 5th Army Division from its camps in central Ireland to a line along the Boyne, facing north. But world war provided for the death of Home Rule—and in turn for the frustrations that helped produce the Easter Rising in 1916. It was on July 1, 1916—the old-style date of the Battle of the Boyne—that the Battle of the Somme began, and men of the 36th Ulster Division went over the top wearing orange ribbons, shouting "No surrender!" and "Remember 1690!" as they plunged into the German machine-gun fire.

That year, after the Somme debacle, there was no Orange parade in the North. But except for that single omission, each July has seen an anniversary celebration of the Boyne victory. In Belfast the parade takes two and a half hours to pass a particular spot, with drums throbbing and the flutes playing their shrill tunes. On this day of sashes and banners the ministers preach and the politicians pronounce as to God's own, a Chosen People. A notable example was the speech made on July 12, 1934, by Sir Basil Brooke, then Minister of Agriculture in Northern Ireland and later the Prime Minister of Northern Ireland, that illustrates what Catholics in the North were up against for so many years. Sir Basil said, "Many in this audience employ Catholics, but I have not one about my place. Catholics are out to destroy Ulster. . . . If we in Ulster allow Roman Catholics to work on our farms we are traitors to Ulster. . . . I would appeal to loyalists, therefore, wherever possible, to employ good Protestant lads and lassies."

Possibly it is a sign of progress that, despite the last ten years of Troubles, that sort of statement, reflecting fairly widespread feeling at the time, could be made by probably only one Ulster MP today. And the Twelfth parade itself is no longer quite so fraught with religious or tribal hostility. Some young Protestants are forbidden to take part in it by parents who regard it as a manifestation of bigotry; some young Catholics begin to think of it as a sort of carnival. An increasing number of people are perhaps coming to share Conor Cruise O'Brien's feeling that the Irish have often in the past behaved "like sleepwalkers, locked in some eternal ritual re-enactment, muttering senselessly as we collided with one another." For that reason O'Brien chose not to atttend a ceremony commemorating the landing of arms from Erskine Childers's yacht *Asgard*—a ceremony, he thought, that merely underlined the ancient rivalries and passions.

ON THE GRASSY SLOPES of the Boyne, on a warm afternoon, topography is more impressive than history. This land is unlike so much of Ireland—a country broken up into areas of poor soil, barren mountains, and bog. The geographical fragmentation of the country has in the past been intensified by the use of the land and by a system of inheritance, in the words of the geographer E. Estyn Evans, that entailed "reallocating land periodically among close kinsmen, and subdividing already scattered plots among co-heirs." Evans and others believe that such practices, over the centuries, have contributed to the violent feeling that lies just below the surface and has brought about so much internecine bloodshed in Ireland.

IN THE LATE AFTERNOON I abandoned my hilltop perch, my petty kingdom, and made my way across the fields to the lane again. It was two miles of country road work into Drogheda, a sizable market and manufacturing town built on both steep banks of the river. Drogheda is famous for its fortified walls, which the English Commonwealth troops of Oliver Cromwell stormed during the civil war in 1649, proceeding to slaughter the Drogheda garrison. Cromwell said, "Our men getting up to them, were ordered by me to put them all to the sword." Cromwell saw himself as not only attacking royalists but also acting as the instrument of divine vengeance against those Irish who had rebelled in Ulster in 1641. He wrote from Drogheda: "This is a righteous judgement of God upon those barbarous wretches, who have imbrued their hands in so much innocent blood." The effect of the death of the 3,500 Drogheda men was to emblazon his own name in Irish memory as a butcher, and to associate his country with the act.

Drogheda is also noted for disputes about the pronunciation of its name, the English—including the Earl of Drogheda—going for "Drowda," which to me sounds Irish, and most of the locals calling it "Drockeda," which is direct enough. Until recently communication from one side of town to the other was via a pair of narrow bridges, which had to carry not only local vehicles but much of the coastal road traffic between the North and Southern Ireland. Two years ago a new, wide road bridge was built, and named Peace Bridge by the Drogheda Town Council. In December 1976, shortly after it opened, a rally was held on the bridge by the Northern Ireland Peace Movement—whose founder members Mrs. Betty Williams and Miss Mairead Corrigan won the Nobel Peace Prize the following year. Ten thousand people turned up from North and South and in two columns, almost two armies, surged across the bridge from either side of the Boyne to meet in the middle, embrace, shake hands, or greet one another. The peace movement has been criticized for failing to get support from the city ghetto dwellers or for dealing in cosmetic solutions. But it seems to me that its dramatization of the possibilities of friendship has been important in a country where the last years have seen rather the reiteration of terror and animosity. Added to which, the peace movement has put some of its funds to very good use, by, for example, lending money to small companies that have been unable to qualify for loans from the government or banks. And it may be that one of the "solutions" for divided Ireland is the willingness to try all sorts of proposals, and to analyze and question all deeply ingrained attitudes and beliefs.

I walked across Peace Bridge and along the main shopping street of Drogheda. The fortification, the cathedral, and the Boyne salmon coracles (the last basketwork-and-skin boats in Ireland, I'd been told) would have to wait for another day. I was all tramped out. I inquired the whereabouts of the railway station, and on learning that it was half a mile out of town, asked about buses to Dublin; they, it appeared, were just down the hill, by the river. There, indeed, a bus was loading up. I had just time to buy some chocolate and apples from a nearby shop, and to take a last look, as the queue of passengers moved forward into the bus, over the footpath railing at the Boyne.

Afterword

IN DECEMBER 1979, Finiston School is still there on the Oldpark Road, but only just. The army pulled out of the front building several years ago. That structure and one wing of the modern school have since been destroyed by arson. (In 1976 there were five attempts to burn the school down.) What is left is the central wing and six classrooms. The total enrollment is now roughly fifty pupils. Dorothy Elliott is principal, and teaches as well; she has a teaching staff of two. David Russell has become the head of a thriving primary school half a mile away, with five hundred pupils. The Oldpark Road has been further devastated by the demolition of slum houses, though some rebuilding is going on in the lower part of the road. The area is now mostly Catholic. Finiston is being kept open, it seems, because the remaining local Protestant families insist on it, as a gesture.

ERSKINE HAMILTON CHILDERS, fourth President of the Irish Republic, died of a heart attack in November 1974—between the writing and publication of this piece. When the President's body lay in state in Dublin Castle on November eighteenth, 11,000 people filed past to pay their respects. The President's funeral took place in the twelfth-century Protestant cathedral of St. Patrick in Dublin, the prayers read by English-accented Church of Ireland clergymen, the Beatitudes recited by Mr. Liam Cosgrave, the then Prime Minister, while in the packed congregation Mr. Harold Wilson, the British Prime Minister, sat near Mr. de Valéra, and from the walls hung the faded colors of Irish regiments that had once served in the British Army.

PUBLIC OPINION: In 1973 a referendum in the North supported the continued tie between Ulster and Great Britain. In 1979, a survey in the South showed that a majority in the Republic favored unity—but only a minority was prepared to accept it if it meant a tax increase. In the summer of 1979, a poll among Catholics in the North found that only a third of those questioned supported a proposal to take British troops out of Ulster. After the explosions in late August 1979 that killed Earl Mountbatten, several members of his family, an Irish boy, and eighteen British soldiers, the London *Daily Mirror* (which had previously been backing the movement to withdraw the troops from Northern Ireland) suggested that the many Southern Irish who live in Britain no longer be allowed to enjoy the special privileges of voting in British elections, of British social security benefits, and of the right to enter Britain without a passport. But no legislation for such changes has been introduced.

IN THE LATE AUTUMN OF 1979, Marie Boyle and Matthew Ferguson were married.

ANTHONY BAILEY was born in Portsmouth, England, in 1933. He was evacuated to the United States in 1940 and spent four years in Dayton, Ohio. Since then his life has been almost evenly divided between Britain and the United States. From 1952 to 1955 he read history at Merton College, Oxford. Since 1956 he has reported for *The New Yorker* and written two novels and numerous poems, short stories, and works of nonfiction. He lived for ten years in Stonington, Connecticut, about which he wrote the highly praised book *In the Village*. He now lives in London with his wife and four daughters.